Wyoming Folklore

COLLECTED BY THE FEDERAL WRITERS' PROJECT

Reminiscences, Folktales, Beliefs, Customs, and Folk Speech

Edited by James R. Dow,
Roger L. Welsch,
and Susan D. Dow

Introduction by James R. Dow
and Roger L. Welsch

UNIVERSITY OF NEBRASKA PRESS • LINCOLN & LONDON

Library of Congress Cataloging-in-Publication Data
Wyoming folklore : reminiscences, folktales, beliefs,
customs, and folk speech / collected by the Federal
Writers' Project ; edited by James R. Dow, Roger L.
Welsch, and Susan D. Dow; introduction by James R.
Dow and Roger L. Welsch.
    p. cm.
ISBN 978-0-8032-4302-6 (pbk. : alk. paper)
1. Wyoming—History—Anecdotes. 2. Folklore—
Wyoming. 3. Legends—Wyoming. 4. Wyoming—
Social life and customs. 5. Frontier and pioneer
life—Wyoming. I. Dow, James R. II. Welsch, Roger
L. III. Dow, Susan D. IV. Federal Writers' Project.
F761.6.W97 2010
978.7—dc22
2010011716

Set in Dante by Bob Reitz.

Contents

Introduction

Folklore is not history, but a good deal of folklore is historical, and only the most self-assured sophomore is able to draw without question the line between the two disciplines and between the two bodies of information. This volume contains a good bit of historical fact, included by the editors to provide a matrix for the folkloric data which is of main concern. We will start by briefly surveying the panorama of Wyoming history in order to set the scene for all of the state's folklore.

The state's history begins with the rich culture of the Native Americans, although there is some speculation, best expressed in Henriette Mertz's book, *Pale Ink* [Chicago: Swallow Press, 1972], that in the dim past the east slope of the Rockies in Wyoming was explored by the Chinese! But the bulk of that history has been lost or destroyed to the white man's shame and to the sorrow of us all.

In 1743 the Verendryes and their party were the first white visitors to travel as far as the Big Horn Mountains, and in 1803 that same virtually unexplored country became the pig-in-the-poke of the Louisiana Purchase. It is hard to imagine the mountains of Wyoming as a peripheral bargain tossed in along with New Orleans, but that was indeed the case.

In 1806 John Colter was the first native-born American, other than the Native Americans, to enter the present boundaries of Wyoming. It was during this or the next year that he tried to describe the land to his cronies in St. Louis, and failed so miserably that they thought him mad. Once his discovery was proven to be real, it was called "Colter's Hell," and then later "Yellowstone Park."

The first resident of the Big Horn Basin, Edward Rose, moved in 1807, and by 1809 eastern Wyoming was under heavy exploitation by fur trappers, who sought especially the heavy beaver furs of the higher altitudes. As a part of that same interest in furs John Jacob Astor sent Wilson Price Hunt across the state in 1812.

1812 saw Robert Stuart and his party discover the South Pass, and ten years later General William Ashley established his trading post on the Yellowstone River. Perhaps Ashley's greatest contribution to Wyoming's history and folklore was that he brought with him the legendary Jim Bridger, whose biography rivals his own tall tales.

In 1827 ironically and symbolically, the first wheeled vehicle to cross through the South Pass was a four-pound cannon (the first wagon didn't enter the state until 1829, a mere twenty years before the Oregon Trail guided thousands of wheeled vehicles through that same pass).

Kit Carson, a living legend of the West, visited Wyoming in 1830, and in 1842 John C. Fremont passed through Wyoming while surveying the West for a chain of military posts designed to open the area for expansion. Fort Bridger was established that same year. In 1843 Fort Bridger was opened for trade and Fremont crossed the Laramie Plains on his second expedition.

In 1846 President Polk approved the plan to establish a series of forts along the great trail route. In 1847 the first Mormon migrants, under Brigham Young, crossed the state on their way to New Zion (Salt Lake City), establishing en route the Platte River ferry near Fort Casper. As part of this plan the United States government purchased Fort Laramie in 1849 for four thousand dollars.

The famous Gratten Massacre, the beginning of a long, painful, and sordid series of Plains Indian wars, occurred near Fort Laramie in 1854 over an old Mormon cow. In reality it was not the cow that triggered the wars but the crossing of a "pain threshold," for it was clear to the Indians that the pressures of settlement were their doom. In the seasons of 1858 and 1859 sixteen million pounds of freight passed through Wyoming on the way to Utah on the Oregon Trail.

In 1860 the short-lived Pony Express crossed Wyoming on the way to the west coast—"short lived" because in 1861 the transcontinental telegraph line was completed across the state.

The Indian troubles increased throughout this period as the pressures increased on the Plains tribes. The troops extended their occupation area and became ever more savage in their attitudes, culminating in the infamous Sand Creek, Colorado Massacre in 1864 and the Fetterman Massacre of 1866.

1867 saw the founding of the city of Cheyenne and the County of Laramie (by the Dakota Legislature). The Union Pacific pressed into Wyoming that same year and the Indians continued to resist with the much romanticized and overplayed Wagon Box Fight in the Big Horns. Estimates of Indians killed ranged from six to 1,500.

1868 marked a turning point in Wyoming history, for treaties were signed with the Sioux, Crow, and Arapaho at Fort Laramie and the Bannock and Eastern Shoshone at Fort Bridger. The Shoshone Reservation was established, and on July 25 Congress established the Territory of Wyoming.

The first Territorial Legislature met on October 12, 1869 and on December 10 of the same year the Legislature enacted the radically innovative bill of women's suffrage, the first in the nation. Also in 1869 the Union Pacific Railway was completed across the state.

Wyoming's progressive attitudes toward women continued in 1870 with the appointment of Esther Morris as the nation's first female justice of the peace. That same year the first homestead was proved up. The census listed Wyoming's population as 9,118.

Despite the state's modest population count it continued to be innovative on the national scene: Yellowstone was designated the first national park in 1872, four years before General George Armstrong Custer led his troops through northern Wyoming on his way to a fateful battle on the Little Big Horn.

The national census of 1880 listed the state's population as 20,789, which was twice what it had been a decade earlier, but still less than any eastern city, a condition that remains unchanged.

On September 6, 1887 the University of Wyoming was opened, and in November of 1889 the state constitution was adopted.

The population tripled during the decade and the 1890 census listed 62,553 citizens of the state, and in 1890 Wyoming was admitted into the Union. On October 14 Francis E. Warren, the last territorial governor, was installed as the first state governor. It was during this same year that the last of the vital Plains Indian bands was butchered at Wounded Knee. The Pennsylvania Oil and Gas Company brought in Wyoming's first oil well in the Shoshone field of the Salt Creek District in 1890 as well.

By 1892 the white man focused his attention away from the Indians and toward killing himself in the ignominious Johnson County Cattle War, and in 1895 a major oil refinery was built in Casper, where the industry still prospers.

The state was still young in 1900 when the national census listed the population of Wyoming as 92,531. The year 1906 marks a milestone of sorts for the state, for it was then that the Devil's Tower was established as a national monument—and the state had its first automobile accident.

By 1910 the state's population was up to 145,965, which was still less than two people per square mile, concentrated primarily in the east and south. The wilderness, it appears, dominated, for the State Guide's singular entry for 1913 reads, "A wolf is trained to carry mail over deep snows."

In 1920 the state's population had again increased substantially to 194,531, and the state continued its progressive attitudes by electing Nellie Taylor Ross, the nation's first female governor, in 1924; in 1933 she was appointed the director of the United States Mint, and was the first woman to hold that post.

In 1930 the state's population had grown to 225,565—215,000 more that sixty years before! The scene was set for the Dust Bowl, the Great Depression, the New Deal, the Works Progress Administration, and the Federal Writers Project.

The Federal Writers Project (FWP), directed on the national level by Henry G. Alsger, was a part of the larger Works Progress Administration (WPA) and like it was designed to put America's unemployed—in this case, writers—to work. Franklin Roosevelt issued an Executive order in 1935 initiating the system of field offices and workers. Its short, frantic history was to be simultaneously gloriously productive and painfully frustrating, and as is always the case with governmental projects, the FWP's supporters primarily saw its strengths while its detractors were blinded by its inadequacies. As is also usually the case, the truth was somewhere in between.

For example, anti-intellectual congressmen saw the FWP as an idle exercise at a time when the country was in need of substantive work, and they pointed to the Federal Writers Project folklore questionnaires, which included such items as "animal lore—how the bear lost its tail," as prime evidence. Even today that would seem a frivolous pursuit to many people, and yet, the FWP workers collected tales, songs, customs, proverbs, and beliefs that can no longer be found today and would be totally lost if it were not for those questionnaires and the workers who used them. Whether that is indeed idle or useful is a matter of values.

It was also in the period immediately preceding the Second World War that political reaction became a congressional watchword. There was thus a constant barrage of charges that the FWP staff was saturated with Communists. There can be little doubt that those charges were sometimes accurate, but it is also clear that many congressmen and bureaucrats confused "intellectual" with "subversive."

In addition to these external attacks there were many internal problems—for example, the fact that the principal qualification for those who sought work with the Project was that they had to be officially poor. At least ninety percent of the staff had to come from the relief roles. This meant that the most successful authors in America were not eligible; many others might have been but would not admit their poverty.

In spite of these ponderous handicaps the Project's ten thousand workers produced 120 publications in less than eight full years of effort. When the Project closed in 1942 as a result of the combined pressures of the growing war effort and increasing political attacks, it had generated a magnificent series of public service publications, notably the state guides, many of which are still in print today, seventy years later. As flawed as they might have been, nothing better has come along in the seven decades since their production.

Even more important perhaps are the thousands upon thousands of files the state offices left behind, unpublished. They lie in library basements, in historical society archives, even lost in government storage buildings. These raw data represent the most thorough survey of American culture ever attempted. Now, three quarters of a century after they were collected, the materials are still capturing the attention of scholars.

This is, in part, due to the timing of the Project—in 1935 it was still possible to interview Civil War veterans and former slaves, Homesteaders and Oregon Trailers, Indians who remembered the Little Big Horn and horse traders who had plied their trade in the days before the automobile complicated everything.

In the case of folklore, the FWP collections take on even more luster because the directors of the national program worked extensively with John Lomax, who was an experienced and accomplished field worker in folklore, especially folk music. Later, Benjamin Botkin, a major figure in American folklore studies, brought to the folklore project new expertise in urban and contemporary lore. Bearing in mind the economic restrictions of the Depression, the stifling atmosphere of the political situation nationally and internationally, and the difficulties stemming from an untrained and demoralized staff, the accomplishments of the FWP are astonishing.

A good deal has been made by modern folklorists of the techniques used by the FWP field workers. In all fairness it must be remembered that the FWP staff members, with rare exceptions, were not professional folklorists before they found themselves working with folklore. In most cases they had not originally been concerned with folklore even in an amateur capacity. With that fact in mind, one must admit that the quality of the collection is extraordinary. Substantial credit for the relatively high quality of the folklore collection must go to Lomax and Botkin for their direction and the questionnaires that guided the workers in the field. The general format was a checklist, a listing of the kinds of items the fieldworker was to search for, such as animal tales, cures and magic remedies, death and burial customs, folk games and dances, jokes, legends, nicknames, proverbs and sayings, superstitious beliefs, signs for planting, weather beliefs and meanings, wishes, etc.

In some folklore areas the questionnaires were more specific and could serve as a direct field sheet that could then be filed only as raw data. The following is a sample questionnaire used to establish a file on Wyoming place names.

QUESTIONNAIRE ON WYOMING PLACE NAME ORIGINS

County:

Date:

Worker:

Address:

1a. Name of place:

1b. By underscoring one of the following terms indicate whether the place is a county, city, village, town, township, post office, old post office, ghost town, river, creek, butte:

2. For whom named? (If for an individual, give his or her full name or initials, identity and title, if any: as, Capt., Dr., Etc:

3. Resident of the community? If not, give address at time of naming:

4. Give his or her connection with the place; as, businessman, officer of a land-holding company, railway employee or official:

5. If place was named for another place, give name and address of latter:

6. If named for neither person nor place, give history and reason for naming (such as coined names) and date of naming:

7. Give full name or initials of person or persons who selected the name and give community connections:

8. Was there an earlier name or names? If so, what?

9. Origin of or reasons for earlier names, if any:

10. Reason for change of name:

11. For cities, towns, or villages, give the following additional information (this does not apply to extinct post offices or ghost towns):

Population:

Altitude (ft.):

Date settled:

State whether incorporated as a city, town, or village:

Date of incorporation:

Give names of railroads (Specify if main or branch lines) that enter the town:

Official number of highways (State, county, or U.S.):

12. Sources of Information (individuals or publications):
13. Remarks:
    Use reverse side for additional information.

Of course, the effectiveness of each state's project depended in large part on the skill and enthusiasm of its staff and the general attitudes of the region toward folklore. Wyoming gets mixed marks in both categories. In his eminently readable history of the Federal Writers Project, *The Dream and the Deal* (Boston: Little, Brown, and Company, 1973), Jerry Mangione writes:

> In Wyoming, as in many other states, the hostility of the citizenry toward the wpa and the Writers' Project was often an obstacle. There was a deep resentment that the government should be using taxpayers' money to pay salaries to writers. The term "writer" coupled with "wpa" connoted everything that the New Deal haters considered scurrilous about the Roosevelt administration. During the fact-gathering trips the Wyoming director and her husband made around the state, she discovered that, invariably, she would be rebuffed if she identified herself as a member of the Writers' Project. Once she hit on the ruse of representing herself as a writer for the Wyoming Stockman Farmer, a magazine to which she had contributed, she had no further difficulty.

Moreover, Wyoming's staff, unlike Nebraska's for example, had little taste or interest for folklore and suffered the same kinds of attack that were the custom in Washington. Again, from Mangione's *The Dream and the Deal*:

> In some states the instructions were received with derision. "We simply could not believe our eyes," recalled Agnes Wright Spring, the former director of the Wyoming Project. "None of us had ever thought much about folklore and when we received an index to folklore subjects listing 'Animal behaviors and meanings, such as a rooster crowing, dog barking, cattle lowing, etc.,' we thought it was the biggest piece of malarkey we'd ever seen." One of her former colleagues, Cal Williams, who had resigned from the Project to work

for the Republican Party, happened to see the folklore instructions and used them to sneer at the New Deal. An editorial he wrote for the Wyoming Tribune began: "The Roosevelt administration is doing things no other administration has ever thought of," and continued: "Animal behavior is being studied intensely and before long our people will know why a rooster crows and a dog barks. . . . Briefly the big idea is this: There is no end to the work to be done—there is no limit to the money it will cost. Boondoggling must go on and you must pay the bill."

It is difficult at the distance of three quarters of a century to judge the competency of the Wyoming staff but there are subtle implications that it suffered from the same kinds of problems that Mangione documents for other state organizations. A glaring example of the kind of boondoggling that put incompetent workers into key positions only on the basis of influence is suggested by a small office note attached to one of the Wyoming folklore documents that is riddled with misspellings, faulty constructions, and downright shattered prose:

Checked for accuracy by Ellen Spear Edwards
Title: Daughter of the late Hon. Willis M. Spear

Despite these obvious problems the Wyoming collection is a rich repository of folkloric data, requiring only the most perfunctory sorting once the six bulging wpa file cabinets and the random materials of thirteen dusty boxes stored in the basement of the Wyoming State Archives and Historical Department had been thoroughly searched. The collection was not as rich or as "pure" as one might like, but most assuredly it was better than many other similar collections.

The editors, James R. Dow, Roger L. Welsch, and Susan Dow came to the Wyoming Federal Writers Project files from different directions. Welsch, who taught folklore in the English Department of the University of Nebraska, had written *The Treasury of Nebraska Pioneer Folklore*, published in 1966 by the University of Nebraska Press and based on Nebraska's fwp files. He had found that state's files to be a wealth of folklore materials and had based two other books on the material and had been casting about for other similar collections in neighboring states. Dow, a German linguist and a trained folklorist at Iowa State University at Ames, had previously been on the faculty of the University of Wyoming, so it was logical that the subject of the Wyoming FWP files should come up in a conversation between Dow and Welsch at a meeting of the American Folklore Society. Theirs was a collaboration made to order: Dow had surveyed and culled the Wyoming files under a grant from Iowa State University but had found himself in an academic schedule that made further processing impossible; Welsch had just finished a book on tall-tale postcards and was ready to begin another project. Susan Dow helped select the items to be included and edited the manuscript. Thus the concept of this book came to be.

While the editors will not—need not—apologize for the materials included here anymore than the scientist needs to apologize for the personality of the phenomena he studies, it may help the reader to understand the nature of the materials included, and to know the processes of selections through which they have passed. It must first be realized that the material reproduced on these pages is not at all the sum total of Wyoming's folklore, nor of the Wyoming FWP files.

First there was the selection process exercised by the Federal Writers Project field workers in Wyoming. As Mangione stated above, they were not particularly interested in folklore and so the data collected are far less than they were, for example, in Nebraska, where enthusiasm ran high, largely because of the able work of accomplished folklorists like Louise Pound and Lowry Wimberely. Wyoming had no such professional folklorists. Moreover, the Wyoming workers seem to have been drawn to legend, local and oral history, and pioneer reminiscences, rather than to songs, traditional beliefs, or foodways. Nothing can now be done about such gaps in the basic materials; the alternative, which has been chosen here, is to take advantage of the strengths of the collection rather than lamenting the weaknesses. It is conceivable that, given more than its meager seven and one-half years, the Wyoming project would have developed a comprehensive collection but the abrupt termination of the program exercised an arbitrary selection process on the Wyoming fieldwork: whatever had not yet been collected was not to be collected.

In much the same way the youth of Wyoming as a state exerted a powerful restriction on the development of folklore there. Tradition does not require a specific amount of time to grow and yet it is clear that time is directly related to that development and the accumulation of a body of lore.

A function of the same factor is population. One of the results of Wyoming's youth and of its geography (which is in part also a factor of its youth) is the state's low population density, which may in turn have its effects on the density of folklore.

A further factor in every state's collection was the very nature of the fieldworker. Germans from Russia in Nebraska maintain a close, closed society; there were few German-Russian field workers, and therefore there was little collection of German-Russian folklore materials. The same must be said of the Indians in Wyoming; there were no Indian FWP workers and so little authentic Indian data were collected and those that were collected were filtered through a series of white mentalities.

Finally, there is no way for us to know how complete the basic files are now. Seventy years is not a long time, but there have been several intervening wars and thousands of disinterested bureaucrats. The editors found several obvious gaps in the Wyoming files and there could certainly have been more where the discontinuity was not apparent.

In addition to the historical filters, the ethnic skew, the fieldwork biases, and the physical influences on the collected material, some selective influences have been exerted on the FWP materials. It will help the reader understand Wyoming folklore to keep in mind the rationale for all of these selections.

The first level of selection was done by James Dow, and then by Susan Dow, who used a very broad discretion and tended to include material even if there was any question attached to it. Welsch then screened the texts several more times, applying several additional criteria: initially he omitted materials that represent "high" culture, i.e., literature, whether popular or elitist. Newspaper accounts and personal reminiscences were included where they seem to occupy the margin between history and folklore or where they provide background and context for the folklore texts. Wyoming texts that are common to other areas or that are readily available in print elsewhere were screened out next. For example, the slim file folder of folksongs offered nothing that could not be found in any number of previously published collections and therefore were not included in this volume in order to concentrate on prose narratives. Finally, while a few of the texts tell of a Wyoming citizen's adventures in another state or begin or end outside the political boundaries of the present state of Wyoming, the focus of the final selections is clearly on Wyoming. It should be noted, however, that only a few texts were excluded on the basis of this consideration. It was clear that the Wyoming workers had used the same criteria in their own collecting.

Two final points must be made, one for the professional folklorist and one for the nonprofessional reader. The folklorist will understand that the data printed here are, in every case, a written record of what various people—from cowhands to penniless FWP workers to folklore scholars—have conceived to be the folklore of the state of Wyoming. It was recorded mostly by nonprofessionals who worked from a guide list and their own biases, of course, which were often extremely romanticized. They did not have tape recorders, they recorded minimal biographical data, and they were obviously totally unaware and unconcerned with questions of "texture, text, and context," "storytelling events," structural typologies, and folklore as "performance." For much of contemporary folklore research the data presented here then are minimally useful, exactly because none of the research orientations just listed were used. Nevertheless, the FWP collections are substantial and need to be published (and thus subjected to active criticism). They often represent, as in the case of Wyoming, the only systematic surveying of the folklore of a state or region, and they stand as something of a monument to both the only direct involvement the U.S. government had ever had in folklore up to that point and to the hundreds and thousands of people who worked at recording what they and their informants felt to be the folklore of their state. For most readers such statements as the preceding ones may well appear to be meaningless professional jargon. To the folklorist it is necessary for putting the research data into its proper perspective.

The other point to be made concerns materials in the texts as they were recorded by the FWP workers. There is no question that some of the characteristics of the Wyoming collection are offensive when judged by contemporary standards. Paternalistic or even openly prejudiced attitudes toward Wyoming Indians and African Americans, for example, are especially troublesome to the editors of this volume, but it would constitute a serious and unnecessary compromise of the folklore to "clean up" the texts. It is therefore necessary for the modern reader to exercise maturity and to view the implicit slurs as cultural indicators of seventy years ago. They do not represent the attitudes of the editors or the publisher.

Where it is clear that the stylistic anomalies—misspellings, faulty or confusing constructions, gratuitous commentary, conclusions, or stylistic remarks—are the work of the FWP workers rather than an integral part of the actual texts, they have been omitted or corrected. Where, on the other hand, such problems seem to be a part of the actual text, they have been left as is. Nor has there been any attempt to regularize the style or format of the texts, which display differences that result from the fact that they were collected and transcribed from different sources by different workers in different areas at different times. Such changes would constitute an unnecessary compromise.

No book is the result of only its writers, and nowhere is that more true than in the case of folklore. The editors therefore offer their sincere and profound gratitude to the following: Professor Wayland D. Hand (of UCLA), who originally inspired James Dow to undertake this research; Katherine Halverson and her staff at the Wyoming State Archives and Historical Department, who enthusiastically aided the search for, then good-naturedly stood aside and let Dow plow through, all the WPA materials stored in Cheyenne. Finally, we thank the numerous people of the state of Wyoming who served as FWP workers and as informants to the project. It is their folklore.

I

Pioneer Memories

"Oral history" was an unfamiliar phrase to the Federal Writers Project workers (and unfortunately, still is to many of today's academic historians), but that is precisely what they were collecting when they interviewed old-timers and copied down in their notepads, with the greatest accuracy they could exercise, the pioneer accounts of what it was indeed like during the years of territorial exploration and settlement. Because of the incredible but dubiously benevolent advance of technology during the past seven decades, we have come to think of those years as being but distant memories, almost prehistoric. But we are today, in reality, only a few generations removed from homesteading, and when these materials were being collected in the late 1930s, the memories of the settlement of the Wyoming Territory were still vivid in the minds of many.

It is to the inestimable credit of the Federal Writers Project administrators (and the eternal thanks of these editors!) that the work of the agency was not simply directed toward further investigation of governors, railroad magnates, and other prominent historical figures, but concentrated instead on the accumulation of information from the very people who had lived the history directed by the governors and magnates—the pioneers themselves.

Here, by including in this collection some of the excerpts from the interviews, we can better understand not only the history of Wyoming but also the folklore that sprang from (and sometimes gave birth to) that history. Perhaps by virtue of the folklore, readers will be able to understand more clearly both the economic and political history of Wyoming as well as its common-man history.

The selections we have included are, above all, restricted by the limited selection of materials in the FWP files—and now, of course, the sources of these transcriptions are no longer available to us. We would have preferred to have interviews with trappers, prospectors Shoshones, or sheepherders, but those choices are simply not available. The glimpse we will have of Wyoming's pioneer life then will include a story of three cowboys on the trail in 1879, a hair-raising episode from a frontier wife's life, two examples of frontier originals, a conversation with an Indian chief, and finally, some fine-grained anecdotes.

1 Cowboy Days with the Old Union Cattle Company

Life Notes of Thomas Richardson.

In 1884 my father decided that he had had enough of the Niobrara [River] (in northwestern Nebraska). Mostly, we had known hard times, strife, and disappointment there. In June we loaded up two covered wagons and started out on a long trek to find a new location.

We traveled south to Kearney, Nebraska, and went on into Kansas and Colorado along the Republican River. That country was similar to the Niobrara, so we returned to Kearney and spent the winter. On the first of April, 1885, we resumed our wandering, but headed north that time, traveling up the UP [Union Pacific] Railroad through Cheyenne and Laramie until we came to Rock Springs. We crossed the LaBonte Mountains and came down on the Platte River at old Fort Fetterman. From there we turned north and came through Buffalo towards the Pumpkin Buttes and looked the Belle Fourche Country over, but my father could not find a location to suit him. Either the water was scanty or bad or something was the matter, so we kept right on traveling east through Sundance onto the head of Stockade Beaver Creek to the L. A. K. Ranch. Bill Smith ("Elk Mountain" Smith), who had been our neighbor on the Niobrara, had come to this country before us and was then nicely settled on a ranch at Elk Mountain. We decided to look him up and pulled on about eight miles farther to Elk Mountain.

In that vicinity our journey ended, for at last we had found the ideal location for which we had searched so long. In all our journeying we had not seen anything better than this. A huge spring gushed forth a stream of water large enough to take (care) of a thousand head of cattle, and there was grass and pasture land galore. There we set about building up a ranch.

For a couple of years I stayed at home and helped my father but I had always dreamed of becoming a cowboy and working on the great roundups. This was a wonderful stock country then. It was all one, big, open pasture with a luxuriant growth of grass and water in nearly every draw. There were cattle droves everywhere, it seemed, in the little valleys and scattered all over the hills. Many big outfits ran cattle over the far-flung range that as yet knew very few fences. One of the largest outfits was the Union Cattle Company that was formed (by) the merger of three big ranches, the S & G, the Bridle Bit, and the 70s.

On the 4th day of May I went to work for the Union Company. My first job with the outfit was far from the exciting life that I had pictured. Some of us younger men were detailed to roll wire in the mud. If there is one thing a cowhand hates it is riding or making any kind of fence. We loafed on the job until the boss came and gave us "thunder." He sent us to the bunkhouse and we thought sure we were going to get our time, but instead he just gave us another good "bawlin' out," and said, "now, go on back and (loaf) as damned little as possible." Well, we finally managed to get the fence fixed and on the 10th day of May the big roundup started.

One morning my horse threw me and took off across the prairie, bucking for all he was worth. My stirrups were flying in the air and some cowboy threw his lariat and caught my stirrup, right up close to the saddle, ripping the strap loose. Such instances were common and very often a bunch of us had to get together and do some repair work while the rest would be halfway to the head of the creek on circle.

Sometimes we ate dinner at ten o'clock, sometimes at two. Supper was generally at four and right after supper we went to bed, if we didn't have to stand first watch on night guard.

The only recreation the men got while on the roundup was card playing and they didn't get much time for that. Some of them snatched a few games between circles.

"Old Ginger," so called because he was red-headed and bad tempered, was the cook of the Bar FS. The boys loved to pester him because he flew into such terrible rages. They would make some remark about his cooking and then Ginger would take after them with a butcher knife and run them around the mess wagon. He had a deck of cards and was continually persuading the boys to play *Monte* with him and of course he always fleeced them good and proper. He kept his winnings on the top shelf of the mess box and anybody that came near that box was in danger of getting carved, so the money was about as safe as in the bank, or so Ginger thought.

But one time a big, tough fellow by the name "Mizzou" joined the outfit. Every time he got a chance he played *Monte* with Ginger and of course the old cook won every time. It looked as though Ginger had taken in all of Mizzou's money, for there was a big pile of bills on his side of the blanket, when suddenly the cowboy jumped up and pulled his six-shooters. He shot into that pile of money and blew it all to pieces.

Ginger was pretty surprised and scared at that and he made a run for the wagon with Mizzou right behind him. Mizzou said, "You get up there and hand me out the dough from the mess box. Be damn quick about it too," and to hurry things along he began prodding Ginger in the ribs with his six-shooters.

Ginger was trying to climb the wagon wheel but he was so scared that he kept slipping off. "Well, damn it," he shouted as Mizzou kept poking him with the guns, "can't you see I'm hurrying." He took a bag full of money out of the mess box and handed it to Mizzou, who promptly pocketed it and proceeded to shake the dust of the camp from his heels.

Of course there was always plenty of excitement right in the line of duty and the boys didn't have to go to town looking for any while the roundup was on. After the general roundup that summer of '87 our horses being all ridden down a new string was brought in for us. These new horses had been brought from Goshen Hole near Cheyenne and were supposed to be broken but they had only been ridden a little the year before. We drove them within seven miles of Dewey in sight of Elk Mountain on ground now owned by myself. Here we selected our bronchs (*sic*) and prepared to break them. The boss asked us to choose our own horses so he would not be responsible for broken bones and necks. We went into the cavvy and picked our horses until each man had six mounts.

The next morning an old cow hand by the name of Soaper was up before anyone else. He had selected a nice brown horse with a white blaze (*sic*) in its face and he woke the rest of us talking to the cook about the horse. He says to the cook, "Don't you think he had a good sensible head on him?" We got up laughing, ate breakfast, and prepared to saddle our new mounts.

Of course we all had some trouble but Soaper had the most of all with that horse that "had such a good sensible head." Every time he went to set foot in the stirrup the horse reared and fell over backwards and every time he fell over Soaper got a little paler.

I was having a good deal of trouble with my horse too. It took two men to help me bridle him and we tied his front feet together and yet he lunged around over the prairie dragging us with him. Finally I managed to get mounted, and still Soaper was on the ground.

Then we all went to roasting Soaper and telling him that only about twenty men were waiting on him and his sensible horse. The horse fell over about five times and Soaper was getting more and more scared, but he decided that he had to ride that horse or lose face in front of the whole outfit.

When he did mount of course the horse keeled over on him and then got up and ran while Soaper just laid there, plumb knocked out. One hand that was an exceptionally good man with horses caught the bronch (*sic*) and gave him a workout that took some of the orneriness out of him. Then Soaper came to and got on the horse and rode him all afternoon.

He didn't ride him again for quite a while until the boss asked him what he had done with his horse that was so sensible looking. Soaper said, "I'm jest a-goin' to ride him today."

He caught and saddled the horse and tied him to the wheel of a big bed wagon and then went to breakfast. The boss had ordered some young tenderfoot to grease the wagon the afternoon before and the tenderfoot had forgotten to put the bur of that particular wheel back on. While breakfast was going on, something "goosed" Soaper's horse. He reared back, jerking the wheel off the wagon, and went through the sagebrush with the wheel hitting the high spots behind him.

Well, of course that caused a lot of fun and we razzed Soaper again about his sensible horse. Something like that was always going on.

When the roundup camps moved it was a wonderful sight. The great herds of cattle and cavvys of horses spread out over the prairie for miles. The roundup cooks jumped in their wagons and raced each other for the best camping grounds. They wanted to get under trees near to the water as possible.

For one thing we always had plenty of good wholesome food and hot coffee. All cooking was done over the coals in big Dutch ovens and no better method of cooking has ever yet been devised. Huge coffee pots stood full of hot coffee nearly all the time. Our meat was the best to be had. Every day a fat yearling was selected from the herd and brought up near the cook wagon. She was killed and skinned right there and only the hind quarters were used. When the boys got hungry between meals they would take the ribs and roast them over the campfire (and) then stand around gnawing on those bones.

The old-time cow hand had to be alert every minute, for emergencies were continually arising and those who weren't equal to the situation or who hung back either lost their lives or were looked upon as tenderfeet. We worked, and the rain never poured down too hard, the gumbo never got too slippery or the blizzards too fierce to stop our work. The floods never raised the streams too high but what we were supposed to cross in the line of duty.

It really rained in those days. We wore our slickers and rode in a downpour most of the time. The ground was sodden with moisture and every so often floods came down the creeks and turned them to raging rivers.

I recollect when a flood came down Beaver Creek when we were working near where Dewey is now. Our herd of cattle was on the other side of the stream and we had to cross to get to them. We were swimming our horses across and one big, young puncher failed to make it. As his horse made a desperate leap to climb the bank its legs sank so deep in the soft sand and mud that it fell over backwards. The saddlehorn struck the boy in the stomach, knocking him breathless. The horse drifted down the stream without a rider.

We saw the cowboy's hat come up above the water several times but we couldn't see him. His hat was tied on with a gee string but no one seemed to know that and in spite of all the cowboys gathered there as eye witnesses to the scene that boy lost his life. On account of the water being so swift and muddy we never saw his body until it drifted out to where the current was more shallow.

We recovered the body then and two cowboys riding real close together made a stretcher for him. We laid him across the two horses in front of the riders and in that way brought him to camp. By this time the body was so stiff that they took and stood him up against a wagon wheel and those hard-boiled, devil-may-care cowhands would go up to the corpse and talk to it, offering him cigarettes, etc., and then cuss because he didn't answer. It was a little too thick for me in spite of all I had seen with the vigilantes.

The cowboys showed little pity or consideration for a tenderfoot and still smaller consideration towards death, either for themselves or someone else.

I remember when we were working at the 3,9 (*sic*) Ranch on the mouth of Lance Creek a young fellow, relative to Sturgis or Goodall, the owners, came out from Cheyenne on a visit. The young man was an office worker, little used to riding or life on a ranch. Naturally he wanted a horse to ride and help in the roundup.

We were driving the cattle into a big corral and somehow that young fellow followed the cattle into the corral, and that onry Mizzou, who was one of the meanest men that ever lived anyway, shut the bars behind them. A big, black steer with long, sharp, mottled horns began "rimming" the fence—that is, circling the corral and running his horns along the poles. Every time he bumped into a post, he got a little madder.

The boy was sitting on his horse among the cattle and when the steer caught sight of him he made a dive at the horse and ripped it up the stifle (*sic*). The horse reared, throwing the boy to the ground, and like a flash the mad steer whirled and before anyone could do anything to prevent it he had plunged his bayonet-like horns through the young man's stomach.

The boy died soon afterwards and the steer was still circling the fence with the striffen (*sic*) of the stomach drying on his horn. Finally one of the punchers climbed on the fence and shot the steer down.

The Union Cattle Company had a great, fenced pasture of government land near Dewey. It was thirty-three miles around that pasture and every day it was one man's job to ride the fence. As we cut out the beeves that were going to be shipped we threw them into that pasture. When we had gathered up the required number of cattle, men were detailed to drive them to the railroad.

I will never forget the fall of 1888. Eight men that were supposed to be the most trustworthy employees of the Union were detailed to take the beeves to the railroad at Orin Junction, the nearest shipping point at that time. I was one of the eight men detailed to go.

We drove seven hundred head of cattle from the big pasture and set out on the long trek. We were well equipped for the journey with one big wagon that served both as a cook and bed wagon and plenty of provisions. A good cook that could drive four horses was provided and a day wrangler and a night wrangler, or "night-hawk," went along to take care of our string of forty-eight saddle horses.

We had traveled about sixty miles towards Orin Junction when a terrible, driving storm came up. The rain quickly developed into a blizzard and struck us about two o'clock in the night. Everyone got up and we were all busy trying to keep the cattle, and four of us at a time would go back to the wagon to change horses and get a bite to eat.

About four in the afternoon four of the boys went to the wagon and stayed there. They claimed that they did not have clothes enough and that they were actually freezing to death in the storm. They turned their horses out, ate, and crawled into bed to get warm.

They stayed so long that we sent another man after them and he stayed too. There were only three of us left—Matt Brown, Chas. "Big" Smith, and myself—trying to hold those 700 head of cattle. The storm increased but we stayed in the lead of it for twelve long hours, without a change of mounts or a bite to eat. We were cold and wet, nearly freezing in fact, but we would have held those cattle until we dropped.

The boss at the S&G Ranch, knowing that many thousands of dollars was at stake in that blizzard, started out to overtake us on the trail. He hitched up to a light buggy and drove the sixty miles without stopping to feed or water his horses, pushing through that blinding storm at an average of nine miles an hour. On reaching the mess wagon he found out about the state of affairs and kicked those five quitters out, ordering them to our relief. After riding twelve hours in the blizzard our horses were played out and we ourselves had stood more than ordinary men could bear.

About the time we were relieved the storm broke and ceased all together at sun up. The cattle had scattered over three miles of country but we had held them so well that they had managed to travel only about four miles from the wagon and we hadn't lost a one. When the sun came out the cattle stood quiet with the snow melting from their back in little rivulets.

After we were relieved we still had to ride the four miles to the wagon on our exhausted horses, but when we got to camp did we ever fill up on beefsteak and coffee! We only got to sleep about three hours and then we had to get up and help the cook move the outfit.

The rest of the trip was made without any (complaints), for such things were all in a day's work for the cowhand. When we returned to headquarters, the fall work being about over, I called for my time, only the oldest hands were kept on through the winter.

The average cowhand of that time was a happy-go-lucky sort of fellow. He lived from day to day with no thought of the future or no ambition. When he drew his time in the fall he usually hit for the nearest town and gambled away his money in one night. I have heard many-a one tell what a tough time he had to get through the winter, often living on one meal a day, or less, and picking up a few odd chores to eke out an existence. They would exchange their experiences on the next roundup and laugh over them.

After two years on the roundups I had enough and decided that I wanted to join a surveying crew on the new line that was going through.

2 Tale of the Southern Trail

As told to A. F. Dow by Jim Enochs.

The spring of 1878 found our outfit in feverish haste gathering together many thousand head of cattle preparatory to starting up the trail. . . . Our herd contained about 3,000 head, 2,000 of which were aged steers, the balance mixed stuff.

Everything went serene 'til long in September. Our herd had cropped the grass pretty close, necessitating a move. We had a neighbor herd just above us on the Saline Rio; they moved up the Rio for fresh pasture while we moved down. That was a lucky move for us and a fateful one for our neighbor, as we will explain later.

The serenity of our Kansas plateau was fast breaking up, experiencing many terrific electrical storms accompanied by torrential rains, which did little good as the rich buffalo grass had cured up, but did much damage to us, lightning killing a number of our steers and causing the rest to become very nervous. Along in the latter part of September all guards were called out on account of an approaching storm—a northwester—that struck us with a double-dyed-in-the-wool-vengeance.

Rain in torrents. Lightning. Words fail to express that inferno of electricity while the herd left the bed grounds in a sweeping trot headed for the Saline Rio, which was a small, shallow creek. Hastily plunging into the small stream, we commenced the ascent of a long, sloping bank, as we realized the hopelessness of stopping them until they reached the beyond.

Just two of us seemed to be on the job when the steers tackled that bank, as we were hurrying our horses the best we could to beat them to the top. Just then we were enveloped in a terrible flash of lightning. Down went my horse, flat on his stomach. He floundered to his feet instantly, and before I was able to lift a leg to mount him I was bloated worse than an alfalfa cow, but this stuffy feeling passed off almost as quickly as it came, and I mounted my horse and was back on duty. On reaching the plateau the herd, doubly frightened by that dreadful shock, was in full stampede.

Just myself and little Jack Londay and those 1,800 head of maddened beasts, thundering across the uncharted plateau. Our lives trusted to God on high and our noble horse. Try as we might we could not change their course, as we were trailing one behind, another some yards apart, trying to force them to run in a circle, bend them we could not. We were guided almost wholly by the almost incessant flashes of lightning.

Suddenly I saw steers almost under my stirrup. I pulled my horse to the right to escape those maddened steers; another flash revealed the gallant little Jack Londay just behind me.

A brilliant flash of lightning revealed the herd going pel-mel downhill, water splashing, mud flying. We spurred our horses at break-neck speed down that treacherous hill (and) soon we were in company with (the animals) again. The herd was badly winded after that ten-mile spin.

The storm having subsided we finally slowed them down, then let them scatter somewhat and graze to avoid another run. Morning came dawning—and mightily welcome too. We soon saw horsemen galloping swiftly toward us. The boys had spotted the herd and hastening to relieve us, warmly congratulated us, "Boys, you stayed with the ship."

We at once started for camp and by the merest chance rode up on the scene of our troubles in keeping clear of the herd the night before: the herd had run up on a great cut bluff from sixty to seventy feet high, we should judge. It was perpendicular, or rather, laying over, being in a great semi-circle. Fortune certainly favored us that we were on the opposite side of the herd from that dreadful cut-bluff.

No doubt, if we had been on the fluff-side of the herd, we would have been crowded over that . . . precipice, thus hitting nothing but air until we landed many feet below.

Nearing camp we saw a big steer laying dead where my horse had been stunned (by lightning). This big steer had been killed about ten feet from where I was riding and that accounted for my fall and swollen feeling. An old adage, "A miss is as good as a mile," but just the same, that stroke of lightning was too close for comfort. All is well that ends well.

All seemed serene. Wrong again. A few days later the men, instead of the herd, received a shock that sent us into a panic. As the crew was eating an early supper by daylight and was changing horses preparatory to night-guard, we saw a rapidly approaching horseman. As he pulled up we noticed that his horse was covered with perspiration.

We gave him a hearty welcome, greeting him with (the words) "You are just in time to get in on the eats."

He declined with thanks, saying he was on a more important mission as a courier sent out to notify people that the Cheyenne Indians had broken away from their reservations in Oklahoma and were headed north on the warpath. They were supposed to be in our vicinity right now but the preposterous (nature) of the report lacked both rhyme and reason because it was unbelievable that Indians could be on the warpath in Kansas. After delivering his message he tipped his hat—Stetson— said, "Adios," which means "goodbye," and galloped away, headed for Wakesney, six miles south on the Kansas Pacific Railroad.

Our first thought was defense. An inventory of our arsenal listed one old cap-and-ball shooter, so defense was out of the question in case of attack. Flight was our only salvation, so every man was requested to catch his speediest horse and saddle up, ready for an attack. . . . A vigilant watch was maintained throughout the night but morning dawned clear and bright but still no Indians, so the foreman ordered the herd grazed south towards the city of Wakesney. It was my guard on herd that day and three of us were on duty.

Ordinarily all hands are kept pretty busy holding up the herd so they will start to graze but on this particular morning instead of holding them up we helped them along until within a mile or two of Wakesney. The foreman had gone to town to learn the facts in the matter and he returned shortly afterward, stating that the reports of Indians on the rampage (*sic*) was only too late. By this time we were along the railroad track. The foreman had told me just before he left town a troop train had pulled in from Fort Riley. I was in some doubts as to the truth of the whole story until a shrill whistle warned us of an approaching train but in a few moments our doubts were dispelled as that long train thundered past loaded with men, guns, and horses galore.

That was the straw that broke the camel's back: I was scared before, but I was terrified now. However, the presence of Uncle Sam's fighting squad at least sent a degree of solace.

Wrong again. That fighting force disembarked and picked up the Indian trail, but that was all they did do, except to tell Slim Holstein, a cattleman who had organized a real fighting bunch of one hundred bronzed-faced cowboys, to go home, that Uncle Sam would take care of his wards.

History would have recorded a different story if Holstein and his boys had got away in the lead of Uncle Sam. As it was, it devolved upon some other troops sent from Nebraska to annihilate part of that renegade band near old Fort Robinson, just west of Crawford, Nebraska. If Holstein and his boys had had their way there would have been a fight before those blood-thirsty demons had ever crossed the Republican and without any help from a foreign troop.

The survivors of that band who had separated from the others are today our neighbors on the Rosebud and Tongue River in Montana. I mentioned our neighbor herdsmen who moved up the Saline Rio while we moved down earlier in my story. Well, he was caught directly in the path of those blood-thirsty demons. Part of the crew was killed and pillaged while part escaped.

He no doubt thought that they were friendly Indians, because he made no effort to escape. Those were real exciting times in western Kansas.

The Indian scare had finally subsided but the prairie fires did not. About the last of September we sent around about 1,400 head of steers up on Beaver Creek in western Kansas to be wintered, leaving 400 head to be shipped or sold to feeders. I was put in charge of this small herd, which was to be a stepping stone, provided it was handled properly. I felt the responsibility keenly and used every precaution to see that no harm befell them. I will admit that the promotion made me feel a little bit chesty. I was just a kid; you could not blame me. I entertained visions of a trail boss and a big herd. All went well until one day there appeared a dense smoke some forty miles north of us. A north wind was blowing, driving fire and smoke eastward.

We watched that smoke carefully, fearing the wind might change, and if it did there was no stream large enough to guarantee safety. Night enveloped us, revealing a huge fire illuminating the whole heavens, which increased my anxiety. I took the authority bit square in my teeth and ordered every horse tied or put in the rope corral (some forty head). All hands were sleep dressed and ready for action; every guard was requested to report any change in the wind.

All went well until the third watch went on duty, which included Jack and myself. We imagined we smelled smoke and galloped up on high elevation to see if we could determine anything as to the fire, and we discovered what we dreaded—a brisk wind and dense smoke headed directly toward the camp. There was not time for delay; we sent our horses back at full speed to camp yelling like a Comanche Indian, "Fire! Fire!"

All the boys were on their feet at once. I asked two men to stay with the cook and to try to save the wagon and horses while the balance of us would tackle the herd. They were resting placidly, and we could not get them started off the bed ground.

We lashed them with quirts, slickers, ropes, and the like. I asked one of the boys that carried a pistol to fire a few shots. That settled things. They must have thought it was lightning again, for they left the bed ground on a two-forty gait, knocking about all the water out to the little old Saline River; plunging through that water scared them badly and a veritable stampede followed.

Jack and I were at the lead when they crossed the Rio, trying to hold them up. Our task was hopeless. The dense smoke enveloped us. That was a terrible ride, through dense smoke, over uncharted territory, with only a small stream to check the fire, and we resigned our soul to God and our faithful horses.

We stopped the herd a mile or so from the river. They bunched together, which was a bad omen. If they did not scatter, we were afraid they would in all probability run again.

We rode off in opposite directions from them, say a distance of one hundred yards, and waited results. The fire had reached the river and checked. Just as far as we could see east and west, just one inferno of flames. We did not know what minute firebrand might blow across the river and sweep up on us. Laboring under the most intense fear, panic-stricken, two little youngsters, "some mothers' sons," out in the smoke.

Our horses had just gotten their wind, when off went the herd thundering down that grade, headed straight for camp and that wall of fire, absolutely uncontrolled and uncontrollable. We kept abreast of them the best we could, hoping they would stop at the river's bank. For once our hopes were realized, but they milled for hours, compelling us to stand by and take that dreadful smoke.

Morning dawned, found us all alive, cattle, horses, and men. The boys charged with having the wagon and horses had a real man's job. As we looked back where we knew this camp had been we could see nothing but fire. We did not know the fate of the men or camp for hours.

Thus ended my first boss job. It started rather badly, but it ended better because my vision of a trail boss and a big herd came to pass. Today I am thankful that I saw service in those older and better days and that I was permitted to add my little might toward the onward march of civilization.

3 Life in a Line Camp

From an Interview with Harry Williams of Basin.

It is late fall on the range. The spring and summer roundups long since have been completed. The beef drive is over and the beef deliveries have just been made. The boys are all back at the home ranch, some wondering what now and others knowing what is ahead. It is a time of necessary adjustment between summer and winter.

Some of the riders who are not needed are given their checks and laid off until spring. These men pass their winter in various ways. Some have jobs waiting that they return to every winter—clerking, tending bar, or helping in the livery stable, while others drift back home for a visit, and still a few who just wander.

Those cowboys who were kept on at the ranch the years 'round were men who by their former work have established a reputation for honesty and dependability. It was not uncommon to find riders who had spent eight or ten or twelve years in the employ of the same ranch.

With the seasonal riders on their way it was the task of the foreman to assign the winter's work to those kept on. It is the foreman speaking:

"Harry Williams, your old pleasant job is waiting for you. See that all the M L stock is driven out of the mountains. You will winter at the Horse Ranch on Trapper Creek. Bob Vestal, you and Bill Dikeman will put in a new camp on the Stinking Water, above Coon Creek. The rest of you will work out from the home ranch."

In those few words we had received our orders for at least four months. We were expected to know, and did, the work laid out for us.

Each camp had its separate, distinct territory to look after. It extended a length of 25 or 30 miles. In general it was their duty to see that water holes were open, that the cattle were feeding on the best forage grounds available, and in case of bad local storms it sometimes became necessary for them to be moved to a more favorable location, to prevent loss in weight and loss in numbers of cattle. If the winter proved to be a warm, open winter, some of the camps were discontinued, as there would be no need for them.

If you had been with us thirty minutes after we received our orders this is what you would have seen: Bob and Bill in the saddle room getting packs, saddles and blankets, extra cinches, ropes, and any other articles they were apt to need in their winter work. The first day was usually taken up making repairs on these various articles. First the pack saddles were repaired, if any repairs were needed, for everything used in those outlying camps was moved by pack horse. So the pack outfits were gotten ready for use, the necessary grub and cooking outfits gathered up and packed and our few personal belongings, including clothing, were also collected.

If a new camp was necessary, the campsite was selected with great care. Nearby there must be good feed for the saddle horses; it must be close to water and dry wood for camp use. It was the rule, not the exception, to build a dugout for winter quarters for ourselves. First we selected a cut bank that had enough clay in it not to cave easily and that was seven or eight feet in height. Then we dug a twelve by twelve room and a fireplace in the end against the hill. We made a roof of poles, covered it first with grass and leaves to keep the dirt from coming through. The front of the dugout was a shoulder of dirt which we left standing. In this we cut a door, which was made of poles covered with fresh cow or elk hide. The door was hung on wooden hinges, each part of the hinge being three foot long. There were no nails in existence, so wooden pegs were used entirely in building, where nails today are used. A window was cut and covered with a flour sack for light. The fireplace chimney was made by laying short poles two in one directions and two on top running the opposite direction until the necessary height was reached. Then they were plastered with mud.

The simplest possible cooking equipment was used. The outfit consisted of three Dutch ovens, a couple of frying pans, tin plates, tin cups, knives, forks, spoons, and butcher knives . . . Our grub lacked variety. We had breakfast and supper. There was no noon meal, as we rode all day.

I will describe one meal. This meal will be like all other meals for four months. It consisted of beef steak, with an occasional roast and brown gravy. There were always hot biscuits, coffee, and evaporated fruits. Of course we had sugar and the seasonings. There were no vegetables or canned fruits. They made their appearance some years later. Nearly all men that worked on the range at that time were good camp cooks.

During our four months in the line camp our evenings were long and monotonous. Here as in the case of our meals the description of one evening will duplicate all others with rare exception. The large cow outfits did not allow playing cards in any of their ranches or outlying camps. There was an occasional chess or checker board, however.

Occasionally one drew a "drone" for a partner in line camp but usually there were men of some interests or hobbies. Story-telling was common—those we had heard and those we invented. Most of the evenings however were spent working with leather, rawhide, and hair. As one would expect, most of the boys put in their time making the everyday needs, as quirts, and hackamores, mending cinches and worn-out bridles. Yet others turned to items of real art—such as the elaborate hair-made bridle, the fine watch chains and fobs. Some of the products were marvelous creations in their line. One hand worked for two years to complete a difficult and elaborate hair-made bridle and then sold it for $100. Another worked in leather and rawhide and sold his for $75. The only light for this work was that called a "bitch." It was a rag with stone tied in it. The stone was pushed down into tallow with the rag projecting as a wick.

Let us "look on" in a typical line camp. It was getting dark. The boys have just ridden into camp. This means supper to cook and horses to be taken care of. Our rule was, "each one must do his share and then all work is easy." It is Bill's turn to prepare the meal. Bob takes both horses and looks after them, as well as the other four head. The men have three head apiece. Bob heads for his home, the dugout. Riding all day without dinner in the cold weather works up an appetite that can do justice to two pounds of choice steak and hot biscuits cooked in a Dutch oven. (There are no biscuits made finer than those from a Dutch oven!) The meal is complete with coffee and evaporated fruit.

Supper dishes are washed and put away. Then the men are facing a long winter evening—not for the one evening but for four months. They are young, healthy animals full of vitality, built up from a life in the open. They have to have action or it seems they'll explode. The first few evenings they spend telling stories they know or can think of. Then they talk of their girls and the folks back home. The saddle horse was a topic always open for discussion and many debates arose from the question of who had the best horse in the string.

An actual story told by Bill Dikeman in the line camp follows:

"I had come north the spring of '84 and gotten a job with 76. The foreman said, 'Can you ride a rough string?'—meaning outlaw horses.

"'Yes,' I answered, 'I can ride anything that ever wore the 76 brand,' and I was sure I could.

"The next morning when the saddle bunch came in the foreman said, 'We are making a short ride this morning. Bill, you can catch that black striped-faced horse.'

"He was gentle enough to saddle and stood perfectly still for me to climb on. And, Bob, to this day, I don't know what happened. In less than a minute the boys had picked me up. I had a sprained leg and my pride was lower than a snake in the grass. This, my first defeat, hit me hard.

"'Say, Boss,' I said, 'I guess I'll ride on.'

"But the boss said, 'You are on the 76 payroll.'

"I rode their rough string that summer. We pulled into the home ranch the first of July for a two-day clean-up and a short rest. As we sat around talking in the evening I asked if anyone knew where Old Demon was.

"'Yes,' someone spoke up, 'he is ranging, yes, over on Old Pinie. Why?'

"'I have a lot of respect for that old horse. I would like to see him again,' I mused.

"The morning following we run him in and that afternoon I rode him. It took everything I had to do it. I patted him on the neck. 'Don't feel bad, old pal,' I said, 'no hard feeling on my part. We will make this contest two out of three.'

"Then it was fall at the ranch. All of the summer hands were getting checks. The boss handed me mine. 'Say, hold on a minute,' I said. 'I want to buy Demon. How much do you want for him?'

"'Enough to make the bill of sale legal,' the boss replied.

"'How will five dollars do?' I bargained.

"It was agreeable to the boss, so he took it off my check. I went and got him. The next morning we finished one contest two to one.

"Demon was a beauty and a showed thoroughbred. He was black as tar with a white stripe from forehead to the tip of his nose. He was gentle to handle but when you got on him—oh boy!

"The next day was Pioneer Day in Buffalo. We all went in. I got one of the boys to enter Demon as a bucker. We pitied the boy that drew him and another who asked for a change. One of our boys said to the managers, 'I have a friend that would like a chance at the black horse but he has not paid an entrance fee.'

"'Okay,' said the manager, 'bring him along, pay his fee, and then he'll have a chance at the prizes, as well as the black.'

"Demon drew ten dollars as worst bucker; I got ninety dollars for first in riding.

"Doing as well in Buffalo turned my thoughts naturally to Cheyenne, for Frontier Days were just seven days away. I rode into Cheyenne the night of the sixth day. I entered my horse as a bucker. In this class the next morning he again won first money. I entered as a rider and got second. I did not have the good luck to get my horse in the drawing but after the prizes were awarded I asked the privilege of riding Demon in exhibition. It was granted and the old boy sure put on a show. I had ridden him enough to get used to his way of going and did a very good job of riding myself. The crowd cheered and cheered. They boys passed the hat. With its contents, the Black's winnings, and my prizes, it made me more than the boy who won first.

"I sold the black that night to a man from Tombstone, Arizona, for $250. They changed his name to Tombstone, known as the worst bucker in all the west. In the year of 1888 the owner of the Sheridan Inn bought Tombstone and Agate. Both were veterans of many bucking contests. They were now kept at the Inn for the attraction and entertainment of their eastern guests.

"In September the Denver Rodeo was coming off. The riders at this time who were thought good enough to have a chance at first place were few. Miner of Colorado had won the championship twice and Sawder of Idaho had won it once. Knight, of McCloud, Alberta, Canada, got second twice. There were many other riders from the western country who were good enough to be a threat.

"Then Harry Brenum entered the picture. He was a lad whose father died when he was young. He proceeded to run his father's ranch. From the age of 16 to 23 he had worked from the big horse outfits around Sheridan. The men he had worked for and many others including Lord Wallop and Moncrief Brothers backed their belief in the boy with action. Wallop kept Harry on his payroll.

"There were thousands of horses in the Sheridan district, and many hard horses to ride among them. They were gathered and brought to the Wallop Ranch. With these and Tombstone and Agate from the Sheridan Inn, he had a great bunch of buckers to work out on to fit himself for the big day at Denver. Wallop went to Denver with Harry and paid all his expenses.

"As a lover of horses I am paying this, my last tribute, to a 'Grand Horse,' 'A Prince,' 'A Champion,' in his own right. Harry used Tombstone for his last workouts before leaving for Denver. It was Tombstone more than any other horse that put Harry in shape to win first and along with this he won the friendship of the crowd. After the decision of the judges and the prizes had been awarded the cowboys carried Harry on their shoulders from the grounds to the center of the town—'a champion'—in the true sense of the word—a smile that never wore off—and a pleasant word for all.

"You know, these other winners as Sawder, Miner, and others could have ridden the same horses as Brenum, but not quite in the same way. Some of them were so temperamental that the slightest thing gone wrong caused them to be irritable and hateful, revealing the lack of good dispositions, but never Brenum; always he wore the fine, cheerful smile, always a kind greeting and everywhere displayed his winning way.

"He rode Tombstone and Agate while they were at an age that they were bucking their toughest. On exhibition one of his accomplishments was, as the horse was brought up Brenum stepped across him and while at his roughest bucking went down on the left side, touched a toe to the ground, came up, seated again, and down as gingerly on the right, touched a toe to the ground, and was back so nimbly it is difficult to believe, unless you have seen it done."

 A Christmas in the Mountains

Collected by Charles Fowkes from "Aunt" Agnes Baxter of Evanston, Wyoming.

In the year 1879 my husband, John M. Baxter, and my brother, Isaac Smith, went to work in the mountains about fifteen miles west of Bear Lake at Hodge's Saw and Shingle Mill. My brother was getting out logs with a yoke of oxen; the oxen were better adapted for that kind of work. They had what they called drags—sometimes three, two, or one log according to the size, with a chain fastened around them so that they could be dragged to the mill. My husband was working also, packing shingles.

One day when my brother was bringing in a drag the oxen became frightened and ran away. He tried in vain to stop them and in his attempt he got his leg between a tree and the drag, breaking it in two places about six inches apart. They sent to Lake Town for a doctor and he immediately set out for the mill but on the way he encountered four bears; in order to escape them he had to return to Lake Town. The next morning he resumed his journey, taking a friend with him.

I was living at Randolph, Utah, at that time and as soon as arrangements could be made for me to leave Randolph I hastened to nurse my brother. I found him in a very serious condition. My husband and the other men working at the mill put splints of shingles wrapped in cotton batton (*sic*) and bound the limb tightly. They were also pouring cold water on the limb to relieve the intense pain. My brother had suffered so intensely that he was affected mentally. The pouring of the cold water had caused his burning limb to become parboiled.

I had taken with me a bottle of Arnica and with this I bathed the limb thoroughly after removing the splints. I took a tight (*sic*) bandage dipped in flour starch, which hardened almost like a cast. This soon relieved my brother's suffering.

I had never been in the mountains before and this was indeed a beautiful place with its tall pines and balsam trees, service berries and wild currant bushes, the aroma of them scenting the air. I was captivated by the sight.

At the mill there were thirteen cabins clustered among the trees, but so thick was the verdure that we could not see the cabins of our neighbors but we could hear the men at work. This was the most ideal place in the summer. It was so peaceful and calm. The pheasants or pine hens were so tame that they would come into the dooryard and eat crumbs thrown from the table.

At this time the mill was making finishing lumber and shingles for the Logan Temple, which was in the course of construction.

September 10th of the year we had our first fall of snow. It was three feet of the beautiful (stuff) but forced us to move to the U. O. Mill ten miles west of Garden City. It was a lovely place in an open canyon with a large stream of sparkling water where we could catch mountain trout and there was a beautiful grove of timber. Many picnic parties came up from the city of Logan to enjoy an outing in the canyon.

My husband built us a log cabin with two rooms. One was large enough to accommodate twelve boarders who ate their meals with us while they were working at the mill.

At this time we had another of my brothers come to live at the mill. His name was James Smith. He had a wife and baby girl three months old. My brother Isaac had been taken to Paris, Idaho, where he remained until he had fully recovered from his accident. Also at this time there were fifteen men with teams who had planned to haul logs to the mill all winter. Enough provisions had been provided to last many months.

All went well until the 20th of December when a severe snowstorm came. The snow continued to fall for thirteen days and was from twelve to fifteen feet deep. During this storm we did not see the sun. This changed our plans. The loggers returned home to their families, leaving us snow-bound—three men, two women, and a baby. We decided that we could no longer remain there.

Christmas came. Oh! what a lovely holiday season. We could see nothing but snow, beautiful snow—but that was before we saw so much of it. Our cabin was entirely snowed over. The men had to dig a trench from our house to the stream. With those two high walls of snow it looked as if we were buried alive.

We then made skis and when the snow was firm and settled we went out on the hillside and practiced sliding with them until we became quite expert. You can imagine our homesickness when we had no communication from our friends. We at last decided that we could endure this loneliness no longer and we made up our minds that we would get home.

The snow sleighs were made. Then we waited for the weather to clear and for the snow to get crusted before we made our effort to escape from our snowy imprisonment. Oh! how long it seemed just waiting. At last the day came when we could commence our treacherous journey. The men loaded our truck, some bedding, and some food on one of the sleighs and started for the top of the ridge only three miles away, but it took all day to get there and return to the cabin preparatory for our exodus the next morning.

On January the 8th, 1880, at ten o'clock in the morning, we made our start—my brother James, his wife and baby, Sam Smith, a friend, my husband, and myself. We could not use the skis only for about a mile, as it was a very steep climb to the top of the ridge. So we arrived, making our way very slowly to the top without a mishap, except Toby, the cat, ran away from us. He became frightened of a porcupine and climbed a tree. That was the last time we ever saw him, although we were told that he went about five miles down the canyon to where Brother Sam Pike lived.

Night was falling and we had to camp in a little grove of pine trees. We had to shovel the snow away and made a bed of pine boughs. Dry trees were cut down to keep a fire burning all night. We were comfortable but could not sleep, and we were very thankful when morning came.

Immediately after breakfast next morning we commenced our journey anew. The weather had moderated. The snow began to fall again. It was wet and heavy, which made it extremely difficult for us to travel: our skis became so heavy with the wet snow that it was impossible to use them, so we abandoned them and waded through the deep snow, which by this time was waist deep. We had to fight every foot of the way through willows and brush while the snow was beating in our faces, almost blinding us.

My brother James was pulling the sleigh in which the baby was riding and while he was going around a steep mountain the sleigh overturned, throwing the box with the baby down the mountainside. You can imagine our anguish. We hurried to the overturned box and found the baby sitting up smiling. We were indeed overjoyed. The baby seemed to have enjoyed her thrilling escapade.

We traveled this way until sundown. We were worn and weary, making out way continuously on toward Bear Lake and as near due east as we could. We again made a fire and as it burned it was gradually sinking down, down, into the snow until it looked as though we were looking into a deep well. We did not receive any warmth from this fire and we were tired and worn out. Our clothing was wet and frozen stiff. We were very hungry, not having had anything since breakfast. We were not able to carry food with us. We knew that we were not far from a hollow where the Garden City people had a wood road, used in the winter time, leading to the timber.

My brother James, being an expert on skis, and seemingly stronger that the others, started out for Garden City for help. He was not gone long when he returned with help. Two men bringing a team and sleigh returned with him. He had found the wood road about one-half mile from where we were and just four miles from Garden City. They could not bring the sleigh to us, so I was placed on one of the horses and the others took hold as best they could. The horse plunged through the deep snow but I was so exhausted that I was not frightened of falling off the horse. We soon reached the sleigh and it was not long before we reached Garden City. We were indeed a very happy and thankful group of people.

Accommodations were not good in those days. We had just one large room for everyone. We made our beds on the floor and put our quilts under and over us. The men sat up all night. We slept in our wet clothes and with the warm fire we had a real steam bath and awakened in the morning feeling refreshed and none the worse for our thrilling experience.

Two days after this a terrible blizzard came over the valley. Had we come that night, we all could have perished. We waited in Garden City one week before we could get word to our people in Randolph.

5 An Old-Time Christmas in Jackson Hole

Collected from S. N. Leek by Nellie H. VanDerveer.

During the fall of 1888 two young men, not so long from the East, traveled the trail form Henry's Lake in Idaho to Jackson Lake, Wyoming. They had heard of Jackson Hole, of its being a rendevous for horse thieves and so forth. "Beaver Dick," who was camped near by with a hunting party, told them of a good cabin with a fireplace on the bank of the Snake River near by. They occupied and prepared it for the winter.

But unknown to the Nebraska Boys (as they are called in this account) three other men appeared. They located in another cabin some two miles away and prepared to spend the winter. The two parties became intimate and visited back and forth, the second party becoming known as "Arizona George," John, and Bob.

Each party secured their winter's meat from the thousands of elk that passed near by on their way to the lower part of the valley to spend the winter. Each party also secured bear. This gave them plenty of bear fat to fry their trout in, for as soon as the ice formed they had splendid fishing in both lake and river. Some very large trout were taken. These were of the black spotted or cut-throat variety.

As days passed, the snow grew deeper but little fur was collected. Everything seemed to be laying up for a long, cold winter. Prior to this time beaver was all but exterminated.

Christmas time was drawing near. George, John, and Bob called at the beckon of the Nebraska Boys, inviting them over for Christmas dinner. To avoid any mistake in the date, Nick remarked, "Yes, we will be over tomorrow to eat Christmas dinner with you."

"No," George replied, "Christmas is day after tomorrow. We have an almanac, have kept record, and know we are right."

The matter was compromised: the Nebraska Boys were to go over and eat Christmas dinner on George's Christmas Day, then they were to return the compliment by eating New Year's dinner with the Nebraska Boys on their New Year's Day.

Nick and Steve went over, had a nice visit, told wild west stories, partook of a grand dinner, and then snow-shoed home in the evening. Come time for the New Year's dinner the three went over, told some more wild west stories.

Come time for dinner all set around, about to partake of the feast when it commenced to grow dark very rapidly. George remarked, "I didn't know it was getting that late."

Nick replied, "It's not late; it's something else." And all, somewhat alarmed, rushed outdoors and witnessed a nearly complete eclipse of the sun.

During the dinner Arizona George remarked, "You boys are right. Our almanac says nothing about an eclipse on the last day of the old year, so this must be the first day of the New Year."

As January moved along and February came, there was not much doing. Snow was getting deeper. It still clung to the trees. Often during the day or night a loud crack would be heard. Some tree loaded beyond its capacity would break with a loud report. The slight breeze out on the lake was settling the snow there, making travel with snowshoes possible.

Steve would go out, select a dry tree, fell it in the deep snow, cut it in suitable lengths for the fireplace, split the larger cuts, carry them near the cabin door, then call Nick, who would open the door and take the wood away as it shot down the snow slide into the cabin. In the meantime Nick would have the meal ready, the second and last for the day.

Spring came at last. With it the Nebraska boys trekked southward directly opposite to animals and birds, where each located 160 acres. Each built a cabin on one of the tracts and were at home.

I wish our story could end here but there are more cards to deal. During the winter of 1888 and 1889 the snowfall was very light, the summer of 1889 very dry. Quite a number of settlers located in the valley that summer. They witnessed forest fires upon every side throughout the summer. It was they that prevented all the winter range of the elk within the valley from being destroyed by fire that summer. It was started by a camping party from Salt Lake City, who, on being overtaken and asked to return and help to extinguish the fire they had started were very glad to do so.

As one extreme is apt to follow another, the following winter was very severe. This drove the game down in great numbers and as these new settlers witnessed the great destruction wrought by the flames during the summer, for lack of snowfall, they now witnessed the suffering and death by starvation of 20,000 game animals within this little mountain locked valley during the winter because of excessive snowfall.

The number of residents within the valley during this winter of 1889 and 1890 was sixty-seven persons, an increase of about fifty for the year.

Prior to this time no wagon had ever been hauled over Teton Pass. These new settlers camped by the way and built the road ahead as they came—cut trees and logs and dragged them from the way with horses, taking them some two weeks to cross the pass. The load of each wagon was lightened as much as possible, the extra things being packed across on horses. It required eight horses to pull the nearly empty wagon to the top. The wagons were let down the opposite side with rough locks on the wheels and trees dragging behind.

6 Stories of a Round-up

Extracted from fragments of an unlabeled manuscript found in the Federal Writers Project files.

It is a rule of the round-up regimen that after eating each man places his cutlery and cup into a large pan placed there for the purpose—also, the plates are stacked neatly beside the pan. Even if the stranger had not known of this custom he could have learned from the procedure of the other men. However he ignored the detail even after the cook had asked him to follow the rule, as it was so easy to forget equipment carelessly thrown down.

Thus, the boys decided to give him a lesson by giving him a hazing— said hazing meaning to place the offender over a bedroll and proceed to thrash him with a strap, usually a belt, until he admits he has learned his lesson.

This was before the time of the gasoline lantern, and candles were used for light in the mess tent. No one could tell exactly who it was that made the first move. Supper had been over for some time, and the stranger's dishes were still where he had left them on the ground. A bedroll that had no place in the mess tent was placed in the center of the tent and many hands seized the stranger and draped him over the roll, face down, and then the light went out.

There was a few grunts and much action of milling bodies in the darkness before someone relighted the candle. In the sudden light consternation was the principle expression on the men's faces, as the foreman, Jim Atkinson, uncoiled himself from the bedroll instead of the stranger that should have been there, and the stranger was conspicuous by his absence.

It was surprising how quickly the tent emptied after that, each man making for his bed as though it was most urgent that he do so—which it probably was! There was some suppressed laughter, but no audible comments from the bed grounds under the stars, as the men settled down for the night. The night hawk's droning voice as he circled the cattle and sang as he went was the only sound heard in the quiet night.

• • •

There were many stories told among the old timers that were interviewed as they remi-
nisced about those happy days, but it would take a volume to chronicle them all that lost
nothing in the telling. However, there is one more that should be told.

Hal Sommer, one of Charlie Sommer's sons, joined the round-up one
year to help gather in his father's cattle. All of Charlie's children—and
he had twelve—were good riders and well liked. So Hal was received by
the round-up crew with much enthusiasm from all of them. It had been
a rainy season and the men had obtained some liquor for "snake bite."
That there was no snakes on the Plains did not matter; the whiskey was
there anyway in case there might be. Most of the crew came in early
that day and although no one was snake-bitten it was a dreary, wet day
and the bottle was produced and passed around.

They were camped near an old homestead claim that had been abandoned; the buildings were falling apart and the toilet lay on its side, its
two holes cut in the seat looking out at the world that had deserted it
like eyes.

Hal, full of good cheer and more liquor than he should have had, told
the crew that that outhouse was just what was needed for the homestead
that had recently been purchased by his father. It is doubtful just how
many toilets the boys saw as they gravely agreed with Hal that that particular toilet was needed at the new homestead. However, with much
getting in each other's way, they managed to hitch the four horses to
the empty bed wagon and pulled up beside the old toilet. With much
comment from the side lines and suggestions the toilet was placed in
the wagon, but instead of laying it on its side as they should have, they
set it upright.

As it was Hal's toilet they decided it fit and proper that Hal should
sit in it while it was being conveyed to its new home. Like a king on a
throne Hal mounted the seat and two other men in the driver's seat the
start was made. The rest of the men mounted their horses and prepared
to accompany Hal and his toilet and assist in the ceremonies befitting
such an important occasion.

In a loud voice Hal started singing "The Old 97" and as the others
joined them the horses jumped at the sudden uproar and jerked into

a frightened lurch, running madly away over the uneven ground. The jerk proved too much for the unsupported toilet and it fell out of the wagon with Hal still sitting on his throne.

When the now thoroughly sobered men had the horses under control they came back to pick up Hal, who was still sitting in the toilet, unhurt, and still singing "The Wreck of the Old 97." He was finally persuaded to leave his new possession to the elements for the time being and go back to camp and sleep it off.

For a long time the upturned toilet lay on the plains, a mute reminder of a good plan gone wrong, but a lot of fun while it lasted.

7 Last Great Buffalo Hunt of Washakie and His Band in the Big Horn Basin Country

Written by James I. Patten, an early Indian agent at Fort Washakie, and was published in the *Big Horn County Rustler*, March 26, 1920.

It had always been the custom of the Shoshones after settling at their agency on the Wind River Reservation, after raising and harvesting their crops, to make annually during the fall and winter months, a buffalo hunt to the Big Horn Basin for the purpose of eking out the supply of rations issued to them weekly by the government by laying in supplies of buffalo and other game meats and to take and prepare for market the hides and peltry produced from the hunt. The meat was first cut into thin strips, hung on poles, to dry in the sun, then packed in parfleches, which made it easy to pack and kept it free from dust and dirt.

At this time, October 1874, the writer was employed at the agency as government teacher of the Indian youths and was serving as a lay reader under a commission of the Protestant Episcopal church. However, the government decided that during the absence of the Indians from the Agency the teacher must take a vacation for the time and draw no pay, whereupon it was suggested to Dr. Irwin, the agent, that he make application for permission for the teacher to accompany the Indians on their hunt and establish a "roaming school" while the hunt lasted.

The request having been submitted by the agent to the Indian Commissioner it was favorably considered and granted and preparations were duly put under way to carry out the new idea. A commodious tent fifty or sixty feet in circumference was made and to avoid the use of great numbers of tent poles made by the Indians was so constructed as to have but one center pole, standing on end, tied and fastened to the top of the tent. When the center pole was lifted and slipped into the top of the tripod the tent was raised at the same time and was pegged down around the edges, and it made a comfortable place to accommodate 25 or 35 scholars. When everything was in readiness it was found that four animals would be required on which to pack the necessary outfit. Besides the two saddle ponies I had one assistant and furnished all supplies at my own expense, except the few text books.

The Indians set the date of departure for October 16, having drawn their rations the day before. On this morning the Indians pulled out as fast as they could get things packed and their horses gathered in, to meet at the first rendezvous, which was on the Big Wind River, at Meritt's Crossing. Here Washakie, the chief, ordered a halt until some young warriors were despatched along the proposed trail to watch for hostiles and at the same time to ascertain in what direction the buffalo herds were retreating. We stayed here for three days, when the messengers returned, reporting game everywhere in the Basin.

On the 19th we made another move and made the Muddy. There were 1,800 Indians in the procession, including men, women, and children, and as we moved over the wild waste of sagebrush hills, sand dunes, canyons, and dry creeks I felt very much, surrounded as I was with such a remarkable cavalcade, as a sure-enough nomad of the desert.

The next day, the 20th, we crossed a trail of hostiles half a mile wide, which caused Washakie to order a change in the course and strike the Owl Creek Mountains over the Red Canyon Trail and thus avoid hostile contact. The weather until now had been most beautiful. It had now become cloudy and turned cold and disagreeable and by the time we reached the ascent to the foot of the Divide a terrible storm of wind and snow had set in. Reaching a camping place later we set the tents, retired in our robes without fire or supper.

On the morning of the 21st the fury of the storm had increased so that we could make no move and here we stayed four days snow-bound.

The mercury dropped rapidly and there was suffering in the camp. The rations were growing short. No game had yet been taken and the snow was so deep that a few warriors who courageously essayed a short hunt met with misfortune. One Indian was thrown from his horse and severely injured. Another came in badly frozen, all without any game. About this time all the food in the camp was my own scant supply, so I had to divide.

An incident happened at this camp that gave me a better conception of these people than I had had before. I needed wood for the tent and as I was preparing to go out for it at the tent opening lay several armfuls of fine, dry pine supplied by my neighbors. As the atmosphere cleared I wished to go cut with the others and try to kill some game. Washkie ordered me not to go out. In asking Norkett, the interpreter, what the chief meant, I was informed that Washakie was so fearful that something might happen that I must run no risk and said, "If I should go back without Patten, then. . . ."

On the 25th the band again began to move. The snow was deep and the air bitterly cold and I shall never forget the struggles made by the men, horses, and women in climbing to the top of these mountains. The children were crying from cold all around me. Some stopped and built fires for them. Others kept on and eventually arrived on the ridge.

Here we were above the clouds. The sun, it seemed to me, never shone so brightly and I drew up to take a survey of a very beautiful scene that was presented beneath us. The earth was not visible between where we stood and the tops of the Rockies and the entire country was enveloped by a continuous sea of clouds upon which the rays of the sun shone down with such splendor it seemed like gazing at a wonderful ocean of pure milk. We found ourselves that night camping at the Red Springs, and there was just a suspicion of snow. It was mild and the springs not frozen. This was the beginning of my first experience in the Big Horn Basin.

Striking Owl Creek we stopped for one day. I saw at this camp the Indians in another light. They were not the same who a few days ago had left the agency self complacent and mild. Huge fires were burning throughout the camp. Harangues were made by the old men, incantations made by medicine men, drums were beaten and rattles shaken.

Washakie himself seemed on this wild and weird camping ground like another being. His voice, loud and clear, rang out on the night air as he addressed his people. His face lighted up and caused great enthusiasm among the young and old and they joined in singing their old war-hunting songs and the drums beat louder as one and then another of the old men took the speech, enumerating a victory here and then there over their enemies, their own bravery and their success on the hunt, and asking that success be given them at the present time. Their exercises then coming to an end, the younger and older boys rushed together to the great fire, plucked from it the burning faggots and with these in their hands different bands rushed toward other bands likewise armed. These they hurled with great force at each other, as if to kill.

They armed themselves again and again made charges back and forth, back and forth until the faggots or they themselves were exhausted. All did not escape injury and when any were knocked heels over head the elder ones whopped and yelled as encouragement to the youngsters to keep at it. While the play lasted it seemed to me very brutal, yet it was one of the wildest, most weird and exciting nights I have ever experienced, for I saw not the tame but the wild, untamable warriors of hundreds of years ago.

Washakie had sent out runners again to find the buffalo. They were reported near Gooseberry Creek. The game was found, it was said, about forty miles above the mouth of the creek. As we approached within a few miles of the herd, Washakie rode up and invited me to go with him. Riding to a high point, where we could see far and near, he took out his field glasses, scanned the country around, and then handed the glasses to me for a look. He then asked me what I saw.

I said, "Buffalo."

"Yes," he said, "heap."

When again we joined the hunters, and as we had now come quite close to the herd, I noticed that some of the men struck off by themselves, saw them quietly ride around small herds and turn them into the general herd. I also noticed that many of the men had led two horses this way. These they were now changing, the ridden to be led and the others to be ridden. The latter were the buffalo horses, never used in common, but skilled in coming upon and avoiding the attack of the game.

Finally, when the herd had been pretty well centralized, the old Weraugough, who was in command, like the general that he was, rose in his stirrups and in a low voice, never to be forgotten, gave command to charge in a body.

Mine was a very good horse and I jumped with the rest, but found I was nowhere, for in an instant one hundred had passed me. The whole army plunged into the band of several hundred animals, scattering it in all directions. The firing was terrific. It seemed like a long while, but I presume it did not last more than three quarters of an hour. The division had been routed and the field was covered with a hundred and twenty-five dead. The hunters killed at least one each, others two to three each, and one or two more expert from five to seven.

From Gooseberry we came straight across country, crossing the Greybull about where Otto now stands, thence down to the Stinking Water, or as the Indians called it "Timp-pe-shen-nak-ko," which is now called the Shoshone, striking it at the old Bridger Crossing and following down that stream to its mouth, making camp on the Big Horn River.

Here the writer was taken ill, caused by the change of diet, and Washakie held the camp there until my recovery. Comanche, an Indian doctor or medicine man, said to me, "You are very sick."

I said, "Yes."

He said, "Your medicine doesn't seem to cure you."

I said, "It doesn't seem to."

"Well," he said, "come to my camp, and I can cure you."

I went and he told me to remove my hat, which being done he laid his hands on my head, commenced an incantation which lasted about fifteen minutes. He then produced large vegetables or dried roots and with a sharp knife shaved off a number to thin slices, directed his wife to bring a cup of water, into which the slices were placed, allowed to stand a few minutes, and then renewed the incantation ceremony. This being completed he gave me the cup, directing me to chew and swallow a few slices of the root, after which he took the cup and with the liquid and balance of the roots bathed and rubbed my breast and bowels. This treatment being completed he produced a fine white powder, added a small quantity of water and directed me to drink it all. After a few minutes he spoke to his wife again, who disappeared and returned shortly, bringing a small sack, from which he took a teaspoonful of very small, black, shiny seeds. These he gave me and directed me to chew and swallow them. These commands being followed, another ceremony of words and gestures was indulged in. He sat down by me and informed me my ailment was caused by eating fresh buffalo meat and instructed me just how his treatment would affect my system.

I then returned to my quarters and laid down and soon felt the soothing effects of the medicine. A glow of warmth was diffused through my body, producing a profound slumber and I arose the next day feeling my illness gone. The old medicine man's remedies had reduced my complaint quickly when my own remedies had failed.

It was well into November now and as the Indians were constantly on the move and doubtless would so continue for a long while, it was foreseen that no results could be obtained from conducting a "roaming school" under such conditions. Consequently preparations were made for my return to the Agency, and the next day the band departed one way and I, homeward bound, followed up the Big Horn. When near the mouth of Shell Creek and the Graybull River, we fell in with the Hon. J. D. Woodruff and Tom Williams, who had been employed by the commander of Fort Washakie to come down into the Basin to watch for and report the incursion of any hostile demonstration and who at the same time had trapped and hunted for poultry and were now also bound for home.

Together with our combined outfits, composed of eleven pack animals, we continued on up the Big Horn, passed over the sites of the now prosperous towns of Greybull, Basin, Manderson, and Worland, until we reached "Big Horn Hot Springs," as they were then known, and where has since grown up the beautiful and thriving town of Thermopolis, which is located near the springs on the ten-mile square of land set apart by the generosity of the government for the purpose of preserving to the use of all mankind the benefits of these healing waters.

... The next year, when the annual hunt began, a small number of braves were sent over into the Basin and the following year still a smaller number. The Indians, noting that the herds of buffalo were disappearing, spent more of their time going after other game—deer, elk, antelope, etc.

The following fragments and short narratives represent the most frustrating segment of the Wyoming FWP files. It seems from the format that they are transcriptions of oral narratives, but there is virtually no documentation to support this contention. Worse yet, the fragments that we have are numbered pages 35 through 48, and it is clear that more narratives follow. The editors moaned and agonized, "Where are the other pages?" but no answer came. The processes of transcription, duplication, and archiving have obviously caused gaps to appear in the FWP materials.

8 A Stampede

There has been much written about the dangers of the long drives but there were no more dangers to be faced going up the trail with a herd of Texas longhorns than there was in any other pioneer adventure. It was adventure and we took our chances—the same as we do today. That's just life.

The first night out a nigger cowboy flicked his slicker and this caused the herd to stampede and it stampeded every night for 26 nights. The first night it ran five miles but we got it under control before it ran that far again . . .

9 Civil Strife

From the *Sheridan Post*, June 23, 1892.

Last Friday night a collision occurred between the colored soldiers encamped about four miles from Suggs and the people of the town, in which one soldier was killed outright, several others wounded, and one citizen shot through the arm. The report came up here Saturday and Sunday morning Sheriff Willey and Deputy W. H. Wood started for the scene. Several parties arrived Sunday who confirmed the report and yesterday morning Sheriff Willey returned, from whom we learned the following facts:

On the night of the 17th a colored soldier and a cowboy got into an altercation over a fast woman of the town. The cowboy pulled his gun and the soldier skipped out for camp with the threat that he would burn the town. Sometime in the night he returned in company of a number of comrades and stationing themselves in the street opened fire on the buildings. The fire was immediately returned by the citizens and one of the soldiers fell dead, while several others are known to have been wounded and are now under the physician's care at the camp.

The firing was heard by the officers, the camp was aroused, a roll call was had, and 44 soldiers failed to answer to their names. Two companies of cavalry with their ordinary arms and a Hotchkiss gun then marched down and surrounded the town but no further acts of violence were committed by either side.

When Sheriff Willey arrived he visited the militia camp and learned that the colonel commanding the regiment had just arrived from Fort Robinson. The colonel assured the sheriff that if discovered the guilty parties would be turned over to the civil authorities as soon as he could connect with the War Department and that in the meantime they would be safely kept. The sheriff then returned to consult with the county attorney and what action would be taken is not known at this time.

From what we can learn the whole trouble seems to have grown out of a personal difficulty between one soldier and one citizen and the midnight attack on the town was an outrage entirely inexcusable. The guilty ones should be made to suffer the extreme penalty of the law. These colored soldiers have long had the reputation of being a tough outfit and a wholesome lesson should be administered to them.

10 The Fleur-de-Lis Cocktail

A Story that took place in Buffalo, Wyoming, in 1880, as told by Abe Abraham.

I was in the Occidental Hotel which had a bar in connection and while I was talking to the bartender a man stepped up to the bar who was comparatively a stranger in that town. He said to the bartender, "Make me a fleur-de-lis cocktail."

Now it happened that this bartender was an old cowhand and knew no more about mixing fancy drinks than he did about preaching a sermon, but he was game. "Yes sir," he says, "I'll mix you one."

Taking a big glass and putting a little gin in it, he took every cordial and bitters that he had on the back-bar and to top it off he put in a whole jigger of Jamaican gin.

The man who had ordered the drink was a remittance man. They called them remittance men because the people in England wanted to get rid of them for some reason so they sent them to America—not to make their fortune but so they could get away from whatever had happened in England. Every month the folks in England would send them some money—remittances they were called.

Now, this remittance man picked up his glass, looked at the bartender, and swallowed the drink, smacking his lips. Then putting down the glass, he smiled at the bartender and said, "Make me another one, just like that."

The ex-cowboy bartender thought to himself, "I'll give you a good one this time," so he doubled the doses of everything he put in before and handed it to the remittance man.

"Ah yes," says the remittance man, "that looks good."

"It is good," says the bartender.

Before any of us dreamed that the remittance man was the least perturbed, he drew his .45 and says, "All right, drink it."

Well, the bartender looked at that Jamaican ginger cocktail and then at the .45, then picked up the cocktail and downed it, and he never batted an eye.

 ## 11 Putting on the Style

Another story told by Abe Abraham, from about 1885.

Jim Swisher was shipping some cattle to Omaha and asked me to go along. I accepted the invitation readily. When we reached Omaha of course we had a couple of drinks—maybe one or two too many. But we were carrying them all right when we went into a restaurant and there was a man at a table next to us who had just received his order for fresh oysters, so we ordered oysters.

Then the man began to prepare his oysters to eat and put a drop of some hot potpourri on each one. Jim looked at him out of the corner of his eye and when Jim's oysters arrived Jim picked up the bottle of potpourri and soused a lot of the mixture on his oysters. I nudged him and said, "Not so much, Jim, not so much."

Jim kept on sousing his oysters with the hot stuff and said, "Hell, if a little is good a lot is better."

Then Jim put an oyster in his mouth. I watched him out of the corner of my eye and I never have seen anything funnier. Jim clamped his jaws tight on the oyster, then looked around as if he would find a means of escape, then he opened his mouth, then closed it again, and then the tears began to run down his face. The man next to us, who happened to be the only customer in the restaurant besides ourselves, looked at Jim with a puzzled expression.

Of course it takes lots longer to tell than it took to happen. Jim just put the oyster in his mouth, shut his mouth, opened it again, looked around the room in desperation, shut his mouth again, and then his eyes began to water.

And then without more ado, he rose to his feet, grabbed the offending oyster, and throwing it across the room yelled "Blaze, you son-of-a-bitch, blaze."

12 American Class

Told by Ed Salesbury.

I was cook for an outfit that was owned by two sons of an English lord. Their foreman was an American and was under contract to the two Britishers for a term of three years.

One day the foreman was talking to me when the Englishmen rode up and dismounted. I went on about my work because I knew that the Englishmen had come to talk to the foreman, but I was in hearing distance, and I heard one of the Britains say to the foreman, "You will have to bow when you meet us."

The foreman replied, "I don't bow to any man."

"But we are the sons of English lords!"

"Well, sons of lords and son-of-bitches are all the same in this country."

The Englishmen paid him three years salary and fired him.

Also told by Ed Salesbury

About 1890 I was cooking for an outfit near Edgemont, South Dakota, when we came to a river that was so shallow that a person could walk across it. We made camp opposite to a camp of Sioux and after we had had supper three Sioux squaws walked across the river and sat down close to where the cowboys were lolling around on the ground.

Well, of course the cowboys began to make some pretty rough remarks among themselves about the squaws, most especially about the middle one, who was quite pretty.

The squaws just sat there, sphinx-like. After I had finished washing the dishes one of the squaws, the pretty one, got up and came over to the wagon and said, in good American English, "Will you sell me a pound of coffee?"

Well, if the shallow stream had suddenly filled its banks and overflowed I wouldn't have been more surprised. We were all buffaloed; we had never dreamed that the squaws could either speak or understand the American language. The cowboys jumped to their feet and beat a hasty retreat.

The foreman told me to give the woman a pound of Arbuckle's coffee, which was considered the best grade of coffee in the country. I poured a pound of coffee in the coffee mill and while I ground it I talked to the Indian woman and she told me that she was a white woman, the wife of Sitting Bull, and the other two Indian women were her maids. They had run out of coffee and she had been sent to our camp to purchase a pound. She also told me that she liked life among the Indians.

When I finished grinding the coffee and gave it to her, she thanked me and joined the other two squaws and they walked on across the river to their camp.

13 Packer, the Man-Eater

Lamentably, perhaps the most notable of the personalities that have marked Wyoming's history and folklore is Alfred Packer, whose story still excites rumors and is good for a few column inches in Sunday human-interest sections. This version was composed by Malcolm Campbell and appeared in the *Casper Tribune-Herald* in 1926.

My first acquaintance with Alfred Packer, alias John Swartz, was in January 1883. At that time Clark DeVoe and his father were prospecting up in Spring Canyon and, as this man Packer was also a prospector, the three men camped and worked together.

In January Packer made a trip to (Fort) Fetterman, and shortly after getting in he proceeded to "get a jag on." While at supper that evening in the hotel he ordered the waiter to bring him a glass of water. The waiter, being quite busy, did not bring the water right away. This of course angered Packer and as the waiter was passing on the other side of the table Packer jerked out his six-shooter and said, "Damn you! Ain't you going to bring me that water?"

The waiter said, "Yes, I'll bring you the water right now."

Packer said, "You better be damn quick about it or I'll plug you one."

The waiter, as soon as he had served him, ran to where I lived, a very short distance from the hotel. He was some scared man, while telling me what had taken place. I threw my coat on, grabbed my gun, and went over to the hotel with him. When we got there Packer had gone into the saloon part of the hotel.

I took no chances, pulled my gun, told him "hands up," and disarmed him. He always carried his gun shoved down in the belt of his pants, right near the front, so it was handy to get when he wanted to use it. I took Packer over to the old government jail and locked him up. The next morning I sent for Judge O'Brien, who lived six miles up on the LaPrele.

After the Judge came the waiter didn't want to file a complaint against Packer, so the only thing for me to do was to turn him loose. This arrest, of course, made Packer very bitter against me, according to what

I afterwards heard. The very looks of Packer intimidated the waiter, and that was the reason he withdrew the charge. Packer looked as if he could butcher anyone who crossed him in anything.

At that time there was a little Frenchman (John Cazabon) who used to peddle goods from Cheyenne through to Fort Fetterman. He drove a large span of horses (sic) to a covered wagon and carried different kinds of goods. He would make all the ranches along the road and all places along the road. Towards spring, while on one of his trips to Fetterman, Frenchy stopped at John Brown's road ranch, later the Bert Elder ranch on LaPrele Creek, now owned by Jake Jenne of Douglas.

Here Frenchy had stopped for the night, and while in an adjoining room he heard a man talking and recognized the voice as Packer's. He went in and commenced looking for marks by which he would know Packer. One was that the forefinger of the left hand was off at the second joint and another was that two upper front teeth were gone. Packer had had these replaced with false teeth. Frenchy was sure that it was Packer. He asked Frenchy to bring him some baking powder the next trip he made that way. Frenchy told him that he would do that and asked where he should leave it. He told him to leave it there with John Brown and he (Packer) would have Brown settle for it.

In those days nearly everyone carried his bedroll with him. If traveling by buggy or wagon it was hauled. If not it was carried on a pack-horse. It was the custom for men to unroll their beds at night on the barroom floor. Lots of them would sleep all night, while others would be drinking and gambling all night long. These places were known as road ranches. All had a bar in connection with them, where all kinds of tobacco and liquor could be bought.

The next afternoon Frenchy came on down to Fetterman and came over to our house. He nearly always hauled his wagon close to our back door for the night. We had him eat supper with us. After supper he asked me if I knew the man Swartz. I told him the only thing I knew of him was that I had him in jail for pulling a gun on Jimmie, the waiter at the hotel, a short time before.

Then Frenchy turned his little, beady, brown eyes on me and said, "Mr. Campbell, You know where he came from? How long will he be here?"

I told him all I knew was that he came down from Buffalo, Wyoming, with a bull outfit belonging to a fellow by the name of Bill Williams of Tie-Siding. Then he ask me, "What will he do here?"

I told him he was prospecting up in Spring Canyon.

Frenchy dropped his head and studied a while, then asked me the same question over again. I knew by this time he had something on his mind that he wanted to tell me, so I asked him, "Do You know anything about Swartz?"

He studied a while longer, then raised his head and said, "Well, yes." Then he told me the whole story.

He said, "In 1883 there were twenty-one of us prospectors got together, including Packer of Salt Lake City, and started for Hinsdale County, Colorado. Before we got to the mountains we came to a camp of Ute Indians in a nice valley. We told them where we wanted to go and they pointed to the mountains and said, 'Heap snow,' and so we camped there close to the Indians.

"Packer wanted to go on over the mountains, and finally he got five of the men to go with him. Frenchy and the balance of the men stayed where they were until Spring, then started and went over the mountains and came to the Indian agency where General Adams was the Indian agent.

"In April, on arriving there, they found Packer and, of course, the first thing they asked him was where were their five comrades who left with him. He told them, 'On top of that big mountain.'

"Then they began to inquire of Packer when he got in there. They found out he had been drinking and gambling and had lots of money, and they knew that all the money he had when they left Salt Lake City was a twenty-dollar gold piece.

"Their suspicions were aroused and they insisted on Packer going back with them where he last saw the men, but they couldn't get him to go. Then they went to General Adams and told him that when Packer left them the winter before there were five men with him and that Packer said he left them up in the mountains.

"General Adams sent for Packer to come to his office. He asked him what had become of the five men who started over the mountains with him. Packer told him the same story that he had told Frenchy and his party. General Adams insisted that Packer go back with those men and show them where he last saw these five men. He put the outfit in charge of his chief clerk to go back and search for them. They all got their pack outfits and started back for the mountains. When they got to the foot of the mountain Packer said he was lost and didn't know where he had left them.

"By this time it was getting late. They pulled into camp for the night. It was a bright moonlight night, and the chief clerk and Packer slept together. At about eleven o'clock that night Packer arose up in bed and raised his hand with a big dirk knife, ready to kill the chief clerk, but he had not gone to sleep yet. He saw his danger at once and bounded out of bed at the same time, yelled, and the rest of the men jumped up. He told them Packer was about to kill him. They tied Packer up and brought him back to the Agency.

"Then Packer told General Adams a story of how they had run out of provisions and with the snow so deep and no game to kill they ate rosebuds and roots to keep from starving. One day, he said, he had been away from camp. While he was gone one of the men went crazy from hunger and killed the other four. So he attacked him and shot him. But when the bodies were afterwards discovered in June by a photographer at Cristoral Lake, it was seen that four of the bodies were lying in a row and the other one had been clubbed to death and his head severed from the body. Packer said he cut steaks from the men's bodies and ate all he could and packed away considerable about his person to eat on the way down, but threw it away when he came in sight of the Agency. He also said that the meat cut from a man's breast was the sweetest meat he ever ate. He had lived on it sixty days and had become quite fond of it.

"The only jail building to put him in was a log one and a poor excuse for a jail. Packer was shackled and put in. The sheriff was called away for six days and in his absence he left his son, a boy about sixteen, to look after the jail and Packer. When he returned Packer had made his escape, leaving his shackles in one corner of the jail.

"The supposition was that Packer had given the sheriff a bunch of money to fix it so he could get away, for he had got lots of money off the men he had killed. Some of them were known to have several thousand dollars on them. Packer had told Frenchy at this time that if he ever got a chance he would kill him, so Frenchy said that during the seventeen years that had gone by since Packer had threatened him it was always on his mind that he might meet him on the road somewhere and kill him. Frenchy said, "He could-a killa me vit a club, I be so lettle and I know so vell how bad a man he be, so I no sleepa any last night at Brown's place where we all had our beds made down in the same room (*sic*).'

At this time I was deputy at Fetterman under Sheriff Louis Miller of Laramie City. I sat down the same night while the story was fresh in my mind and wrote it to Sheriff Miller. I kept cases on Packer until I heard from Sheriff Miller.

In the meantime Packer had left Spring Canyon and had gone over on Wagon Hound on to the cabin of Crazy Horse, another old prospector. In those days the mail and passengers were taken about three times a week to Rock Creek and then on by train to Laramie City, so mail came very slow.

I could have telegraphed, as the Government had an agent at Fetterman at that time, but I wanted to know the particulars in the case. I knew he had been a prospector himself and might by chance know the circumstances in the Packer case.

"In about a week I received a telegram from Sheriff Miller, saying, 'Arrest Packer, alias John Swartz, at once, and take no chances whatever. Identification marks: the forefinger of his left hand off at the second joint and the little finger of the same hand off at second joint; the two upper teeth gone and replaced by artificial ones. Wire me at once.'

"The evening I got the telegram I hunted up my brother Dan and told him I wanted him to go with me the next day to get Packer. We started early the next morning in my spring wagon for Wagon Hound and Crazy Horse's Cabin.

"When we were about half way there we met Crazy Horse coming to Fetterman. I asked him if Swartz was at his cabin yet. He said he was, but was talking of going over to the Hartville mines, and he didn't know if he intended to go that day or not.

"We drove on, and through the Douglas Wellin place. Within probably a hundred yards of Crazy Horse's cabin we saw a man standing in the door. We turned our buggy around facing a haystack and jumped out, Dan on one side and I on the other. By this time the man was coming toward us and had got near enough so that I recognized him and told Dan, 'That's him.'

"I pulled my gun on him and told him to halt, that he was my prisoner. At the same time Dan covered him with a Winchester rifle. When I went to get my handcuffs Packer dropped his hands like he was going to get his gun.

"Dan hollered, 'Throw up them hands or I will put a bullet right through you,'

"Packer said, 'What are you fellows fooling about?'

"While I was putting the irons on him, after searching him, he remarked, 'That's the first time in twenty years that I didn't have my gun on. If I had had it on you fellows never could have taken me, for I would have got one or both of you.'

"Dan said, 'What in hell do you think we would be doing all that time?'

"I read Sheriff Miller's telegram to him, saw the marks, the fingers gone. I raised his upper lip, saw the two teeth gone, replaced by false ones.

"We hooked up the traces and drove over to the cabin. We had oats for the team and while Dan watered and fed the team I took Packer to the cabin. I made him sit on a bench near the door. I asked him where his gun was. He pointed to the shelf. I saw the gun, a .44 self-action, fully loaded.

Packer insisted on helping us get some dinner but I told him to sit on that bench and sit there until I told him to get up. I made some coffee, and there was some cooked food left from the dinner. Packer had eaten shortly before we got there. By the time we had eaten our dinner the team had finished eating oats and we started back to Fetterman, a distance of twenty miles.

Packer sat with me. I drove the team while Dan sat behind me on a bedroll with the Winchester rifle across his knees. It was after dark when we got back to Fetterman. We put Packer in a cell in the old Government guard house. I got him something to eat, and made a fire to keep him warm, then went home and got some supper.

"I put a guard in the corridor, for I knew Packer wouldn't stay in a place like that very long if I left him alone, as the guard house was just a crude, wooden building.

"This was Friday and the next stage wouldn't be going to Rock Creek until Monday. On Monday I started with him. The first night the stage made it to the Point of Rocks in Downey Park. I slept that night with Packer, or rather cat-napped. He was rather an uncomfortable bed-fellow, for every time he moved his shackles would rattle.

"There were lots of snow drifts on the way, some of them fifteen feet deep, and the four-horse team frequently broke through and floundered around, got down, and we would have to get out. I left Packer standing with a lady passenger at one side while I helped shovel out. Then we would load up and go on until we would hit another drift and have to go through the same procedure.

"We didn't make it into Rock Creek until after dark. Then we had supper at the hotel. I asked the landlady to give me a room upstairs with two beds. I didn't sleep that night, but I think Packer slept fairly well, as he didn't seem very restless.

"The next day we took the train to Laramie City. When the train pulled in the sheriff was there to meet us, also a crowd of people anxious to see the man-eater. They crowded around as close as they could to get a look at him, much to his disgust.

"We stayed there that night. Next day, accompanied by Sheriff Miller, we left for Cheyenne, where I was to turn the prisoner over to Sheriff Claire Smith of Hinsdale County, Colorado. When the train pulled into Cheyenne there was a big crowd there at the depot to get a look at packer. Some crowded into the train when it slowed to a stop and stood and stared at him. It made him so mad he said to me, 'I wonder what the damn fools are looking at me like that for?'

"The Cheyenne sheriff met us and went with us to lock Packer up. The next forenoon the Colorado sheriff and General Adams, from the Indian agency, came and took him, leaving that afternoon for Denver, Colorado. I went with them and, while going I sat with Packer. He told me it was the third time he had started for Hinsdale County. I asked him why he didn't go on. He turned it off by saying, 'Well, I go so far, then turn off and go somewhere else.'

"He was asked while on the way to Denver if he knew that little French peddler, but he had told Clark DeVoe, when he went back to the camp, that he knew that little Frenchy, that he met him at Brown's ranch and that he was an old prospector.

"Packer was taken back to Hinsdale County, Colorado, to be tried for the murder of those five men. He was tried and found guilty and sentenced to be hanged. I received an invitation to attend the execution, for Sheriff Smith, as follows:

Lake City, Colorado

May 2, 1883

Mr. Malcolm Campbell:
You are respectfully invited to attend the execution of Alfred Packer, at Lake City, Colorado, on the 19th day of May, A. D. 1883.

Claire Smith
Sheriff of Hinsdale County
Colorado

The laws of Colorado had changed after this crime had been committed, so his lawyers got a new trial for him at this time. Colorado had done away with capital punishment. He was retried and sentenced to serve eight years for each man he had killed. This meant forty years in the pen.

Packer evidently had no brotherly love for me, for word came straight to me that he had told DeVoe if he ever got a chance at me he would kill me and cut my heart out and eat it. This shows the cannibal in him again. His face showed he was a hardened killer and would kill a man almost for pastime.

While Packer was in jail at Laramie City, Sheriff Miller had a boy in jail for some little offense. The boy could look right straight into Packer's cell. The boy said as soon as the officers would leave the jail Packer would, with the aid of a fine wire, take off his shackles and throw them in a corner, and when he heard anyone coming he would put them back on.

Many times now I think of the chance I took with that big, powerful man, when I even slept with him at Point of Rocks. I did not realize that he could have got the best of me and what might have happened, but I didn't know what fear was in those days. Dr. J. M. Wilson used to say, 'Campbell ain't afraid of God, man or the Devil,' but that is putting it rather strong, I think.

When Packer broke jail the state offered a reward of five thousand dollars for his capture. Afterwards, a body of a man answering the description of Packer was found in the mountains and the reward was withdrawn but I did not know this. Neither did Frenchy.

Some time later I went to Denver to see a lawyer, Patterson, to see if he could get the reward for me that was offered. I told him if he could get it I would give him half. He made the remark that since it had been so long ago he would look it up. I never heard from him, but afterwards learned that he had been hired at the time of the trial by Packer's sister to defend Packer in the case.

After Packer had been sentenced I received a letter from a friend of the Packer family, saying Alfred Packer had always been the black sheep of the family. He stated that the Packer family were very prominent and wealthy and that Asa Packer was once Governor of Pennsylvania.

Packer tried repeatedly, while out on parole, to get permission from the Governor to come up into this part of the country where he once prospected, but was refused. He died sometime about 1908 in the hills, seven years after he was out on parole.

II
White Man's Tales

When the contention is made that folklore cannot persist in a technological age, the proof that is most often put forth is that the folksong in America has been reduced to a commercial commodity and the folktale has faded away entirely. There may indeed be a case for the transmutation of the folksong over into the area of popular culture, but the folktale is far from dead. To be sure, the folktale form most frequently considered, the fairytale, has faded away to a mere whisper in American tradition, but the fairytale is not all there is to the folktale after all. Today, as well as in nineteenth-century Wyoming, the folktale prospers in the subcategories of the jest (or joke) and the legend.

Little explanation is necessary for the jest, because it is vividly distinct from its social and cultural matrix. Everyone knows what is happening when someone is telling a joke, when it has begun and when it has ended. It does not take a trained folklorist to characterize the nature of the traditional joke. But a legend is another matter altogether. The true legend rarely has a distinct opening, like "There was this bug . . ." in the case of the joke, or "Once upon a time . . ." for the fairytale. Nor does it usually have a true closing like the joke's punch line or the fairy tale's "and they lived happily ever after." Neither the form nor the language of the legend is so distinctive that it gives away the genre (such as a wicked stepmother, three tasks, or talking beasts and living objects in the fairy tale). The legend, on the contrary, just drops into the conversation, told as fact, rumor, or gossip. It has no distinctive opening or closing, no commonplace expressions, no set number of brothers, tasks, monsters, or episodes. Professional folklorists often cannot recognize a true legend until they have collected several different versions and thereby ascertain that it is not truth, rumor, or gossip they are hearing but a story passed from person to person with no discernable truth or substance other than the pressure of tradition.

The Wyoming WPA papers suggest that the legend constituted a substantial proportion of pioneer folklore too, for the predominant percentage of the tales in that collection are legends, and a major part of those legends in Wyoming's collection are stories of lost mines.

Lost Mine Tales

It is not surprising that a story about a lost mine—with its traditional components of incredible wealth, an isolated or distant locale, a hidden entrance, and a death curse—can claim a few column inches of newspaper space as a human interest story. Stories of immense wealth available for the very taking are somehow magnetic to the very nature of man. Imagine then what it must have been like in those days when the Wyoming mountains teemed with men desperate with gold fever. Not only was the likelihood of the lost mine legends' truth greater, but all the more did men want to believe the tales and cling to them as hope for yet another grubstake.

14 The Lost Treasure of the Haystacks

Alice C. Guyol collected this tale from Mrs. E. H. Green, George Houser, H. T. Miller, Minnie Harphoff, and others of the town of Guernsey, presumably the result of a collation of their versions. Guernsey lies in the east central part of the state, not at all in the gold-rich mountains of the west.

Fort Laramie was the outpost of outposts. It seems strange to find mention of the site in 1835 when the missionaries Parker and Whitman stopped here, or in 1836 when the travelers Whitman and Spalding visited the fort, or 1841 when Brigham Young stopped on his way to found Salt Lake City, while the white frontier was just beginning to cross the Missouri River 500 miles to the east, but such was indeed the case.

While most Americans have heard of Fort Laramie—in western movies if no where else—the name Spanish Diggings will be familiar to far fewer readers, and yet in many ways it is an even more fascinating eastern Wyoming historical site. The quarries of the digging were worked for many hundreds of years before, and after, the advent of the white man on the continent, and until metal arrow points and gun powder were readily available to the Plains Indians. The quartzite, jasper, and agate points and blades from the thirty-foot pits scattered across the four hundred square miles of the Spanish Diggings have been found a thousand and more miles to the east, and it is therefore presumed that the Diggings were a center for the mining and working of such weapons. Even today rough, imperfect, and broken fragments of stone knives, hammers, axes, grinders, knives, and spear and arrow heads can be found where their frustrated makers discarded them, carrying away of course the successful artifacts. The Digging acquired the qualifier "Spanish" because it was believed early in the nineteenth century that the pits, furrows, and trenches were the work of Spanish explorers searching for Cibola.

Eureka Canyon and its present occupant, the tiny village of Hartville, lies a few miles north of Guernsey. Its history is short but convoluted. Long before the white man's arrival around 1881 in a copper boom it had been an aboriginal campsite. A second boom at the turn of the century— iron this time—brought more wealth, disaster, and disappointment. The gold of the legend was a boom that never really materialized.

Even today the name "Slade" carries with it a sinister chill, and with good reason, for even in the days of the birth of this legend Slade was notorious. As was so often the case, his notoriety was less earned than bestowed, but he merited his share, dying dancing at the end of a vigilante rope in Virginia City, Montana, in 1864. Slade Canyon was believed to be a favored rendezvous for the Slade gang.

Tourmaline is a semi-precious silicate used in jewelry, and some optical instruments. Corundum is second in hardness only to the diamond and is therefore very important in industrial processes requiring grinding, cutting, and polishing; there are some precious and semi-precious forms of the mineral, notably ruby, sapphire, and topaz. Beryllium is an important alloying metal for several metals including copper and nickel. Mica, also known as mineral isinglass, forms as thin transparent sheets and was used as window material, especially in ovens and stoves.

From the earliest time that prospectors entered the hills on the north side of the Platte River there have been tales of gold in the Haystack Mountains, that range of low, dark mountains lying east of the town of Guernsey and to the south of Whalen Canyon. These tales have never varied much: sometimes they have been of an old prospector who would drift into Fort Laramie at intervals, during pioneer days, and would pay for his provisions with gold dust. No one was ever able to discover the place where he mined the gold, although he was known to operate in the Haystack range.

Another story was that of an old prospector seen driving his burro along the road to the fort. A traveler going in the same direction noted that there were several canvas bags hanging from the burro's pack and asked what they were. In answer the prospector invited the other to see for himself. The traveler thrust his hand into one of the bags and withdrew it—filled with gold dust. Asked where he had found the gold the old prospector pointed to the Haystack Mountains and said, "Over there."

Over a period of years other prospectors continued to search for gold in these mountains but with no success. Finally it became known as "lost gold" and is thus called today.

One of the most interesting experiences in connection with this search for the lost gold was that of Joseph Stein, one of the best known mining men of the district. Joe Stein discovered and named the Spanish Diggings; he developed a number of valuable mineral bodies; and although he made no fortune from his many mining ventures he retained until the time of his death his enthusiasm for and his faith in the mining future of the district.

Stein came into the area from South Dakota, where he had been prospecting for gold in the Black Hills. He drifted into Eureka Canyon, where the town of Hartville is now located, and, although he gives the date of his arrival at 1881, it was doubtless the following year, for in 1881 Eureka Canyon was a wilderness of almost impenetrable trees and undergrowth and could only be explored as far as the Indian Spring. In 1882 however, the mining camp in the Canyon was in full swing because of the copper strike in the nearby hills.

In Eureka Canyon Stein made the acquaintance of a desperado who was known by a number of names. At this time the man was calling himself Johnson and he claimed to have been one of Slade's outlaws who had carried on their depredations from Slade's Canyon, located on the northwest from the mining camp. Johnson repeated the story of the lost gold to Stein. In fact, he claimed to have been the traveler who had met the old prospector with his burro and the bags of gold. He also claimed to know of buried treasure, presumably hidden by Slade's men, and he persuaded Stein to form a partnership with him in a search both for the gold and the treasure.

The two men went into Whalen Canyon and located a claim near the Haystack Mountains. Johnson insisted that they build a wall around the claim, supply themselves with a quantity of ammunition, and be prepared to hold out against all comers in the event that they should strike gold. This done, they spent their time in prospecting for gold and for the cache of buried coin.

They had no horses but Stein owned a burro and one morning after they had been living at the place for some time Johnson asked the use of the burro, saying that he wanted to make a trip to Fort Laramie, a distance of some fifteen miles, for the purpose of buying more ammunition. Stein readily agreed and Johnson left, riding the burro. Ordinarily the trip would have taken two or possibly three days but the week passed and Johnson did not return.

One day however a cowboy appeared at Stein's place leading the burro. The cowboy claimed to be on his way to the old 4-J ranch, which was located north of Eureka Canyon. He said he had brought a message to Stein from his partner. Johnson had said to tell him "goodbye." He had signed a contract to go as a scout with a government train and he would not return.

Stein immediately thought of the buried treasure and he felt that Johnson must have located this before leaving for Fort Laramie. He had confidence in his partner to such an extent that he believed that Johnson would have sent him a part of the treasure if this were true. He asked the cowboy if Johnson had not sent him a letter or a package. The cowboy answered no and left the place as fast as his horse could carry him. A friend who had been stopping with Stein during the absence of Johnson remarked (sic) the nervous and excited condition of the rider, which Stein had also noted, and Stein decided to go at once to Fort Laramie to see if he could trace his missing partners.

He was obliged to walk the fifteen miles to the Fort and here he discovered that Johnson had been seen in a saloon outside the military reservation where he had spent large sums of money, treating everyone to liquor. He had, however, left the place and no one knew where he had gone.

Stein again set out on foot, this time to the 4-J ranch, a distance of nearly forty miles. The men at the ranch were astonished when he reached the place to see him arrive on foot and heavily armed. When he explained his mission he learned that the cowboy who had brought the burro to his place was unknown at the 4-J, but he was furnished a horse and one of the men went with him to try to locate the cowboy. Scouring the country toward the north Stein and his companion at length spotted the man they were after. They rode near enough to identify him but upon seeing them approach the cowboy put the spurs to his horse and raced away so rapidly that they were unable to overtake him.

Stein then returned to his claim, still firm in his belief that Johnson had met with foul play, that he had discovered the buried treasure and had been murdered and robbed, possibly by the cowboy who had returned the burro to prevent Stein from searching for his partner. Stein could never bring himself to believe that Johnson would have kept all of the money for himself had he discovered the treasure, so for many years he hunted the surrounding country hoping to find some sort of grave where the body of Johnson might have been concealed. Once he heard a report that Johnson had been seen leaving Fort Steel with a government train but was never able to ascertain that the report was true.

Since that time a great deal of prospecting has been done in the Haystack Mountains. Tourmaline, corundum, and beryllium have been discovered; mica and copper have been mined in paying quantities, but the lost gold, if it ever existed, has never been found.

15 Lost Gold of the Big Horn Basin

This tale and the next were collected by Orville S. Johnson of Basin, Wyoming, who did not list his informants in the WPA files. It is significant that even he found the distinction between the legend and truth blurred and it is refreshing to find that he spends little time worrying about the dividing line, for after all, what is truth about what we believe is truth.

Lovell and Big Baldy (now Bald Mountain) are in the extreme north central area of Wyoming, directly on the Montana border, while Thermopolis is approximately one hundred miles to the south. Captain Bates Battleground is where Captain Alfred Bates, on July 4, 1874, fought an Arapaho encampment to an ignominious victory. Thermopolis earns its name from the hot mineral springs that abound in the area. The Bighorn Basin of course encompasses this entire region.

The Black Hills are in South Dakota but lie only 150 miles to the east of the Basin and are therefore considered an important and constant landmark in the western Plains and mountains, where a few hundred miles were—and often still are—nothing at all.

Fort Bridger was established in 1842 by the legendary trapper-explorer-mountain man Jim Bridger. It lies in the extreme southwestern corner of the state, about 35 miles from the Utah border to the west.

Placer gold was "easy" gold that had settled in concentrated pockets in stream beds (or in ancient stream beds long abandoned by water) and which could be extracted by any of the hydraulic systems—pan or cradle usually—and, most importantly, required no tedious, dangerous mining. It was here, in the placer, that nuggets were found—a fortune in a minute. Or, in this case, in three days.

There were seven Swedish prospectors from the Back Hills district came into the Basin looking for gold where there was not so much competition as in the Black Hills right then. The time is set in 1856, or near that date.

The seven Swedes found their gold at a point somewhere between Big Baldy, which is almost due east from Lovell, and Captain Bates' Battleground, which is in the Big Horn Range east of Thermopolis. The first point of location is in Big Horn County at present, and the second is in Washakie County. Old timers on the west slope of the Big Horns claim that there is more evidence in favor of the strike having been made on that slope. Old timers on the east slope laugh at such a notion. The strike was made over in the middle of Johnson County north and a little east of the present town of Kaycee.

Wherever it was, it was a rich strike. The Indians attacked the Swedes and killed five of the seven. The other two escaped and when they reported at Fort Bridger, or wherever it suits the mood of the yarner to have them report, they had around eight to ten thousand dollars worth of coarse placer gold which had been gathered in three days.

16 The Lost Soldier Mine

Basin lies in northernmost central Wyoming, on the eastern edge of the Big Horn Basin, after which it is named. Worland lies thirty-five miles to the south.

It happened when the soldiers were after the Indians and camped somewhere in the Big Horns between a point east of Basin and one east of Worland. Two soldiers became separated from their companions in the evening when they were strolling around at leisure. Suddenly one soldier gripped the other's arm and pointed at an ancient pick and spade lying in the sand at the base of a low ledge. They went and investigated and learned that the ledge was rich quartz. Gold stuck out of every little piece chipped off like somebody had been there and melted it in a frying pan and then hurled it at the ledge.

The two soldiers vowed to keep their secret until later and then return to the place and reap the harvest of immense riches waiting there for them. A battle with Indians followed. One soldier lost his life. The other became sick from exposure later on and when about to die told his story to a companion, who passed it on to two others.

The three made a trip back but found no old spade or pick or gold. They did not even find the place where the camp had been. The country did not look the same as the two soldiers had said it would. The three new explorers had not been with the company at the time the mine was found.

Many years later three men were hunting elk in that same territory.

One was a young man with seeing eyes. The elk killed, he was returning to camp when he stopped at a tiny stream for a drink. A friendly
sheepherder came up as he dropped to his stomach and gave greeting.
The hunter smiled and stooped to drink. In the stream beneath his eyes
were nuggets of gold as large as wheat kernels. Many such nuggets. He
dared not pick any up for fear the sheepherder would understand what
had been found. He would return the next day and with his father and
brother stake the richest claim the Big Horn had ever heard about.

Back at camp the father was sick and had to be rushed to town.
Snow started to fall. There was no chance of getting back to the little
creek before spring. And when spring came the young hunter found
the whole face of the mountain at that point changed from the ravages
of a forest fire. For two weeks he searched without success. Every little
stream was swollen then, but he spared none and there were hundreds
of them, and still no gold.

That was twenty years ago. Today anybody approaching him at the
garage where he works in Billings with the suggestion that he be one
of a party to look for that gold he found, he will throw down all work
and with a sudden glint of hope in his old eyes climb into the car and
screech, "Head 'er for Lovell this time!"

17 The Lost DeSmet Treasure

The Wyoming WPA files also included this letter with an early reference to the
incredible wealth of the mountains, and especially of the Black Hills, whose
magic, long known to the Indians throughout the northern Plains, was also
soon a blessing and curse combined for the white men sick with gold fever.
The letter is from Stewart Van Vliet, an army officer, to Thurlow Weed.

Father DeSmet is one of those remarkable figures like the Roubideau
family, Jim Bridger, or Bill Cody, who show up again and again in the
most disparate situations and most certainly during the most dramatic
years of the frontier. Father Pierrre Jean DeSmet came west with an
American Fur Company party in 1840 and celebrated Wyoming's first
Mass on July 5 of that year among the trappers and Indians. Think of
it: the United States was less than 75 years old, the Civil War was thirty

(*sic*) years in the future, and the Missouri had not yet been reached by the frontier, and yet here was Father DeSmet, a familiar figure some 600 miles further to the west!

Head Qts. (*sic*) Dept. of the Missouri
Office of the Chief Quartermaster
Fort Levenworth, Kansa

April 17, 1875

My Dear Sir-

I read with great pleasure your remarks on our old friend Father DeSmet. Over twenty years ago my home was on the prairies. I passed several years between the Missouri River and the Rocky Mountains, and it was while leading that life that I became acquainted with Father DeSmet. I only refer to this in connection with the precious metals in the Black Hills. One day in 1851, at the dinner table of our friend, Col. Robert Campbell of St. Louis, the conversation turned on our wanderings in the mountains, when Father DeSmet related the following incident, which occurred in the Black Hills beyond the Cheyenne.

One day, while among the Indians, a chief came to him and showed him some pieces of metal which he had in his bullet pouch. As soon as the Father saw it he recognized it as platinum. In company with the chief he visited the place and discovered a large mine of this metal. He said it was of great extent and of untold value. He made the Indian promise never to divulge the secret, for if he did the white people would drive the Indians out of the country. He also promised to keep the secret. He told us that he had carefully described the location of this mine, and that when he died the secret would be with his church.

Father DeSmet could not have been deceived, and I firmly believe that there is a valuable platinum mine between the Yellowstone and the Cheyenne. As this metal is worth $115 per pound avoirdupois, and the silver only $18, you can well understand the fortune that awaits some lucky man.

Yours truly,

Stewart Van Vliet, U.S.A.

18 Indian Joe's Gold

Nor was the dream of the lost Mine only a pioneer dream. The Wyoming FWP files include the following tale from a 1938 issue (August 10 and 11) of the Saratoga, Wyoming, newspaper.

Much of the nomenclature of the story will be familiar enough to current Wyoming citizens but "outsiders" may have some trouble. The Continental Divide is, of course, the imaginary line that is drawn down the country's backbone; the rain that falls on one side flows to the Pacific Ocean, on the other to the Atlantic.

The town of Saratoga lies at the extreme south edge of Wyoming on the Colorado Border, to the east of center. The Grand Encampment is nearby, where every season the mountain men gathered from their lonely Rocky Mountain haunts to exchange news, hides, and vices.

The Green River flows southward near the western border of the state, while the North Platte loops up through the south central part of the state up to Casper and then heads westward into Nebraska. The Sierra Madres Range mentioned in this story is not the famous Mexican range but rather the small group of peaks poking up into the south central border of Wyoming from Colorado.

A "Sluice" was a large box through which a gold-bearing stream was diverted or into which crushed gold ore and water were run. Small riffle bars ran across the floor of the sluice box and the heavy gold settled behind the bars exactly as it might do naturally in a placer. The gold could then be retrieved from the sluice by panning or using mercury to form an amalgam, from which the gold could later be separated.

According to Indian tradition there is a place on this slope of the Continental Divide, within twenty miles of Saratoga, where big gold nuggets have been found and coarse particles of the precious yellow stuff can be scooped up by the hands full. "Old Jim" Baker took so much stock in these stories that he spent a great deal of time in hunting over the country between here and the Grand Encampment, trying to fix the location of these rich deports. His faith that such treasure could easily be attained was based on the stories told by the Indians and on seeing for himself some of the nuggets they brought away with them from this mysterious store house of riches.

It was many years ago that Baker once rode into a camp of the Utes and Snakes over on Green River. He was friendly with these Indians, for he took a wife among the Utes, and the Snakes belong to the same family. While visiting with them he noticed a red youngster playing in front of a tipi, who was tossing about a chunk of something as large as an English walnut that at first he took to be brass. But it glittered so in the sun that his curiosity was excited to examine it closely. He satisfied himself that it was gold and then set about making inquiries to find out where it came from. The papoose said his father, who was known as "Joe," had given it to him. Joe was not around then but Baker was so much interested that he tried to get some information about it from Joe's squaw. Either she did not know much about it or was afraid to tell. All the satisfaction Baker could get was that when Joe came back from a hunting trip here in the Platte Valley a short time before he brought that nugget with him. The woman said she had never seen it before then.

After a while, when he had made several long trips to Joe's camp on purpose to see if he could get some clue as to the origin of the gold, he became convinced that it had come from this side of the Sierra Madres. The Indian was very secretive about it, and Baker had a hard job to get any information at all. He was so persistent in his inquiries and attentive to Joe's family that finally he got from him this story in installments.

Joe was after mountain sheep on this side of the big river, as the Platte was known among the Indians, and tracked a band high up in a canyon just this side of the little river, as they called the grand Encampment. These animals, as is well known, make their haunts in rough, rugged sections and the sheep that Joe went in pursuit of led him a long chase over steep declivities and up and down the sides of the canyon. Tired out, he sat down to rest by the side of a little wet-weather water course that ran down from a backbone.

Nearby in a little basin worn out in the rocks, Joe caught sight of a glittering object. There he picked up the nugget which he subsequently gave to his youngster, who used it for a plaything until Baker saw it. Questioned closely about the find, Joe grew suspicious at Baker's interest in it. He promised to guide the old frontiersman to the place where the nugget was picked up, but refused to fix the locality so Baker could go there by himself.

Appointment after appointment was made by the Indian to show the way but usually he failed to turn up at the specified time. When taken to task for his failure to keep his promise, Joe always protested that something to detain him had come up at the last minute. The more often Baker was disappointed, the more eager he became to solve the mystery surrounding this gold deposit. With or without the guidance of the discoverer, "Old Jim" determined to make a hunt for that receptacle of gold. Joe had told him just enough to be misleading, for in those days band after band of mountain sheep roamed over the range to the west of the Platte Valley, and nearly every bold canyon, the entire length of the Sierra Madres, afforded them feed and shelter. It was hard to pick out the particular canyon where Joe hunted.

Baker had an idea the best chance for finding the place where gold was so abundant was to search in the neighborhood of the Grand Encampment. The most favored section to his mind was between there and Cow Creek, for the Indians were partial to that stretch of territory because the numerous little parks furnished good feed for their ponies and all kinds of game were to be found there in abundance. Visit after visit was made to that locality without getting any trace of the mineral in such quantities as Joe described. He claimed that there was not only one basin, but a series of them where big nuggets glistened in the sun and "heap little" ones also showed in so great quantity that his two hands would not hold them, as he estimated it.

"Old Jim" enjoyed the confidence of the Utes generally and was in a position to prosecute his inquiries to an extent that would not have been possible on the part of any other white man. Through the women too he was usually able to get at information he desired on almost any subject. But as regards this gold each additional item of interest he collected was merely in the line of corroborative evidence that Joe had not overestimated the extent or the value of his discovery. Baker set women and other Indians to watch Joe but he succeeded in eluding their vigilance after getting out of camp.

On several occasions "Old Jim" got together an outfit and took Joe along with him to make the search. Before they reached the valley or got into the mountains they ran into hostile Indians and had to turn back. The Sioux roamed over this country then and it was dangerous to venture into the mountains when they were around. Once on the way to his gold field Joe was all eagerness to make good time. His disappointment on being compelled to abandon a trip was a keen as that of his white companion.

Baker is now an old man but it is not so very long ago that he was seen wandering about in the neighborhood of the ridge along which runs the trail to the Balle Lake country. He had been hunting but an old timer who knew the story of Joe's nugget was convinced that it was gold and not game the "Old Jim" was after.

There is one reasonable explanation that might be given as to why Baker missed finding the nuggets, supposing he ran across the exact location of the Indian's discovery. At that time, when the green timber was heavier and thicker than it is now, the snow stayed on the ground until late in the summer, and in some places never wholly disappeared. Water from these melting banks coursed over the hills, and so numerous were the little streams that landslides were of frequent occurrence along their line, especially when the volume was large. Such slides would not only change the appearance of things, so as to make it difficult to identify or definitely fix a locality, but would likewise hide these basins of which Indian Joe talked.

"Old Jim" was not alone curious about the rediscovery of these natural riffles in Nature's own sluice-way where such a big cleaning was made. He always had a big retinue of Indians, men and women around his ranch and kept up a sort of feudal style. There was a howl raised whenever he talked of taking a trip, particularly among the female members of his following. The old scout was cute in inventing excuses. If any remonstrances were made against an intended absence from home, "Old Jim" would explain that he was going off to hunt for Joe's diggings. That was enough to silence any and all protests. The hangers-on about the establishment would vie with one another in the lavishness and expedition with which his equipment was put in readiness. All knew somewhat of the story of the remarkable find and were eager that the master should sample its richness.

Although this excuse partook at times somewhat of the character of the stereotyped lodge fiction, tried on a trusting wife by a stay-out-late husband, it is a fact that Baker tried time and again to locate these remarkable gold pickings.

Nothing anywhere near approaching such richness has since been found on this slope of the Sierra Madre. The source from which the nuggets came must be somewhere this side of the summit. The coarseness of the gold indicates that it was from one or more ledges that lie higher up near the crest of the range but not far removed. The section where Baker looked most carefully and frequently was between Cow Creek and the Grand Encampment. Rich float is found all over the country there. That is a good field for prospectors now.

Ed Bennett, who knows all about Baker's nuggets hunts, has always had great faith in that neighborhood as a future bullion producer. He expects that someone will stumble over the place, after a heavy run of water, or come on the basins when digging down through the gravel or debris that may have washed over them in the seasons that have passed.

In 1868 when Bennett ran the stage ferry on the old overland trail, eight miles below Saratoga on the Platte, he had a strange visitor in an old-treasure hunter who raised great expectations by the promise of showing him rich gold diggings on this slope of the Sierra Madre and not far away.

It was late in September or early in October of that year that Bennett was enjoying a quiet smoke all alone in the stage station after supper was over. The first snowstorm of the fall, in the valley, had set in that afternoon. That did not worry the ferryman because he had laid in a good supply of wood and had plenty of feed for his stock. There came a knock at the door and, answering it, Bennett was confronted by an old man with long, white whiskers. The stranger said he was sick and he looked it. Inviting him in, Bennett made his visitor comfortable by the fire and then turned his attention to the stock outside. There were two horses and a saddle horse, all slick and fat and in good condition as though they had not come on a very hard or long journey. When the animals had been sheltered and fed, Bennett devoted himself to the care of the old man, who seemed to be in a bad way. He doctored him up as well as he could with the few remedies at hand. Supper had been prepared for the quest but he was too sick to eat anything and simply drank a cup of coffee. The only explanation the patient gave was that he had been at work in the mountains but was forced to leave on account of his feebleness and for lack of provisions, his supplies being entirely exhausted.

The next day the old man showed some signs of improvement. He was not inclined to talk about himself and merely said that he left the mountains on the west side of the valley the previous morning. He stayed at the stage station for several days and then announced that he would set out the next morning for Laramie City. The night before he went away he partially took Bennett into his confidence as to what he had been doing. So far he had not so much as made known his name, and, in fact, that was kept secret. But, in speaking of his intention to leave on the following morning he asked his host how much he wanted for his entertainment and nursing. Thinking that the old man was a luckless prospector or disappointed pilgrim who had taken the back-track across the Plains after a fruitless search for fortune, Bennett, who was nothing if not generous, told him that the account was square. This did not please the old man at all. He expressed his gratitude for the attention shown him and declared that Bennett had saved his life. This was undoubtedly true, for the stranger, besides being advanced in years, was suffering from a severe attack of mountain fever when he found a haven at the stage station.

"I've got enough to pay my way," remarked the old man with dignity and a self-satisfied air. Drawing forth a bag of gold he exhibited it as proof of this assertion and then added, "There's plenty more, too, where this stuff came from."

Bennett, who was a miner himself, was interested at once. He asked where the gold came from. "Over there," said the stranger, pointing in the direction of the Sierra Madre. That was all the information that could be got out of him as to the source from which it was derived. He permitted Bennett to weigh the gold and to examine it as miners are fond of doing.

There was a little over $45 worth of the stuff and when the result of the measurement was announced the old man involuntarily congratulated himself with the comment, "Pretty good for less than five days work."

"Well, I should say so," spoke up Bennett, whose curiosity had jumped several points by the revelation of such rich workings. Then he plied the old man with questions and he became a bit more communicative. They talked a long time together and when the stranger found that his host could be of some service to him in the future, he told a fragment of his story.

Who he was or where he came from the stranger would not reveal. Not so much as his name would he tell. He said that for a long time he had been hunting for rich gold diggings, that he had reason to believe existed on the Sierra Madre next to the Platte Valley. He did not explain what the basis was for this belief that led him to take up the search in the first place. It was enough to say, he seemed to think, that he had found what he was after. The hunt had been long and laborious but he had struck it at last. Success came when the early snowstorms began and the summit was soon coated with what was to become the foundation for the huge banks and drifts during the greater part of the year.

Naturally, having made the discovery he had planned beforehand to accomplish, he was ambitious to see how good a thing he had found. That kept him in the bleak mountains and on short rations. He was taken down with fever but pluckily stuck by his diggings until satisfied that he had big pay dirt. Then he had some thought and regard for his condition, but not until then.

Although he did not say so, in as many words, the inference was strong that the lucky miner may have purposely delayed his departure from his diggings until the snowfall was great enough to hide the place from wandering or other curious prospectors. Sealed by this white mantle his secret would be safely kept till the bonds of the elements were riven in the spring time.

Whatever may have actuated this mysterious unknown to limit his vigil at the treasure-field by his supply of rations he took big chances and recklessly tempted fate. He was more dead than alive when he reached the ferry and had good cause to be grateful to Bennett for his kindly offices. This may in part explain why he told his Samaritan as much as he did concerning his big find.

From purely selfish motives though it became necessary that Bennett should be let into the secret to some extent. The old man said he was going east for the winter but intended to return again in March or April following. He would be certain to get into the mountains before anyone could do any prospecting. All his plans had been carefully laid to guard against any encroachment on his field of operations. He had studied out what ought to be done and how to do it. Some assistance would be needed to do it and as Bennett was in a position to help him, the old man decided to let him know just enough to command his services—and nothing more.

To avoid exiting any curiosity the locator of the placer said he would ship by the railroad to Fort Steel in the spring enough lumber to build a flume and sluice box. Bennett had about twenty-five mule teams and as many as were required were to be set to work hauling the lumber into the valley so as to have it on hand to take into the mountains as soon as the snow went out. The impression was created that extensive works were to be put in when the season opened, judging from the amount of material and supplies for which transportation was being arranged. It was apparent that the need for further prospect work did not enter into the calculation at all. The diggings had gone beyond the stage when an investigation was needed to determine the extent to which they should be developed.

Such confidence could not do otherwise than arouse Bennett and create a longing to become interested in such a big thing. "Wait till I come back in the Spring and I will show you everything," the old man kept repeating.

This was the answer invariably returned to any inquiry as to the location of his diggings or anything else pertaining to them. The only exception he made to this rule was the statement that the new workings were handy to the stage station and in a place in the Sierra Madre on the river slope where there was an abundance of water and extra advantages for washing out the rich dirt. This, he said, covered a large area and the gold taken out there was heavy. So much Bennett was satisfied of from examination of the lot which the stranger said he panned out in four or five days. It was shot gold, some of it quite coarse specimens, weighing more than half a pennyweight.

Leaving Bennett in an expectant and impatient state his strange quest headed his outfit in the direction of Laramie. That was the last Bennett ever heard or saw of him. He did not turn up in the spring and so far as is known there was no placer work done to amount to anything in the Sierra Madre that year. No trace could ever be found of a man answering such a description that had turned up in Laramie. He may have died and with him, his secret.

Diggings where one man could wash out an average of nine or ten dollars a day have never been found since then in this part of the country so far as there is any record. The field is still open for anyone who wants to hunt for it. The place where the old man panned cannot be very far from Saratoga because he said he had made the trip to the ferry since morning. For the last four or five hours his journey must have been slow, as snow was falling at three or four o'clock in the afternoon. His horses did not appear to have been pushing hard and, in fact, it is not likely that in his condition the stranger could have traveled far.

The advent of the aged treasure-trove character in this section was prior to the time that Bennett heard anything about the lost Bradfield diggings. Neither Bradfield nor any of the old prospectors who accompanied him on his expedition search for the Lost Pick and Shovel claim professed to know anything about the mysterious gold-washer.

19 The Lost Sweetwater Mine

The dreams of sudden, lavish wealth were not all idle. This story was also printed in the Saratoga Sun in 1938 (October 6) and was collected for the Wyoming files by Fay Anderson August 12, 1941, shortly before the closing of the Works Progress Administration. The Sweetwater cuts eastward across the middle of Wyoming, joining the Platte at the Pathfinder Reservoir between Rawlings and Casper. Sublette County is in extreme western Wyoming.

Combining modern equipment with fairly well established legend centering in the vicinity of the headwaters of the Sweetwater in Sublette County a party of five men from Seattle, Washington, are closing in on what is thought to be a rich pocket of gold ore, according to the Pinedale *Roundup*.

The story, often repeated, concerns the experience of three early-day prospectors who, some seventy years ago, explored the headwaters of the Sweetwater. Upon returning from their expedition their saddle bags were said to have been filled with a fabulous quantity of the yellow mineral, both in free gold and gold ore. Later, two of the prospectors attempted to return to their diggings and were ambushed by Indians and killed. The third party, a man by the name of Phillips never returned but worked his way northwest to Seattle. Ore in his possession was taken from the rich lode and was recently assayed and found to be valued at approximately $15,000 per ton.

With a crude map of the surrounding territory, drawn by Phillips from memory, a return expedition is at present attempting to locate the lode. The expedition is financed by a group of prominent Seattle business men and promises to be a success with the use of geophysical equipment, and indications are being confined to the location near the headwaters of the Sweetwater from soundings which have been made over the area.

20 The Lost 600 Pounds

Perhaps the only gold trove that could be easier to pocket than a mine where the gold "color" literally lights the walls or a stream with nuggets the size of a walnut, is gold already extracted from the stream or lode by someone else and then lost or hidden and forgotten. This tale was recorded by WPA worker Olaf Kongslie from the Newcastle Newsletter in 1938 and may very well be a true story.

It is related that a party of twelve miners, '49s, from the gold fields of California, were on their way back east in the '70s through the Black Hills, carrying with them 600 pounds of gold which they had recovered from the rich sands of the western coast.

As the party was somewhere in the vicinity of Rotchford they were attacked by Indians and seven of them were killed. The survivors, in order to make their escape, buried the gold and marked the spot by sticking some rifles into the ground. With their loads lightened by the loss of 600 pounds of gold the five did escape and arrived at their destinations. Just why they did not return to get the gold is not told.

An old-time miner named Boch, who lived near Rotchford for a number of years, is reported to have found one of the rifles in 1876 and any number of persons have explored that area in the hope of finding the cache of gold but no one has ever reported any success.

Along about 1900 a nephew of one of the men who had been with the party and escaped visited the hills and he, it is said, found two more rifles but still no trace of the gold was found.

Last fall a party of deer hunters, one of them a sixteen year old school boy from Wall, South Dakota, were after deer in the Hills and this boy, according to the story, found the remains of an old rifle sticking in the ground. He pulled it up and took it back to camp and later it was presented to the museum at Deadwood, where it is now on display. Several efforts have been made to get the boy to go back and try to locate the exact spot where he found the rifle but so far that has not been done.

Tall Tales and Humor

21 The Coney

Wyoming has a reputation for wry frontier humor, represented chiefly in the works of the editor of the Laramie *Boomerang*, Bill Nye. His razor-edged, irreverent wit was timeless and still enjoys a wide circle of admirers today. And one might even say that Wyoming was born in humor, for when John Colter and Jim Bridger returned to Saint Louis with tales of the fabulous Yellowstone region (known then as "Colter's Hell") they found that no one believed their true stories about steaming fountains, mountains of glass, and bubbling natural paint pots, so they decided to "do it up brown" and elaborated their tales to an even more preposterous degree.

For the folklorist the problem then becomes, "What is truth and what is tall tale?" Sometimes the distinction is not at all clear. Was the following tale included in the Wyoming files as a point of biological interest and fact or as a possible antecedent for the famous Douglas, Wyoming, jackalope, the offspring of small antelope and large jackrabbits, ferocious in nature, capable of speaking English and singing cowboy songs, and eluding would-be hunters by shouting "There he goes! Over there."

In connection with the writer's [unidentified] report on the various wild animals which he listed as existing in Carbon County, when endeavoring to get an accuracy check he discovered considerable question was raised as to the authenticity of his report on a rather strange animal, seemingly native in this region, namely the "Coney," or as it is sometimes also spelled, "Cony."

Without question there are hundreds of people in this state who have never heard of the animal and a great many who have heard the name in connection with its value as a fur for wearing apparel who have not the slightest inkling concerning the animal itself. On the other hand there are a good many old timers and outdoor people of the mountains who have been acquainted with the existence of this strange little rodent almost "ever since they can remember." The writer himself has lain quiet for hours at a time in the higher parts of the Sierra Madre mountains of Carbon County and watched the little fellow put up his hay.

He is very hard to glimpse, being very wary and timid, with extremely acute senses of hearing and smell. Natives describe him as being about the size of a half-grown cottontail rabbit, with no tail, a head like a doe deer, large, round ears, activities resembling the chipmunk in movement, living mostly in the rocks, making hay similar to mankind by putting it up to dry, using various grasses, and baling it with a wisp or strand of grass. Its cry is similar to the sound produced when the stem of a squeegee balloon is blown without the balloon attached.

22 Bearing Down

The following two animal tales were collected by Ludwig Stanley Landmichl in the Big Horn Basin.

[That] reminds me of a yarn I heard about a bear hunter who had tamed and trained a bear to lead other bears close up within gunshot of the hunter when he went out bear hunting. He also had the bear trained so he could ride him. Once when he went bear hunting he sent the bear out to find another bear and lure it back so he could shoot it. The bear returned, with four others, all the same size and color of the tame one.

Perplexed, the hunter didn't know the tame bear apart from the others. And while he was trying to decide what to do the bears all got into a furious fight.

Well, the old dodger didn't want his tame bear torn to pieces so he flung himself into the melee to get his bear away from there. He leaped astride a bear and after considerable tussle got the bear started toward the cabin, having a gosh-awful time getting there. But when he got there he discovered that he'd brought in one of the wild ones!

23 Slovakian Rabbits

Which, quite naturally, brings to mind another yarn, not another bear story
but this time an innocent little yarn about rabbits.

In the heyday of Hudson's coal mining industry work about the mines
went on by night as well as by day. In this night work two men worked
together at driving a new slope. One of them was a Slovakian by the
name of Mike Malaski, the other an Irish lad whose name was Bill Flynn.
They always ate their midnight lunch together and Flynn would give
Mike a piece of pie or piece of cake from his lunch, for which in kindly
reciprocation Mike would give Flynn a piece of rabbit.

"Mike," said Flynn to the Slovakian one night, "You don't have time
to go hunting. Where do you get all the rabbits?"

"Oh," replied Mike blandly, "the wife she kill 'em when they come
around the house at night and cry out."

"Cry out?" echoed Flynn in consternation. "Why, Mike, rabbits don't
cry out."

"Yes, oh yes," Mike defended stoutly. "They go 'Meow meow.'"

24 The Prolific Herds

This tale from Jackson Hole in the northwestern area of the state, just south
of Yellowstone Park, was collected by Nellie H. Vanderveer of Jackson, who
brought her field reports into the FWP on horseback: The story brings to mind
Bill Nye's astonishing story, also about an enterprising Wyoming pioneer, who
came to the state with one lone steer and in the invigorating air his herd soon
grew to several hundred head, all off-spring of that lone steer.

This is not an outlaw story. It is a story about one of the leading citizens
of Jackson Hole and the amazing herd of cattle he once owned. This man
was one of the old-time, honest settlers of Jackson Hole and became
quite well-to-do because he knew how to take advantage of everything
the country had to offer to further the increase of his herd. The old timers often tell the story to illustrate the great advantages of Jackson Hole
as a cattle country. The cattle become so prolific sometimes. Of course
they must be the right kind of cattle to start with.

This Jackson Hole cattleman owned a herd of several hundred head. It turned out to be a most amazing herd. The abundant feed, the pure water, the wonderful climate, all combined to make this herd extremely prolific. And not only prolific: this herd upset the laws of Nature.

One season in particular every cow in the herd had at least two calves and a good many of them had three or more. Still more astonishing, these calves were not always the same size or age. There were several weeks, sometimes months, difference in the ages of the two or more calves belonging to the same cow although they were all born during the same season. Such a wonderful herd of cattle could not fail to bring rich rewards to the fortunate owner. Almost every cattleman in Jackson Hole found himself wishing that he could get a herd of cattle that would respond so well to the natural advantage of the country.

Whenever some newcomer wants to go into the cattle business and talks it over with the natives some old-timer is sure to tell him the story of the prolific herd. It is bound to prove a paying proposition if the newcomer takes advantage of the methods used by the owner of the famous herd of some years ago, making the most of the natural advantages of Jackson Hole. Of course he must have the right kind of a herd to start with.

25 Hunting on the Railroad

This tale, collected from the December 7, 1887, issue of the Douglas *Budget* by Jean McCaleb, would have been interesting enough in its own right but the editor of the *Budget* offered an interpretation of the item a week later that would also be worth reading on its own merit, rich with frontier dialect, vivid with wilderness imagery, and filled with historical data.

The customary few hours for dinner at Lusk had been spent and the accommodation train, consisting of a freight engine, a dozen boxcars, a baggage car, and a passenger coach, pulled out for Douglas. All the train hands were, as usual, on the lookout for antelope, herds of which were seen near the track every day, evidently attracted thither by the strange noisy objects that had boldly invaded their feeding grounds. The boys had been emptying their six-shooters at long range without achieving any noticeable triumphs, and interest in the sport was lagging, when the attention of the crew was attracted by a dark object moving along an arroyo some distance ahead on the south side of the roadbed and about three hundred yards from the track. That it was an animal was evident, though opinion was divided as to whether it was a mountain lion, wolf, or coyote. Interest in the matter at once rose to fever heat. The engineer signaled for brakes, the conductor scaled a boxcar and made for the forward end of the train to get the first shot and war was unanimously declared.

A regular fusillade was directed at the animal, which now had crouched close to the ground and seemed to seek shelter in a condensation of its own avoirdupois. The bullets tore up the ground for a dozen yards around and still the perverse creature laid low, unharmed. This went on for an hour; when the supply of ammunition was beginning to fail and the passengers aboard had exhausted their remarks about the marksmanship of the assaulting party and were considering counting the ties to Douglas, one of the attacking force chanced to cast an eye to the rear of the train a few steps away and saw a big-boned, roughly dressed stranger leaning against the steps of the rear platform, industriously chewing a big wad of tobacco and contemplating the actions of the train gang with every sign of cynical amusements. Where he came from or how long he had been there were questions which arose in the minds of the sharpshooters, for no sooner had he been sighted than he commanded the respectful attention of the whole outfit.

The ivory-handled "45" which was slung to his belt in a business-like position might have been one reason for the general cessation of hostilities toward the target, but the remarks inimical to the occasion which this tall specimen of frontiersman made when his presence was noticed was a strong hint to take a vacation.

"Ye're a set o' dandies now, ain't ye?" was the first observation volunteered by the mysterious spectator. "Been shootin' off your nickel-plated tops for an hour an' couldn't hit the blind side o' a sandbank, let alone a pore ol' dorg what's strayed away from camp and ain't got sight enough left in 'is eyes to see what all this blame noise is about. Fellers, that there's my Tige ye're pluggin' at so funny, and if I hadn't knowed ye couldn't come within a mile o' hittin' him there'd been a different kind o' war goin' on about this time."

There's no telling how long this disgusted pioneer would have continued in his contemptuous speech, for by the time it had dawned on the boys what kind of "mountain lion" they had been spoiling their ammunition in an effort to bag they were making tracks for the forward car in inglorious haste, followed by the shouts of the weary passengers, who had heard the remarks. The train moved on, and the canine's proprietor whistled to his property and the dog skulked to his master. The latter case a pitying glance at the dissolving forms of the knights of the rail that would have frozen a can of kerosene.

EDITOR'S EXPLANATION, DECEMBER 14, 1887:
It is possible that some of the *Budget* readers were inclined to doubt the truthfulness of that article on frontier railroading in last week's issue; but it was "straight goods." In fact, the envious down east railroaders used to call the train on the Chadron-Douglas division the "Pot-Hunters' Express," "Sharpshooters' Line," and "Ammunition Train" and things like that. The boys did have a high old time and no mistakes, but they reached the top notch last spring during the young sage hen harvest. The sage hen, when young and tender, is the peer of the quail or the prairie chicken and the most toothsome morsel ever set before a hungry hunter. The adult sage hen, on the contrary, is as tough as a bale of swamp grass and as rank as the breath of a consumptive hired girl. The rolling prairies between Lusk and Douglas were fairly alive with those birds last spring and the boys nailed more'n a million during the season. I made several trips with 'em and thoroughly convinced myself that hunting chickens with a railroad train is great sport. It was done this way: Two brakemen were stationed on top of the cars and these men, with the engineer and firemen, comprised the lookouts. On sighting a covey of chickens the engineer would give a peculiar signal, at which the conductor, expressman, baggageman, mail agent, brakeman, and everybody would sling a cartridge belt over the shoulder, seize a breech-loader, and otherwise prepare for the fray. When the train came to a standstill the hunters would hop off, and the lookout would sing out, "About ten car-lengths to the nor-west'erd." The shotgun brigade would march in the direction given with smoke and flame. Loaded down, and soon the very air

would be filled with dead birds the boys would return to the train, and thence onward in search of another covey (*sic*).

Occasionally the locomotive, contrary to all bird-dog etiquette, would flush a covey hiding near the track and give the boys a wingshot from the moving trains. I got two with each barrel, standing in the gangway of the engine one day, and we were making twenty miles an hour too at the time—for, although the time was slow enough and only one train each way, the boys usually put in from one to three hours a day in this sort of fun, which had to be made up somewhere and somehow.

26 All Aboard!

To the rest of the world the advent of the railroad was thought of as a civilizing feature, bringing culture and refinement with it wherever it happened to go. To the Wyoming frontier, however, judging from the last story and this next one, it was primarily a means of entertainment and amusement. The story is dated June 1, 1884, but is otherwise without identification.

Some of the boys who from time to time frequent the "curiosity shop" on Hill Street have a little quiet fun of their own which is hardly noticed except by the victims of their jokes. When the passenger trains come in there are generally from one to a half-dozen of the passengers who will step uptown for a moment to see how the city looks and occasionally some of them want to buy hats or something of that sort. This is where the fun for the boys comes in.

Just as these passengers start to go back to the train the boys will come out in front and sit around on boxes and benches and, when the passenger has got a good start down the walk across the flat towards the train, someone of the boys will sing out, "All a-b-o-a-r-d!" and then will follow such a scampering down the walk to the train as you don't see every day unless one happens to be down there the greater part of the time. Nineteen times out of twenty it will be from ten minutes to half an hour before the train starts. A middle-aged, well-dressed, man with a tall plug hat on got caught in that way last evening just after the train from the east arrived, and it was worth more to see that fellow run that it was to see Cole's white elephant. The train he wanted to go out on didn't start for more than an hour afterwards.

27 The Fossil Bug

After the settlement frontier had swept across the Plains and washed up against the east slope of the Rockies, other frontiers followed—for example, the technological frontier. When science, self-serious and unsmiling, met the sardonic world of the cowboy and homesteader, science definitely came off second best.

This tale was uncovered in the June 12, 1909, *Riverton Republican* by L. S. Landmichl. Riverton is smack in the middle of Wyoming.

J. B. Bradley, the well known sheep man of the Black Mountain district, was in town the first of the week for supplies. While here he sent a description of a queer find near his sheep camp to the Professor of Entomology of the Smithsonian Institution, at Washington DC.

It appears that about a month ago a prospector named Williams, who during the past spring had been touring Black Mountain in search of minerals, came across the fossil remains of what at first sight appeared to him to be an animal, imbedded in a chalk cliff on the western slope of the mountain. It lay on its back about two hundred feet up from the base of the cliff, which rose abruptly and towered fully a thousand feet from base to summit. The chalk had separated from the fossil and it lay in a niche or pocket in the cliff's face, just like a sleeping baby in a cradle.

Williams clambered up to it and on closer view it resembled a stone hippopotamus, being about the size of a half-grown animal of that species. But upon closer inspection still he found it to be more like a gigantic bug of the beetle family. So far as he could observe, without moving it, the fossil is entire, not a member being missing. Wings, legs, feet, even the long tenuous feelers, similar to those that protrude from the head of the common black beetle, all were intact.

Visiting the Bradley sheep camp, Williams told Mr. Bradley of his strange find, and the latter's curiousity (*sic*) being aroused he went to the cliff with him. They made measurements and found that the bug, or whatever it may prove to be, measured eight feet in length, five feet three inches in width across the center of the belly and two feet eleven inches in thickness. The legs were a trifle over a foot in length, six in number, and closely folded to the body. Wings six feet nine inches. The antennae protruding from the head measured two feet. The head itself, exact in resemblance to that of a beetle, was found to be a trifle more that a foot in length. Mr. Bradley estimates the weight of the bug to be about 1,200 pounds.

Williams claims that fossil by right of discovery and will try to dispose of it.

28 The Big Snake on Muddy Creek

Riverton seems to have gone through a spell of monster fever in 1909. The July 3 issue of the *Republican* of that year carried this story, specifically designed, it would seem, for the greenhorns in the youthful boom town.

R. P. Kile, who recently took up a claim on the Reservation on the banks of the Muddy, about twenty miles northwest of Riverton, was in town the first of the week with a strange tale. If it were not for the unimpeachable reputation for veracity enjoyed by Mr. Kile in this neighborhood some people might be of the opinion that he either looks at things through a most powerful magnifying lens or that he is not on speaking terms with the Goddess Truth.

The sheep men in the vicinity of the Kile Ranch have been missing lambs for the past two months, and until two weeks ago were unable to account for their strange disappearance. Almost every morning a lamb would turn up missing, the robbery invariably taking place during the hours of the night. They laid the decimation of their flocks at the door of the coyote family, probably because the coyote bears an evil reputation and has an evil inexhaustible appetite for spring lambs.

One morning about a month ago Walter Ferguson, a herder, found he was a lamb short on his count, and on looking around for traces of the missing animal found a long, sinuous trail in the soft dirt adjacent to the sheep camp. He traced it to the bank of the Muddy, some distance away, where it disappeared. The marks in the soil resembled those made by the passage of a large automobile wheel over soft mud.

Ferguson told his fellow herders of the track or trail he had found and they resolved to keep a sharp lookout for the lamb thief. But, while they were vigilant at all times, their lambs continued to disappear and they were unable to catch even a glimpse of the marauder.

A week ago last Tuesday, or, to be more correct, on the morning of June 15, Mr. Kile was out on the banks of the Muddy cutting fence posts. In the middle of the stream opposite from where he was cutting the posts is a big sandbar. Kile happened to glance in the direction of the sandbar and saw what looked like a blackened and charred stump lying on it. While he looked, the stump began to move. He admits that at the same time his hair began to move and assumed an upright position. Slowly the stump began to disintegrate as a stump and to take on the form of a serpent of enormous proportions. As he looked the snake stretched out to its full length, slid into the water, swam to the opposite bank of the Muddy and disappeared in the undergrowth of willows and weeds. Kile did not go out onto the sandbar to investigate. He came to the conclusion that the bar belonged to the snake, and he does not believe in trespassing. However, he had a good look at the reptile while it was uncoiling and says it was fully sixty feet in length and as large in circumference as a beer keg. In the center of the body was a lump about the size of a two-months-old lamb.

Kile is endowed with the deductive reasoning of an A. Conan Doyle and he at once put its forces to work. He had heard of the mysterious fading away of the sheepmen's lambs and it did not take him long to make connection between that snake and the little ones that are accustomed to following Mary. He went over to the camp of the Yellowstone Sheep Company and told the herders what he had seen in the Muddy. They gave him some antidote for loco weed and advised him to go home and put mustard plasters on the soles of his feet.

On Friday night of last week Orville M. Winterbottom of Lost Cabin, who owns a small band of sheep on the Muddy, was awakened about eleven o'clock by a disturbance in the sleeping flock. He tumbled out of his wagon, grabbed a Colt's (*sic*) automatic, and ran to the restless sheep. He saw a long round glistening object swiftly undulating through the sage-brush carrying a lamb in its mouth. He opened fire and emptied his gun at it but was afraid to go close enough to take a good aim. The reptile dropped the lamb, which scampered back to its hysterical mother. Winterbottom ran back to the wagon for his Winchester but when he returned the snake was gone. Clots of blood along the furrow-like trail to the Muddy testified that at least one of the revolver bullets had taken effect. The Winterbotom camp is nearly two miles form the Kile Ranch.

Mr. Winterbottom more than corroborates Mr. Kile with regard to the dimensions of the serpent. He saw it in the bright moonlight and it looked to him to be about seventy-five feet in length.

It is difficult to account for the appearance in this part of Wyoming of a reptile of the size affirmed by Mr. Kile and Mr. Winterbottom. No circus with a menagerie attached from which the snake could have escaped has ever visited this section of the country or has come nearer than five hundred miles to the Shoshone Reservation. The largest snake heretofore seen in these parts was the twenty-six foot bull snake killed near Fort Washakie last September while in the act of carrying off an Indian papoose.

The reptile seen by Mr. Kile is still at large and as there are many spring lambs gamboling on the braes (*sic*) of the Muddy, and, as wild mint grows in profusion along its banks, spring lamb with mint sauce will probably be on his a-la-carte until he retires to his winter quarters for his long comatose snooze.

29 Wyoming Fauna

The newspaper editor was the resident intellectual in frontier boomtowns that had too few children or too many gunfights to attract a schoolteacher. The editor was, in truth, the village wit, or at least it is the result of his efforts that survive for us to appreciate. Since he usually owned more books than anyone else in town—even though it might be only a dictionary—he also acted as the librarian and general reference and information center. Letters that might now be addressed to a chamber of commerce, tourist agency, or mayor's office went to the newspaper editor, and he gave the letters his undivided attention. This was collected by Fay Anderson from the January 23, 1903, issue of the *Grand Encampment Herald*.

In spite of all that the editor of the Dillon *Doublejack* can do to attract easterners to the mineral fields of Wyoming, he receives an average of a half dozen letters each mail asking about hunting and game in the Sierra Madre. He therefore wishes a public announcement made to the effect that these hills abound in game of various and strange kinds. We have the Cogly Woo (*sic*) which is a six-legged animal with a sharp, stiff tail. It has the faculty, when closely pursued and cornered, of standing upon this tail and whirling rapidly around, thereby boring a hole into the ground. Into this hole it disappears; the hole also disappears. This animal has been faithfully described by a noted naturalist who has written for several eastern newspapers.

We have the deadly Backaboar (*sic*), which is a four-legged animal with short legs on the left side and long ones on the right—adjusted admirably for mountain climbing. This animal courses its swift way around mountain peaks with its four legs always touching the ground equally, no matter how great may be the slope of the mountain. It can be captured only by turning its course to the opposite direction when its long legs become uppermost, when it suddenly falls off into space and is lost.

We have the One-Eyed Screaming Aemu (*sic*), which is a terrible bird inhabiting the highest peaks. It has the faculty, when closely cornered, of casting back upon its pursuers a look of mingled scorn and derision as, with one mightily, sickening gulp, it swallows itself.

30 The Capture of a Sea Serpent

As incredible as it must seem to the provincial easterner, the region between the Missouri and the Rockies apparently teemed with water monsters. Huge reptilian creatures were reported in Nebraska in the Platte River and Big Alkali Lake and now the species is traced several hundred miles further to the west to Lake DeSmet and Sheridan, on the north central border of the state, just a few miles south of the Montana line. Fort Phil Kearny lies approximately twenty miles south of Sheridan.

Frankly, I was out on a limb. Several months ago, in my weekly letters to flour brokers all over the United States, I had told them of the terrifying sea monster which lived in the murky depths of Lake DeSmet, and which at various times had swallowed Indians, road graders, missionaries, and various other delicacies (*sic*). For some reason those flour brokers, living a soft life in the effete east without even a hankering for the raw adventure to be found in the west, scoffed at me.

So it was up to me to make good. I immediately posted a reward of $100 for the capture of this monster, and I even went so far as to make arrangements to have it exhibited at the New York World's Fair in 1939.

Then I sat back to wait, certain that the monster would be brought to the Sheridan Flouring Mill where we had constructed a special tank and were prepared to fatten it on Tomahawk feed. I was even experimenting with a special laying mash, in the hope that I could produce some baby monsters to be given to the brokers for pets.

The reason that I was certain that the monster would be captured was because it had been seen this spring by Art Hufford of the Sheridan Meat company, whose reputation for veracity is unquestioned. He admits that he would have attempted to capture the awesome creature himself but he was in a hurry at the time to get to Buffalo to attend a Rotary Club meeting. The reason for his hurry was the fact that he had not missed a Rotary meeting since the club was founded by Chief Red Cloud in an attempt to foster a brotherly feeling between his braves and the troops in Fort Phil Kearny.

But the days dragged into weeks, and the weeks into months, and still no serpent. "By the Great Horn Spoon!" I finally declared, "I'll capture that beast myself—even if it takes all summer."

Being a man of action I immediately went to my ranch south of Sheridan and began to outfit my hazardous expedition. The items I finally selected were:

A sturdy, non-sinkable boat

Life preservers and water wings

A portable radio set like the one used by Commander Byrd at the South Pole

A cow, fattened on Tomahawk, to be used as bait

My favorite trout pole

A hay rope, to be used as a fish line (sic)

A block and tackle, to be used as a reel

An anchor from the flagship of the Wyoming navy, to be used as a hog

A compass and navigating instruments

My St. Bernard dog (weight 231 pounds, ringside)

Provisions for three months

A book, "How to Fish," by Isaac Walton

Tents and bedding

An Alaskan Harpoon

A pitchfork, otherwise known as a barnyard gaffhook

A case of Coca Cola (not to be taken for its face value).

As I scoured (*sic*) the lake in search of the monster, realizing that death was lurking behind every wave, news of my startling venture spread over the countryside. Finally even the Sheridan *Press* heard about it. As a result, L. L. MacBride, managing editor of that newspaper, and Walter Harris, staff photographer drove out to see if there was a story in it. . . .

Mac, after looking around the camp, expressed a desire to see how the instruments on my boat worked, so I started with him on a circle of the lower end of the lake. Everything seemed calm and peaceful, and I was sitting aft, trolling with some Tomahawk feed for bait.

ZINN-G-G-G-G-G!

My line snapped taut, my reel began to sing, and the boat was tossed around like a chip on the ocean. Thirty-Forty-Fifty-Sixty miles an hour we cut through the water.

"That's Governor Millers speed limit!" Mac gulped (*sic*)—and then, with a roar that echoed from shore to shore, a great monster leaped completely out of the water, snapping viciously with dripping jaws. We had hooked the monster at last.

That desperate ten-hour struggle still seems to me like a nightmare. We gyrated, twisted, turned, and sometimes the boat was actually sailing through the air a foot above the water, now churned to blood-red foam. Suddenly, without warning, the beast whirled around in the water straight for the boat.

It was a tense moment—our lives or his. Mac, who claims to have been raised on a farm, grabbed the pitchfork lying in the bottom of the boat and struck out blindly. Apparently he had been wearing a horseshoe for a tie pin because the blow proved fatal and soon the monster was drifting on its side as we slowly pulled to port. With the help of Walt and Dan, we managed to pull the huge carcass up on the shore and then a curious thing happened: the monster exploded!

The only explanation I can give is that the phenomenon was caused by the difference in pressure of the air and the water. We know that the monster had been living at great depths, where the pressure is much greater than at the surface or on land.

Our only evidence was what we found scattered around after the explosion—12 horseshoes, the wheel of a road grader, Father DeSmet's Bible, 13 Indian scalps, a backless bathing suit, a piece of track from the North and South railroad, and an outboard motor.

31 Vanishing Elk

The following story was collected by Olaf B. Kongslie from Mel D. Quick in Newcastle. It defies comment. The Bear Lodge Mountains are nestled in the very northeastern most corner of Wyoming.

In the fall of 1887 I heard queer stories of a thing that happened in the Bear Lodge Mountains. Some hunters came back from there telling of a mysterious herd of elk. They said they would follow the elk up to a certain place in the mountains and there the animals would disappear. Well, my partner and I decided to go and see for ourselves. We made our camp at the foot of the Bear Lodge Mountains and got ready to hunt.

The very first morning we struck a band of elk. They saw us and ran for the hills. We followed them, but when they struck the timber they were no where to be seen. There were no tracks, no sign of them anywhere. Well, that night when we went back to camp my partner said he'd had enough, but I said I'd try it once more.

The next morning I pulled out and scared up the same herd of elk. I followed them to the timber and they vanished in the same way as before. But this time as I looked carefully about I happened to glance up and there were all the elk perched in the branches above.

Well, I picked out a fine fat buck and thinks I, "I'll do a nice job of it and shoot him through the head," but he kept dodging around the tree away from me and I had to keep going around so fast that I was well nigh dizzy. Finally I did catch up with him and plugged him neatly through the head, but he did not fall to the ground.

Then I went up to see what was the matter and found that when he started around the tree he had caught his foot in a crotch and it had held him fast. But he had kept stretching and going on around to keep me from shooting him, until finally when I did manage to unwind him I found his body was 128 feet long.

32 The Hard-Water Spring

Wyoming's geography is so spectacular in its reality that it almost defies exaggeration—who could conjure up anything as bizarre as Yellowstone?—but a few fertile minds have managed to rise to the occasion. The following was published in the *Sheridan Post* on February 20, 1920, and was deposited with the Wyoming FWP project by Ida McPherren.

There is a cozy corner over at the Elks Home where interesting characters occasionally forgather. Men come there from all walks of life but it is when some of the old-timers get together that the man who is fortunate enough to be near may hear things that are not written in the books. Wyoming is still in her swaddling clothes compared with some of the hoary states of the east and the man who alighted in the land of promise a quarter of a century ago is fully justified in laying claim to the honor of being an old timer. But the real pioneers are the men and women who journeyed westward soon after the Civil War and landed in Wyoming during the late seventies or early eighties. These men are the real goods.

There are not many of them left. Not because they have died off, for these rugged, husky, red-blooded trail breakers do not die young nor do they ever grow old. Most of them moved on when the buffalo left but there are a few of them here, active businessmen generally, but still far enough along in life to occasionally drop into a reminiscent mood, and when one of them does get started, he is worthy of close attention.

"This grumbling and growling about exorbitant (*sic*) water rates and the inadequate (*sic*) supply of water is rather amusing to me when I remember the conditions when I first hit the place where the city of

Sheridan is now located, and for a good many years after," said a real old timer who landed in the Big Goose Valley along in '81. "Of course when I first came there was not much kick about water, for there was no one here to do the kicking. There wasn't any town, but George Mandell had taken up a homestead and had built a cabin down on Big Goose on what is now Smith Street. George could get plenty of water out of Goose Creek, but that was about all he could get. Grub had to be hauled four hundred miles from the railroad and about the only company he had was Injuns and a few stray hunters who happened along.

"George stuck it out a while, then came to the conclusion that the homestead was not worth a damn anyway, so one day he pulled up stakes and left. Harry Sutton, then jumped the claim and I suppose proved up, for later he sold the cabin to J. D. Loucks.

"About that time John Works came rolling in from Iowa and with him was his son-in-law, Dr. Rhodes. The doctor brought with him a few boxes of pills, some castor oil, smoking tobacco, and overalls, and opened up a store in the Sutton cabin, and then we felt like we were right in town, though we still had to go to Big Horn for our mail.

"Afterwards the cabin was moved and the logs went into a building on the corner of Main and Loucks, where J. D. Loucks ran a store. Later the building was sold to E. A. Witney for the first bank in Sheridan and the logs today are in the building now occupied by T. B. Freeman.

"But it was the water I started to tell about. After Sheridan had grown to be quite a town, most of the water came from the Big Goose. Joe Coleson, Jack Jones, and a few others would haul it and it sold for two bits a barrel. Old H. C. L. (*sic*) had already begun to make his presence felt and the water system raised its meter rate to four bits, and then what a howl went up.

"There were a few surface wells where water was reached at a depth of twelve to fourteen feet, but the water was so hard that you had to pound it to pieces with a maul before you could drink it, so little of it was used.

"Finally a bright idea struck Jim Cazien and he decided to dig a real well, so he freighted in a drill and sank a hole just back of the old Windsor, three hundred fifty feet deep. An artesian well was the result, and it flowed about fifty barrels a day, but the water [was] so impregnated with minerals that it could not be used.

"The water tasted so peculiar that McClinton—'Old Mack' we called him—decided it was undoubtedly fine medicine. Mack was getting a little old and really needed a rejuvenating drought, and as goat glands had not yet become fashionable he decided to drink the artesian water. He kept up for a week and then quit. 'What's the matter with the water, Mac?' one of the boys asked him. "Nothing,' Mac says, "The water's all right, but it's a trifle too efficacious. That water is so full of iron,' Mac said, "that after I had drank it a week, every time I would go to expectorate, I would spit out a string of ten-penny nails!'"

33 "Dutch" Seipt's River

In a state with place names like Chugwater, Tensleep, Tie-Siding, Crowheart, and West Thumb, it is not surprising that some traditional explanations for these names have sprung up. This tale was collected by Ludwig S. Landmichl. The Big Wind River runs southeast from the Continental Divide just south of Yellowstone Park.

There is a yarn about "Dutch" Seipt, who owned and operated the Hermitage Lodge near Dubois. Dutch was a very talkative fellow— "windy," some of the boys said, which, by the way, is a highly necessary accomplishment for the successful operation of a dude ranch. The yarn goes that there was a party of surveyors working near Hermitage Lodge. Dutch came along and got to talking with them, incidentally bringing up the subject about naming certain points of interest.

"Why don't you name something after me?" he asked.

"Why, there already is a large stream named for you," one of the surveyors replied.

"What's that?" asked Dutch.

"Big Wind River," was the prompt reply.

34 The Great Discovery

Deep down one would like to believe this tale. The story was published on April 2, 1881, in the *Evanston Chieftain* and was uncovered for the FWP project by Charles M. Fowkes Jr. Evanston, for the information of those readers who would like to join us in organizing a search party for this lost mine, is less than five miles from the Utah border, in the extreme southwestern corner of Wyoming.

On Monday of last week Messrs. A. C. Beckwith, A. V. Quinn, M. V. Morse, and one or two other Evanstonians, together with Mr. D. O. Clark, superintendent of the Union Pacific coal department, started in a wagon for some point of the Bear River. This move on the part of these prominent business men, taken in connection with the immediate prospect of one or more northern lines of railway, created quite a ripple of excitement among the curbstone prophets and speculators of Evanston, and various surmises were indulged in as to the meaning and object of their trip. Some said they had gone to file a claim on all the coal lands in the vicinity of Twin Creek. Others thought they had gone to stake off a city and erect extensive warehouses.

In order to satisfy our own curiosity in the matter and also to be able to give our readers a full, reliable, and trustworthy account of the object and result of this trip, when the party returned we sought and obtained a personal interview with Mr. Beckwith, and what we gathered from the conversation is substantially as follows, and can be relied upon as true and correct.

The party had no higher object than the pursuit of wealth, and they have found it. They were on a prospecting tour, and they have struck it rich. They have found and located the best paying claim in the world. Within twenty feet of the mouth of a tunnel at the head of Twin Creek Canyon they discovered and located a claim of rich gin cocktails of the most aristocratic flavor.

This mine flows about 26 barrels a minute and assays 268 drunks to the gallon. As soon as the discovery was made known, hundreds of men gathered around from all parts of the country, eager and excited, offering to swap coal, lands, railroads, and every other kind of property for an interest in this new discovery, and when Mr. Beckwith and party started for Evanston there were about 8,000 men on the grounds hunting for the extension of Gin Cocktail Mine.

The holders stood firm, refusing to part with any portion of their claim, as they have a grand scheme in view. They are going to establish a line of steamers between the mine and Salt Lake City. They will float the steamers out of the Twin Creek on cocktails into Bear River. This will let their vessels into the Great Salt Lake; this will furnish the company with independent transportation to the lake and from there at intervals along the shore, tin tubes will radiate in all directions, supplying all southern Utah, Arizona, Mexico, all the United States, and Green River City with the choice fluid. The first steamer of this elegant line is to be named "Kit Castle."

35 Love on the Yellowstone

Jackson Hole country is notorious for its brutal winters and wintery summers, lows ranging to sixty-five degrees below zero. The town of Jackson lies at an altitude of 6,000 feet, which, assisted by the northern latitude and mountain shadows, gives rise to the common Jackson Hole saying that here there are only two seasons, July and winter, and tales like that of the old-timer who was asked how he liked the summers in Jackson Hole and replied that he didn't know because he had only been there for three years. Ice in the lakes has on occasion remained solid into July and snow accumulates to such a depth that laundry can be hanged to telephone lines and cattle are driven directly into the second floor loft of the barns. (As collected by Nellie VanDerveer).

But in Jackson Hole, as in the rest of Wyoming, the real interest lies not in weather or geographical phenomena but in the men and women who lived here. It was in their wit that the peculiarities of that geography were transposed into magic. And even more significantly, it was in their wits that the ordinary became worth a laugh. For example, a hunter who visited Jackson Hole in the 1930s got a bill tersely worded: "10 goes, 10 comes, at $5.00 a went."

It was perhaps a gent of like articulation who was the subject of the following item, first published in the *Bozeman Courier*, and reprinted on September 21, 1874, in the *Cheyenne Daily Leader*, from which it was copied for the FWP files. It is a tender story that should put to rest forever the frequent comments to the effect that the harsh frontier spirit had little time for affairs of the heart. (Gallatin County, Montana, lies to the northwest of Yellowstone Park.)

One of Gallatin's fair daughters while returning from Wonderland stopped with her companions at a Yellowstone ranch. They had been there scarcely an hour when one of the proprietors gained the ear of our heroine and informed her that hard by was one of the finest, largest, best, and most skukum (*sic*) raspberry patches he had every seen or heard tell of. "Why, they could just scoop them up," etc. He urged upon her the necessity of the berries being picked immediately, as they were dead ripe, millions of them. She was delighted at the prospect of going for the berries, but when she ascertained that our hero was bent upon acting as guide, her ardor became dampened.

However, they started.

We bid adieu to any further description of this novel scene as now follows the conversation in which the mountaineer wooed the former city belle, whom two hours before he had never seen, showing the absurdity of the old "faint heart" and "frail lady" business.

"Say, do you see them fences?"

"Oh yes. They are nice fences."

"Well, them fences is ourn." (sic)

"Whose?"

"My pard's and mine. Half is mine and half is his'n, and those fields is our'n too, and the houses and stock and chickens and all on the ranch is our'n, half is mine and half is his'n."

"Ah, indeed."

"Yes, and you do not know how much we got in the bank besides and if I was to get a wife you bet I would get more than half. And I suppose you don't know I'm the best hunter and guide in the Rocky Mountains. Well, I am, and what is more, I have enough of quartz to buy out all the post offices in Montana, and pay for running them besides. Why, I have a fortune just in one mine alone. The boys tell me it's gold, sure, and if it ain't, that it's good quartz anyhow, and—don't—don't you think I ought to get married?"

"Most assuredly I do. A young man possessing your wealth and good looks should not hesitate a moment about entering into matrimony. I am surprised to think you are still single. Are you?"

"Well, yes, I suppose so. But say, do you see them granaries? Well, I just have enough grain over yonder to last two years, and so you see I can stand off the grasshoppers one year anyhow. And you needn't be afraid of Injuns up here. They don't come this high up, and say, don't you want to marry me? There now?"

"Oh, sir, why—why, this is so unexpected, you know, and besides, I—I should deem it my duty, while thanking you for honoring me with your hand, to inform you that I am engaged to be married to a gentleman in the States. I regret that your affections are not bestowed upon some young dandy (sic) who is heart free. Please do not refer to this subject again."

"Well, I wouldn't have done so now, only I heard as how you didn't talk pretty to a nice got-up Boseman chap, and told him you didn't want to marry him no how, and I supposed after that I stood a good show of catching you myself. And—and (raising his voice) there's the raspberry patch over there, and come to think of it, I don't think they are as damned thick as they use to be."

36 The Dying Cowboy

Cowboys were the subject of a good many humorous tales, in part because their lives when viewed by town folks—that is, when the cowpokes came in wild and wooly after a drive, loaded with money and short on inhibitions— lent themselves to humor, and partially because cowboys are not afraid to tell stories about themselves and to laugh at them. These tales were recorded by Alice Guyol, a field worker for the Federal Writers Project in Hartville, in conversations with old-time cowboys.

The great ranches of early days located in the area north of what are now the towns of Hartville and Sunrise were the famous Keeline and 4J holdings, and one of the best known practical jokers of this times was Harry O'Hair, cowboy on the Keeline ranch, who later became a prosperous ranchman in his own right. Tales of Harry O'Hair are still told, although he has been dead for many years.

O'Hair was also past master in the art of prevarication when it came to describing his experiences and exploits. On one occasion a party of ladies visited a round-up camp, with their escorts, and O'Hair, never adverse to the spotlight, approached the visitors. Casually rolling a cigarette he offered to give them any information they might desire.

"What was the most exciting experience you ever had?" demanded a lady, a visitor from the East.

O'Hair immediately launched into a description of an occasion when on foot and alone in Slade's Canyon he had found himself surrounded by a least fifty Indians. He had started to run, but they pursued him— drawing closer and closer—until he had reached the head of the canyon. Here he was confronted by a solid wall of rock, impossible to climb and with the hills closing in on either side. The Indians were also closing in, and he knew that his hour had come. His auditors were quivering with excitement, as O'Hair paused in his telling.

"And what did they do to you?" gasped the lady who had called for the story.

O'Hair, with a dramatic gesture, answered, "Lady, they killed me."

37 Getting the Tenderfoot

Not infrequently the practical joke was turned on the joker and when this occurred the story was told with the same gusto that would have been felt in relating the success of the trick. The cowboy was sportsman enough to enjoy a joke on himself, and it would lose nothing in the telling. Any tenderfoot visiting the west was a logical recipient of these somewhat crude attentions.

An incident of this type is still related when a few of the remaining knights of the range foregather. It concerns a tenderfoot who visited a cow camp in the old days and who was unwise enough to let it be known that he was obsessed by an insane fear of snakes. At the first opportunity some of the cowboys killed a large rattlesnake and, attaching a string to it, waited until the tenderfoot had retired, when they placed the snake on his bed. They awakened the man with cries of "Snake! Snake!" and as he raised up they pulled the rattler along with the string. With a blood-curdling shriek the tenderfoot leaped from his bed and rushed out into the night.

Through cactus and sagebrush, across gulches and over rocks raced the tenderfoot, with the cowboys panting and gasping after him. They eventually succeeded in surrounding him and with him returned to camp.

Here they explained the joke, which the tenderfoot accepted good-naturedly.

He departed however the following day, leaving the jokers to nurse sore feet and bruised shins and to vow that they would never try to play a joke on another tenderfoot unless they hobbled him first.

38 Jerky Bill's Funeral

One of the most popular stories of the entire district is told by a small rancher known as "Jerky Bill," whose escapades are still remembered. It was during a fall roundup attended by all of the cattle owners in the area that a camp was made near the town of Douglas The campsite was located close by an old graveyard with many deep, sunken graves.

Most of the men went into town to celebrate when night came on, and among these was Jerky Bill.

Returning in the wee, small hours, Bill missed his way to camp and upon dismounting his horse stumbled into one of the old sunken graves. Too drunk to rise he simply slept there until dawn, and, at daybreak, the men at the camp heard a great whooping and shouting.

Rushing to the spot they discovered Jerky Bill sitting up in the grave. "Whoopee," he shouted. "Whoopee! It's Resurrection Mornin' and I'm the *first one up!*"

Characters, Big and Little

39 The Wake of the White Swede

It is precisely the singular and sometimes awe-inspiring character of these people who are truly representative of the attitudes and emotions of the frontier culture as a whole that made them as eligible for legendary treatment as geographic features like Devil's Tower. Indeed, the parallel is more than literary: how much like that uncompromising shaft of basalt towering over the surrounding prairie are the frontiersmen! Wouldn't it be a joy to spend an evening at the campfire of John Colter or Father DeSmet or Jim Bridger or Chief Joseph, to hear from their mouths what it was that drove them on their unique historical paths?

Sometimes it is not one man or several particular ones that leave the reader wondering, but the actions of several nameless ones simply acting in accordance with a cultural standard that we no longer embrace. It is difficult to know how to react to the following story, one of the best and most widely known of Wyoming legends. Is the gamblers' cavalier attitude toward death an admirable irreverence, or is it a callous disrespect? The editors prefer to accept the former.

This version of the story was collected by Alice C. Guyol from four Hartville sources: Jack Welsh, Dan Hauphoff, Mrs. N. Catlin, and J. J. Covington.

One of the strangest wakes ever held at any time or in any place occurred during the riotous mining-camp day of Hartville, Wyoming in 1902. This wide-open camp with its saloons, dance halls, and gambling joints had become a Mecca for an assortment of characters that have now almost entirely vanished from the American scene, including a number of tinhorn gamblers. Among these was one known as the "White Swede." He was not in fact a Swede but in addition to being very light in complexion he had a dead white face that contrasted strongly with the sun-tanned visages of his associates.

One night this man died suddenly from natural causes and, as there was no undertaker in the community, the corpse was laid out on a cot in his room. Three of his gambler friends agreed to sit up through the night with the dead man and this they did. Coming to the place at dusk they made themselves comfortable. Then they moved a table up beside the cot, raised the head of the corpse as high as they could, placed a cigar in his mouth, and a glass of whiskey on the table beside him with the bottle nearby. Pulling up chairs for themselves they started a poker game which was to last throughout the night. News of the game was carried about and occasionally other men dropped in to note the progress of the play.

The corpse was dealt a hand, which was played for him by the other gamblers, and thus the game was carried on until dawn, with drinking and laughter.

Every effort was made by the authorities in the mining camp to locate friends or relatives of the dead man but no one was every found to claim the body. He was buried in the old cemetery near Hartville. It was said at the time that the winnings of the corpse in his last game were used to help defray the funeral expenses.

40 Disappearing Johnny

This story was collected and collated from several sources by Olaf B. Kongslie. The tale is set in the locale of Newcastle in the extreme northeastern part of Wyoming.

For two generations the youths of this locality have searched for the cave of the robber recluse who for years successfully evaded the early day sheriffs in the strangest sort of a hide-and-seek manhunt ever carried on. This story-book drama took place some forty to fifty years ago and the circumstances are now so little known or remembered that it has taken a legendary character and few even give credence to the tale of the mysterious cave.

They say that a certain man, known only in these parts as "Disappearing Slim" Johnny, came to this country when the Black Hills were still a part of the forbidden land of the Sioux. He had selected a beautiful spot on the Limestone Plateau, and here in a tiny upland meadow had built himself a home.

The Limestone Plateau, on the border line of South Dakota and

Wyoming, is one of the most rugged regions of the Hills. It is a land of steep, jutting cliffs, deep, narrow canyons like gashes in the terrain, winding caves and tunnels washed out of the limestone formation by the action of water, and great castle-like rocks protruding from forest of pine and quake-aspen so dense that in many places only a small animal can penetrate the thickets. This region of the Hills to this day remains little known or frequented.

For years Slim lived the life of a hermit, hidden away in the forest of the limestone. He had built himself a crude log shelter and a stable and corral for his horses. Game was very bountiful and in summer he raised vegetables in the rich soil of a little clearing near the shack. In the winter when the deep snows of the region piled up to the very eaves of his cabin he hibernated somewhat like a bear.

He was lost to the world in this wilderness, lost and forgotten, as he no doubt thought and certainly desired to be; but back east the law remembered, as it always does, those who trespass against it, and Slim Johnny had been a serious offender. It is said that he had murdered a wealthy old man and stolen his money, some ten thousand dollars in gold and paper. That is why he had sought refuge in this wilderness, miles away from his fellow beings.

Still trespassing against the law, hidden away in the heart of Indian Country, which white men were forbidden to even enter, Slim felt himself secure from discovery and he probably thought he could live free from worry and care the rest of his life on ill-gotten fortune. A trip once a year to the trading post at Pierre could supply him with all his needs and this trip he made with his two horses, loading them down with all they could carry. Needless to say, he took precautions to disguise himself before he entered the trading post and if anyone had been looking on they would have seen a tall, slender man with long, blond hair and beard suddenly change to a stoop-shouldered, dark complectioned (sic), black-bearded person with a lame leg. By such subterfuge (sic) Slim Johnny was able to fool the law for many years. He had even guarded against chance discovery by wandering scouts and prowling Indians, for he had a secret cave somewhere near his abode, into which he could disappear at a moment's notice, and here he kept his stolen riches.

He had taken care of himself very well but there was one thing on which he had not counted. That was the rapid advance of civilization. Before he realized what had happened the land had been wrested from the Indians, and white people were pouring into the country looking for gold and digging in every hillside for the yellow dust. Soon ranches dotted the banks of Beaver Creek that flowed at the foot of the plateau and it was becoming increasingly difficult to maintain his policy of isolation. The towns of Custer and Newcastle were built and soon the whistle of locomotives penetrated even his lonely retreat.

Then he found that he could not keep away from the towns. The hustle and bustle, the excitement and color of the young, growing communities attracted him in spite of himself, and he found himself drinking at the bars and "playing the wheels" all too often. He was extremely lucky at poker and often put back twice as much money in his strong box in the cave as he had taken out. He avoided his neighbors as much as possible, but they would come and intrude on his solitude and gradually his attention began to drop from him until he even discarded his disguises and went about quite openly.

But he was such a tight-lipped, odd-acting fellow that people could not help but regard him with suspicion, and eventually the truth filtered through that he was a hunted man—a criminal. Then began the queerest game of fox-and-hounds ever played, with Slim as the fox and the officers of the law as hounds. For some years the game continued, for Slim always managed to give the hounds the slip.

He never came to town after that any oftener than was necessary, then he would hurry into Custer or Newcastle in some disguise and be gone again before the officers had time to learn what it was all about. Sometimes they hounded him almost to his lair in the woods, but he always turned the corners ahead of them and when they arrived at his cabin he was no where to be found. They fine-combed the ranch and adjoining woods but not a trace of his retreat could they find. They tried to take him by surprise but never, night or day, were they able to find him at home.

One time they arrived just at dark and saw a light shining from his cabin window. They thought surely they had him and sneaked to surround and pounce upon him but cautious as they were Slim's dog, a wild beast half coyote and half dog, raised an alarm and when they rushed to the cabin and threw open the door no Slim was to be seen. An inviting aroma of bacon and coffee greeted them. Hot cornbread and bacon steamed upon the table and the coffee pots sang on the stove. It was a home-like scene but the host was absent from the board. Nevertheless the hungry posse sat down and enjoyed the meal and when they left they pinned a note on the door that read, "Thanks for the supper, Slim. You sure can make good cornbread. We'll be seein' you."

And so it went on for years in spite of the fact that there was a sizeable reward offered form Slim's capture. And it might have gone on for some years to come but for one thing—and that thing was an apple pie! You might say that the apple pie was what captured Slim, but of course the sheriff got credit for it.

One evening Slim was out looking for one of his horses that had gone astray and had found it at the ranch of his nearest neighbor. As Slim rode past the house the owner came out and greeted him most hospitably. The man engaged Slim in conversation about the straying horse and acted so friendly that Slim, as suspicious as he was about all people, lingered on the road in front of the ranch house door. A flood of lamp light issued from the open door and a warm, delicious smell of freshly baked bread wafted out upon the cool autumn air. The man of the house had invited Slim to stay for supper. "Aw, come on in, Slim, and have a bite to eat with us. You must get darned lonesome way up there by yourself. What's your hurry? Come on in."

"Aw, thanks, Bill, but I've got to be gittin' on home."

Slim started to back away but at that crucial moment the good housewife appeared in the door with a great, fat apple pie in her hands, bubbling hot from the oven. She set the pie on the shelf by the door and a tantalizing fragrance of cinnamon spice drifted to the nostrils of poor Slim. Hypnotized he gazed at the pie, for its aroma had cast a spell on him, a spell that seemed to carry him back to the long ago when he was a boy at home and led the life of a normal human being, not that of the hunted outcast he now was. All his resistance and caution gave way and some how he found himself dismounting and on the way to the barn with his host. There they gave the horses a good feed and then returned to the house.

It was years since Slim had known neighborly friendliness or hospitality. The hard shell of his reserve dropped from him and he found himself conversing freely with his host and hostess. It seemed like a dream to sit down to a table with a clean white cloth and sparkling china dishes and the food seemed like something from paradise. After all, cornbread, even the best of cornbread, could not compare with fresh home-made rolls and apple pie. Rose-cheeked children ringed the table and it all seemed so happy, so natural somehow, after the long years of isolation. One thing he did not mark however was that one of the children was missing.

They were sitting in front of the fire when a clatter of hoofs sounded in the yard, Slim knew instantly what that meant. He realized that he had been betrayed—baited like a fox. His rare mood of friendliness flashed to fury and with a venomous oath he whipped out his gun and turned on his host. But the man was on guard and knocked the weapon from Slim's hand so that the deflected bullet struck in the wall. For an instant the two men wrestled desperately until the posse entered and overpowered Slim. Then he gave up and went along with them quietly.

He pleaded guilty to his crime but nothing could make him reveal the secret of his hidden cave. He boasted that he had thousands of dollars stored there and piles of gold dust that he had dug from his secret mine, but to all queries regarding it he had but one answer, "Damn you, you will never find it."

He died in prison, an old man, but never once did he reveal a single clue to the whereabouts of his mysterious hideout. And it looks as though the mystery will go unsolved, or has the treasure already been found and confiscated by someone who can keep a secret as well as Slim Johnny?

41 The Lynching of Walters and Gorman

Bad men have traditionally captured the Anglo-American imagination. Of course that is in part due to the alleged romance and daring of the elusive outlaw, but often ignored is the fact that the most admired of those robbers have been those who directed their attentions to the railroads, the banks, and the government—the very agencies that the people felt were the thieves who dipped into their pockets with impunity. Jesse James, then, was not seen as a violator of the public morality but rather as an agent of social justice.

Those bad men who preyed on the common man were not celebrated in song and legend but instead received summary justice at the end of a rope. Today it is the fashion to show in television westerns how the innocent (and sometimes even the guilty) are saved from the rope by a brave and righteous sheriff, but that was rarely the reality. More often than not the sheriff was a corrupt, unreliable, quasi-legal figure whose loyalties were questionable, as was also the integrity of his jail. Moreover, a gang member in jail might be the cause for a raid from his compatriots, and while a corpse was not worth any risk, vengeance carried little profit. The grim spirit of vigilante justice and something of the incredible guts all men—good and bad—had to have to face the forward edge of the frontier, glare out from a historical story that became Wyoming legend. The story, recorded in the Big Horn *Rustler* in July of 1903, told of the lynch-executions of murderers held in the Big Horn County jail in the town of Basin. Deputy Clark Earl Price was in charge of the jail holding Joseph Walters, accused of murdering Agnes Hoover of Thermopolis, and James Gorman, who had been convicted of killing his brother. Even more importantly to the mob, Gorman had been twice convicted, had yet one other appeal pending, and had escaped once for two days.

A mob of 35 to 50 citizens advanced on the jail from across the Big Horn River on the east side of town and threw a cordon of pickets around the jail to keep away idle sightseers. They began to batter down the jail door and shot a volley through the door, inadvertently killing the clerk, Earl Price.

Next the mob's attention was directed to opening the steel door and grating separating them from the prisoners. Tools were brought from a near-by blacksmith shop and at the end of some ten minutes these were opened, giving access to the corridor containing the cage and cells occupied by the four prisoners in custody. An endeavor was made to open the cage but its material and workmanship proved too strong.

Old Man Walters was first of the prisoners to fall. He lighted a candle and gave it to the men hammering at the door, saying, "Take this; you can do better," to which the party addressed answered, "Much obliged, old man."

Walters met his fate bravely, saying, "Boys, if you are after me, here I am. Don't destroy the jail." His suggestion was followed: they shot him down in his tracks, he falling in the door of his cell.

Gorman, who had a cell-mate in the person of a suspected horse thief arrested three days before, next fell a victim to the mob's vengeance. According to Gorman's companion's story he pleaded with his assailants for mercy, saying he had a mother and a sister who would mourn his death. He was answered that he had shown very little consideration for them. After dodging around the cell for some little time he was shot down in position where he could be killed without danger to others. Gorman received five wounds in all, from which he died after lingering until 8:30 Sunday morning. He made no statement, though he claimed to have recognized some of the mob.

After finishing their terrible work the mob assembled north of the courthouse at the command of their leader and marched quietly in close order to the river bank, taking a southeastern direction on leaving this vicinity. . . .

 Jim Baker's Revenge

Summary justice was not always fatal for the defendant and sometimes in the narration the effect is more humorous than didactic. This tale was published in the *Saratoga Sun* on January 23, 1939.

Jim Baker, who came to Wyoming country in 1838, built in 1873 over in the Little Snake River Valley the picturesque cabin which now stands in Frontier Park at Cheyenne, and who died in 1898 after sixty years on the frontier, came out of the Medicine Bow Mountains in 1866 with three horses loaded with furs he had taken during the preceding winter. He thought he was through with the west and intended to take the money the furs would bring in Denver and retire to his native state, Illinois.

The forty-eight year old mountain man reckoned, however, without his passion for gambling and the thorough crookedness of gamblers with whom he consorted at Denver and the nearby settlement of Golden. Soon the sizeable sum for which he sold the furs had gone into the pockets of the gambling gentry and his vision of a life of ease in Illinois was gone with the wind. This made him right peevish and he wasn't a pleasant person to be around when he was in a peevish mood. In fact, proximity to him on such occasions might be downright dangerous.

Jim, confronted with the harsh necessity of returning to the peril-infested mountains to gather more skins, brooded upon his evil fortune, decided that among those who had contributed to it most reprehensibly was a gambler who held forth at Golden. Forthwith he sought out the slippery gent and without dismounting his Indian pony upbraided him in English, Sioux, Cheyenne, Arapaho, Ute, Crow, Shoshone, and Spanish, selecting from each tongue with a fine discrimination the most opprobrious epithets of its lexicon. Incensed to the point of infuriation by this polyglot tirade and his inability to phrase retort discourteous save in inadequate English, and being at the moment, as was his tormentor, destitute of a device with which an explosion of gunpowder might be caused to impart to a leaden pellet a lethal velocity, the gambler, with more courage than discretion, seized upon clods of earth and hurled them at the vituperative victim of his manipulation of the cards.

This childish display of temper was displeasing to Jim. So displeasing, in fact, that he felt constrained to do something about it. Loosening his riata he deftly heeled the prancing dirt slinger, whipped the slackened rope over the projecting ridge pole of a cabin, and elevated the squirming corporeality of the object of his disapproval until it was suspended a man's height above the ground. Then, while his trained pony kept the rope taut, he gathered brush, built a fire beneath the dangling gambler, and smoked him until he pleaded for mercy.

None who looked on moved to interfere, Jim's demeanor suggesting that interference might be inimical to the health of the interferer (*sic*). Finally, after a homily on the virtue of holding one's temper and also holding only those cards which chance and chance alone bestows upon one engaged in a game for stakes, Jim kicked the fire aside, lowered the half suffocated sharp upon the excessively hot spot where it had been, disengaged his rope, and departed, his good-humor fully restored by the divertissement (*sic*) in which he had engaged.

43 The Piano Tuner and His Hallet Canyon Hunch

When Dow combed the Wyoming FWP papers, he labeled this item "legendary?" and Welsch had the same question in mind. Is this a factual news report? Is it some one writer's fancy? Or is it, as hinted in the phrase "it is said . . ." truly a Wyoming legend? We have included it here on the basis of that phrase and one other factor: the documentation for the item reads "September 14, 1904, Laramie, Wyoming, *The Boomerang*." Now, the *Boomerang* was Bill Nye's great newspaper, named after his favorite mule, and that alone is good reason to doubt the fact of the matter. The city of Laramie, incidentally, is not the same as Fort Laramie and is located in the southeastern corner of the state, a scant twenty miles north of the Colorado border.

Out of the head to Trail Creek, in the Halleck Canyon country there is a mining prospect upon which quite extensive work has been done. The shaft is sunk in the country rock—a barren granite, and those who have descended to the bottom, a distance of 150 feet, and who have explored the several drifts, all say that there is not a sign of mineral anywhere.

The manner of the location of the claim was peculiar even when the many curious superstitions of unscientific prospectors are remembered. The locator (*sic*) is a man whose regular occupation is that of a piano tuner but who spends all of his spare time and all of his spare cash in the hunt for minerals. He is superstitious for the extreme and most of his prospects is guided by spirits through various mediums in Denver and Laramie.

It is said that of the thirty or more claims the piano tuner has located in the Halleck Canyon and the North Laramie County alone, not one was prompted by the interference of any surface indications.

The particular location in question was made in the following manner. Two years ago the piano tuner left Laramie early one morning to visit his prospects. When he was a mile from town he noticed a small rough-haired terrier following his buggy. The dog was one he had observed several times in town the evening before and which had appeared to be hungry and homeless. It had tried to make friends with him when taking his dinner at a restaurant.

The piano turner called to the dog and told him to go home. The animal slunk behind a sage brush and he went on. It is forty-five miles to Halleck Canyon from Laramie, where the piano tuner was going, and he unhitched the team to water it and to eat his lunch at Sybille Springs. His astonishment was great when he was busy with his sandwiches to hear a whine and to find that the same dog was sitting a few feet from him, looking at every morsel he was putting in his mouth.

He scolded the dog and called him names, finally throwing it a few scraps, which were eagerly devoured. Before he hitched up again he threw rocks at the dog, driving him some distance back on the road to town.

That evening he slept at the cabin of a prospector and the next morning when he looked out of the door the first object which met his eyes was that same dog lying beneath the buggy and regarding him with a mournful eye. That morning the piano tuner spent in prospecting, the dog following him. As he was about to return home for dinner he was surprised to hear the dog yell and saw him standing on a ledge of rock looking anxiously at him. The prospector called to the dog and turned again but was again stopped by a yell from the animal. Surprised at the dog's actions it struck the observer that perhaps the dog was the embodied spirit of some ancient prospector who wished to do him a good turn or else that he was imbued with the spirit of some astral consciousness which wished to serve him.

He examined the ledge of rock, the dog excitedly wagging his tail the while. It was barren looking as any other ledge of country rock around, but so strongly was the piano tuner impressed by the mystery of the dog's actions that he determined to sink a shaft upon the spot.

The dog disappeared that morning and was never seen by anyone again. But from the time to this the piano turner has concentrated all his resources upon the development of the prospect and the neighbors are just as anxious to see how it is going to come out.

The Man with the Celluloid Nose

This is the stuff fireside stories are made of. Imagine crawling into your sleeping bag and listening to the coyotes sing after hearing this one, collected by Olaf Kongslie.

The man with the celluloid nose was almost a legend, for few had seen or conversed with him. His name was Banks. He and his wife had saved and built a tidy fortune and owned a fine ranch. When anyone stopped at the house Banks would be seen going into the barn or across the fields. They were fine neighbors and gave generously to neighborhood projects, and no Christmas went by without baskets being found on doorsteps of needy families. I heard one prosperous settler in that region say, "The first winter I spent in these parts here would have scared me out for good but 'Old Celluloid Nose' helped me out in so many ways and somehow gave me courage to stick it through. I remember that first spring, the renegade Utes stole my horses and there I was, without a dollar to buy even a donkey, and no way to get my plowing done, and what did "Old Celluloid Nose" do but send over one of his teams with the word that I was welcome to use it until I got my plowing all done. Yes sir, he sure is about the best neighbor I ever had, and yet, do you know that in all that time I've lived here I have never yet seen or spoken to that man face to face."

At frequent intervals his fine black team and buggy would be seen in town but only the wife would alight to do the trading while the man stayed in the buggy, his face hidden in the shadow of the buggy top.

As a lad I often wondered about this man. Old timers had told tales of him but sometimes they conflicted on certain points. I had gathered that he had been a great hunter and would like to have his version of the old days of pioneer life. One time I was thrilled by an opportunity to do an errand for him, and though I did not get to see him he spoke to me in his kind voice. It happened this way: While riding in the woods I came upon a cow belonging to his dairy herd. The cow was a fine Jersey with a young calf by her side. They were a good four miles from home in thick timber and I wondered how they had escaped the hungry wolves.

I rode back to the ranch and told my story. Then from the kitchen came a big voice saying, "Yes, that is the cow I have been looking for all this week. If you will go and bring them home in good shape I will give you a dollar, sonny." Off I went, with that dollar looming before me bigger and brighter than the harvest moon.

I returned to the place where I had seen the animals and found that they had traveled farther on to a little meadow. The cow was feeding peacefully but the calf was no where to be seen. I hunted everywhere for an hour but no calf. The sun was going down and I decided to use a more subtle method to outwit the cow and her youngster, so I mounted my restless horse and pretended to ride away. I only rode behind a hill that overlooked the meadow, tied my horse, and looked over the rim, and sure enough the calf had emerged from his hiding place and was getting his supper with much gusto. I ran back and got my horse and rode back to the meadow so fast that the cow didn't have time to hide her calf again. Her eyes bulged with surprise but she turned in the direction of home, the calf prancing along beside her. If it had not been moonlight I would never have gotten her home, but I herded them slowly along, for the calf was only a few days old, and when the moon was at its zenith I drove them into their own pasture and rode on home.

In the morning Mrs. Banks came over with a shiny new dollar and a dollar bill besides, for her husband thought I had done such a good job that I had earned more than one dollar. I was quite dazzled but a little disappointed that the man had not given it to me himself.

However it was not long till I did see the man with the celluloid nose in person. One rainy, windy night he came to our door, his face so muffled I could not tell who it was, but I recognized his voice. "Would you please ask your Ma to phone for D. Wygend? My wife is terrible sick—pneumonia, I think."

Mother phoned and offered to go over and see what she could do. I hitched the old horse and we went through the fields, as it was much nearer, and Mr. Banks went ahead and opened the gates. The rain fell faster and it got darker except when a flash of lightening split the sky wide open. We were able to keep our bearings by the flashes and trusted the old horse to find the road.

We finally made it and Mother took her medicine satchel and made a run for the house while I managed to get the horse and buggy in the shed. The rain came down in torrents and I shivered in the drafty shed for hours it seemed.

The doctor did not come; no doubt the bridges were carried away by the rising waters of the creek. It didn't matter if the doctor did not get there, for Mother would pull Mrs. Banks through all right. She had helped lots of neighbors even when the doctor had given up all hopes. We could never get home till morning and I was wondering if I would catch pneumonia too, when I saw a lantern bobbing through the rain and soon I heard a kind voice saying, "Well, bless my soul, sonny, if we didn't just about forget you in the excitement. You come into the house with me now but first we'll take care of your good old horse."

After taking the horse to the barn and caring for him we sloshed back to the house through the water and mud. All the time Mr. Banks talked in that kind voice of his, "You know, your Ma is sure a wonderful woman. Why, she knew just what to do, like a doctor. Mrs. Banks feels a lot better already, only she worried a lot whether the little chickens got drowned in the flood, so I went out and got them, and the little beggars were nearly dead, standing in the cold water on the floor of their coop, but I got them in the woodshed now all wrapped up in a wool blanket. Well, when she heard the chickens were all safe she dropped right off into a peaceful sleep."

We changed our wet clothes by the stove and Ma made us drink a big swig of peppermint tea. Mr. Banks hustled around and pulled a chair for me in front of the stove, let down the stove door, and said, "Now, you take off those wet shoes and just put your feet right on that door," He clattered around in the cupboard and brought out a platter with some ham and bread and set a cup of milk on the stove to heat. "Now, sonny, you just eat and warm yourself up! You're a brave lad. How old are you?"

When I answered, "Twelve next September, sir," he exclaimed, "Well, well, you're a regular man," and I felt quite grown up.

He poured me a cup of hot milk and for the first time I stole a quick glance at his face. I had heard his face was terribly scarred but I was not prepared for such a shocking apparition. Great white scars cut across his tanned visage; one eye was drawn almost closed; a great strip of naked scalp showed through his graying hair; and his lips were drawn up on one side to reveal the teeth in a perpetual sneering grin. The worst of all was the nose. That weirdly unnatural appendage to his face was created of celluloid. Its sickly flesh color was a startling contrast to the rest of his deeply tanned features and made his countenance a nightmare.

After the first glance I guess I just forgot my manners and stared, for he noticed my startled gaze and said with a laugh, "Now, sonny, don't get scared. You know, I ain't nearly as bad as I look." I dropped my eyes sheepishly. He went on, "Yes, I know I'm homely looking enough to scare the crows away but there was a time when I was as good-lookin' a man as any."

"Oh, Mr. Banks, tell me how you—you—you had a fight with a bear, didn't you?"

"Yes, sonny, I sure did. Come with me and I'll show you that bear," and taking up a lamp he led me through a hall and into a large room that seemed to be a regular museum. On the log walls of that room stretched a huge black bear skin. The massive head was mounted with jaws agape and the paws retained claws, which were at least two inches long.

"There's the claws that ripped my face to pieces. Do you wonder I'm such a sight of a lookin' thing now?" he asked.

I stood spell-bound before the great pelt until he called my attention to a picture on the opposite wall. It was the likeness of a young and handsome man, dressed in a buckskin suit and carrying a rifle and all the equipment of a frontiersman. To my young eyes he might have been the ideal for all the heroes in my adventure books.

"That's the way I looked before I met up with the bear, and here's the knife I fought that fellow with." He indicated a stout hunting knife with a bone handle that was hanging below the picture. Beside the knife hung an old rifle and a rusty canteen.

"I had those with me at the time, and here is my cartridge belt," he said, fingering a torn and battered strap.

"This strap saved my life, probably, for it protected my breast from the claws of the bear to some extent."

"Tell me about the fight," I urged again.

"Well, you see, I was a trapper for the North West Fur Company. I hunted and trapped all over this country in the early 1880s. Beavers, muskrats, and mink were thick along all the creeks and there were many lynx, mountain lions, and black bears around here then. The bears lived fat on the wild berries in the summertime and in the winter they holed up in caves yonder in the limestone ridge. Their pelts didn't bring much so I didn't hunt them a great deal.

"I lived here on this place, in that little log cabin we use for a chicken house now. I had been married about three months when this thing happened." He stopped and seemed to think for a while, passing a hand over his scarred face and seeming to forget all about me.

"I read once that you never lose a diamond but you find a pearl. I never used to believe that but I do now, for it sure worked that way for me. My wife and I were mighty happy for awhile. I made pretty good on the furs and we had a snug little home. Nell was an awful handsome girl and she was high lifed and loved a good time. I bought her nice clothes whenever we went to the settlement and took her to all the dances at the fort. Folks used to say we were the handsomest couple in the quadrille. But you are not interested in all that. You want to hear about the bear.

"Well, it was early in the spring. I was hunting over there at the base of the ridge. I wasn't hunting for pelts, just trying to bag some grouse for supper. I was walking along the top of a cut bank above a little creek when a big cock grouse flew up into a clump of aspen. I kept walking along, looking up into the trees, trying to get a bead on that grouse, and I wasn't watching my footing. The bank must have been washed out underneath until there was nothing left but the crust.

"When I stepped on that, down I went and slid about ten feet in the soft dirt and landed not far from an old black bear that had been fishing in the creek. We were both mighty surprised but he didn't take it as a joke, and I didn't either. He was still pretty 'gant' and darned cranky from his winter's sleep, and I guess he hadn't had very good luck fishing. Anyway, he let out an awful bellow and reared up on his hind foot. He came wabbling (*sic*) at me and I couldn't find my gun, for it had been buried in the soft dirt. I managed to whip out my hunting knife and just as he fell upon me I buried the knife to the very hilt in his heart, but the first swipe of his terrible claws ripped across my head and face. His other paw caught me with a sledge-hammer force and laid the flesh back from the bones of my right shoulder. His strength failed him then, for the knife had found its mark, and he fell to the ground with a gurgling groan and a few convulsive kicks, and about that time I passed out too.

"I must have lain there for some hours and probably a little more. I would have joined that bear in his last sleep, but lucky for me two homesteaders who were fishing along the creek ran across me and the bear. They said that when they found us my head was resting on the bear's side and my blood was trickling down to mingle with his in little pools upon the rocks.

"Well, they made a stretcher by buttoning their coats over two poles and carried me all the way home. I was still in a stupor and couldn't see through the red mist that seemed to almost smother me but I knew when we reached home by the dreadful screams that pierced even my dull ears.

"It must have been pretty hard for Nell to see me so torn up. She was young and inexperienced in such things. Well, they brought the doctor up from the fort, and he fixed me up the best he could. He had to cut away what was left of my nose and do a lot of sewing on my face and shoulder, and I came out of it gradually. Nell waited on me day and night and did all she could to make things easier for me. My face was kept bandaged for a long time and my shoulder was broken, so I was laid up for months.

"Nell did the chores around the place and tried to keep things going but I could tell a change had come over her. She was restless and unhappy. When the bandages were finally taken from my face I noticed she avoided me. Then she began to come up missing for hours and one night she skipped off with a wandering hunter, and I never heard tell of her since. Things looked mighty blue for me then. I figured I had lost about everything, but I kept puttering around the homestead. I had nothing else to do. I realized I was a horrible-looking creature, and I didn't want to go around other people any longer, so I got to stayin' more and more to myself.

"It was a lonely life, all right, but one day Allie came to my place. She was a poor, starved-out-lookin' kid that belonged to some settlers down the valley. She asked for a cookin' job, and although I didn't need anyone, her eyes were so sad for a seventeen year old I thought I'd let her work for a few days to earn some money. Well, she cooked and cleaned the house so tidy, and when she had gotten a few square meals down her, she was lively and jolly, and it sure seemed nice to have her sittin' across the table and chatterin' so cheerful.

"Well, the upshot of it was that we went to Miles City and got married. She has stayed right by me through all kinds of trouble and hardships, and we have been happy. The only thing we miss is having a boy like to help us out and give us something to think about in our old age."

He was silent then. The rain dripped on the roof, and we were both busy with our own thoughts. I remembered what he had said about losing a diamond and finding a pearl; that was a new idea for me. Finally I nearly fell asleep in my chair.

"Well, bless me," he said, "the boy is tired and sleepy. Come, I will show you to your room. Now don't dream about bears tonight," he said as he put out the light.

The next morning the sun was shining brightly, Mrs. Banks was improved, and mother and I went home, but this was not my last visit to the Man with the Celluloid Nose. It was just the beginning of a fine friendship.

He is gone now and among my most treasured possessions is a hunting knife, but more treasured still is the memory of a brave man whose heart was never scarred by the cruel scars of life.

45 Portugee's Ride

One of the most daring and grueling feats in the frontier history of this region was the famous ride of John "Portugee" Philips—236 miles in sub-zero weather in December 1866, from Fort Phil Kearny to Fort Laramie—to summon aid for defenders of the Piney Creek outpost following the Fetterman massacre.

The story of this ride was retold by Charles D. Schreibeis, caretaker at the partially restored Fort Phil Kearny, in the March–April 1940 issue of *The Western Horseman*, under the title "The Unknown Thoroughbred," thus paying tribute to Philip's horse.

John Philips originally came from the island of Fayal. He was Portuguese. He first landed in America on the Pacific coast and then worked toward Fort Phil Kearny during the summer of 1866. At the time of the Fetterman disaster he was employed by contractors of the post quartermaster to put up hay at the fort and do other jobs. After his famous ride he was employed by the government to carry mail from Fort Phil Kearny to Fort Laramie. Many such mail men were being killed at that work, for seldom did the government detail more than a dozen soldiers to escort the mail through the country, which was more overrun with Indians than was any part of the west.

When Fort Phil Kearny was abandoned on August 20, 1868, Philips followed the little army to the newly established Fort Fetterman on the Platte. This was named after Brevet Lieutenant-Colonel Fetterman, who lost his life in the Fetterman massacre. Later he lived on a ranch on Deer Creek near the present site of Glenrock, Wyoming.

Philips died in Cheyenne November 18, 1883, aged 51 years. Thirty-two years after Philips made his famous ride, Congressman F. W. Mondell succeeded in getting a compensation of $5,000 for his widow. This was in partial recognition of the service of her husband in connection with his famous ride and for the loss of stock stampeded while he was in service at Fort Fetterman.

It was December 21, 1866. Darkness had just settled down on old Fort Phil Kearny. From the direction of Lodge Pole Ridge large wagons were slowly approaching over the Baseman Trail. As they neared the huge pine stockade all ears listened intently, all hearts beat quickly, and as the sergeant of the guard unlocked the massive gate, five wagons filed by bearing forty-nine mutilated bodies. These told the mute but heart-breaking story which all had rather suspected.

Still, thirty-two bodies lay out in the sub-zero weather. No one survivor remained to tell of the disaster which had befallen Brevet Lieutenant-Colonel Fetterman's command of eighty-one men who were victims of Red Cloud's strategic cunning in less than a brief half-hour battle. The situation at the garrison became desperate, for none knew at what moment Red Cloud's three thousand Sioux warriors might attack the fort. The nearest point from which relief could be had was Fort Laramie, two hundred and thirty six miles southeast.

Where was the man brave enough to slip through the Sioux cordon in such an hour of peril and in such arctic weather? No soldier volunteered. Moved by the gravity of the situation, John "Portugee" Philips, scout and hunter, offered to take dispatches to Fort Laramie on horse back. He made but one request, and that was to be allowed to choose his own horse. Because he was a connoisseur of horses he asked for the best horse at the post—General Carrington's own beautiful thoroughbred, which request was immediately granted. Strangely enough the name of this famous horse has never come to light nor has his breeding been traced, which is most unfortunate.

He has always been referred to as a thoroughbred horse, even by Carrington's wife. There is no record of where he came from except that Carrington fitted out his expedition at Fort Kearny in Nebraska. He was one of 37 serviceable horses reported as being at Fort Phil Kearny by Carrinton. Whatever breed of horse he was, his name would be re-membered, for he left Fort Kearny in a blizzard that night and it was 25 degrees below zero when the ride was finished at Fort Laramie.

Little is known about the details of this ride. Philips made no written report and he was not inclined to talk about it. We know that he left the watergate (sic) at old Phil Kearny some time about midnight after the Fetterman disaster. This would have him riding from the first hours of the 22nd of December. Fort Reno, which is 67 miles away, recorded his arrival on the morning of the 25th, and Fort Laramie reports his arrival at about 11 o'clock the evening of the 25th. This would make four days for the journey. Tradition has it that he made the journey in two days. The newly constructed monument to John Philips has it three days and read as follows:

> In Honor of John "Portugee" Philips who December 22–24, 1866 rode 236 miles in sub-zero weather through Indian infested country to Fort Laramie to summon aid for the garrison of Fort Phil Kearny beleaguered by Indians following the Fetterman Massacre. Erected by the Historical Landmark Commission of Wyoming, 1936.

Over the more dangerous portions of the journey Philips rode during the night and hid in some secluded spot during the day. One morning he selected what he thought was a suitable hiding place for the day but the clever horse did not share his judgment in this matter. It became so nervous that Philips decided to look around and try to determine what was the matter. Suddenly he came upon the body of a dead man who had been killed the day before in an encounter with Indians at that very spot. Our brave frontiersman too thought that another hiding place would be more appropriate for both horse and rider.

Fort Reno was warned by Philips but it could do nothing to help the men at Phil Kearny. Reno was inadequately garrisoned. At that time there was a gold rush at Virginia City and other points in the Montana Territory. Men found it more lucrative to go to the gold fields at the end of the trail (the Bozeman Trail) than to enlist in the army to protect the Trail. Many of the soldiers deserted in order to go to the gold fields. After the Fetterman Massacre Colonel Carrington had 119 men left, including teamsters. All were now convinced that Chief Red Cloud was a master strategist and that his 3,000 braves could fight.

There was no alternative for the Portugee but to ride on. He had left the trail at the Buffalo Wallows and gone five miles south of the Forks instead of following the Indian-beset trail over Crazy Woman Fork. One hundred sixty nine miles lay ahead to Laramie but the most dangerous part of the hazardous journey was past. What followed was a test of horse and human endurance against freezing weather. That they won through is still a marvel.

By ten o'clock the morning of the 25th he reached the Horseshoe

Telegraph Station and filed dispatches to Omaha and Laramie, which told the world of Fetterman's tragedy. Both horse and rider were by this time exhausted but rather than chance a misunderstanding of the wires or possibly because the telegraph at that time was not as perfect and dependable as today the faithful scout and his horse continued on to deliver the dispatches in person.

Late that night a weary horse and rider approached the gate at old Fort Laramie. A dance was being held in old "Bedlam" and they could hear the welcome tones of gay music and the fiddle. The Portugee managed to fall somehow from his faithful horse into the arms of the guard, who led or half-carried him to the commanding officer. He had strength enough left to hand over his dispatches before he fainted. Out on the parade ground the unknown horse which had so nobly done everything asked of him lay down and died.

The next three tales do indeed have the ring of the dime western but they were collected and collated from several oral sources by Olaf Kongslie, who was an active FWP field worker in Wyoming, especially in the Weston County area.

46 The White Rider

The exploits of the White Rider were so daring, so romantic, that they seem the wild dreams of some writer's fertile imagination, but many old timers of this section claim that such a character really did exist and that his deeds were truly just as adventurous as pictured.

The mysterious White Rider roamed over a wide region and one of his favorite hideouts was a cave somewhere on the border of the southwestern Black Hills. The Rider had a grudge against the Indians and never missed an opportunity to do them harm. The Indians, therefore, despised him and sought to capture him alive. They had some mighty ingenious and effective methods of torture prepared for his special benefit and they yearned to try them out. However, the Rider usually managed to outwit them and turn the tables in a way disastrous to their pride.

Some old timers declare that the White Rider when hotly pursued by his enemies would make for his cave in the Hills. The cave had a front and back entrance and many winding tunnels leading off the main artery. Into this underground maze the White Rider would pop like a gopher into his hole. He would lead his horse right into the cave with him and enter one of the dark tunnels that branched from the main track. At the end of this tunnel was an opening that he kept covered by a big, flat rock. He would move the rock a little so the daylight would shine through and then go back to the entrance of the tunnel and drop a buffalo robe curtain over it.

Thus he had a neat trap all laid for any Indian intrepid enough to intrude beyond the curtain. He had cut a jagged rent in the center of the robe near the floor and usually his pursuers could not resist the temptation of squatting down to peek through the hole in the curtain. They would see daylight shining dimly at the back of the cave and thinking that the Rider had surely escaped through the opening they threw all caution aside and started to crawl through the rent in the robe. The Rider was waiting for that and with one swipe of his sharp knife he cut off the curious one's head. Then he would seize the luckless Indian and drag him quickly under the curtain. He often killed several that way until the rest of the party, terrified out of their wits at the strange disappearance of their comrades, would bolt yelling from the cave.

The Rider then dragged the bodies of the dead Indians from the cave and buried them. Returning he would seal the opening with the flat rock and scratch tally marks of his kill on the rough sides of the cavern.

47 The Chicago Kid

This story reads like a tale from a Wild West magazine but old settlers in this region say that it really happened some time in the '70s near old Stoneville on the Deadwood-Miles City stage road. It seems a gang of horse thieves had set up a camp in that vicinity near a high cut bank. The bank had been washed out to a half-moon shape and the thieves utilized this to make a corral for the stolen stock and also as a sheltered hideout for themselves. Here they had made some dugouts and felt safe from discovery.

One day in their foraging the thieves found a half-starved boy wandering over the prairie. He was just a lad of about fifteen and he had no gun or any weapons with which to kill game for food. He told the men that he ran away from his home in Chicago and had tramped and begged his way out to see the Wild West where there were cowboys and Indians and plenty of adventure. The men thought that the kid must have spunk, so they took pity on him and brought him home to their camp.

They were kind enough to him in their rough way and called him "Chicago Kid." The Kid made friends with an old trapper who lived a piece up the creek and the trapper gave him an old rifle. The gun was very rusty and the sights were broken off, but as the old trapper remarked, "She's been a mighty good gun in her day and killed a heap of Injuns and other varmints, as you kin see by them there notches," pointing to the stock of the rifle where some fifteen or more small cuts had been made. It was the first gun that the Kid had ever owned and he was mighty proud and elated. Now that he was out west and owned a real gun with notches on it, he had realized the height of his boyish ambitions. He helped the old trapper clean the gun and whittle out wooden sights for it, and even though the rifle was old-fashioned and badly worn, he learned to shoot it surprisingly well. The men teased and poked all kinds of fun at the old "cannon" but they had to admit that the boy was a better shot than any of them.

One day when the thieves were leaving on a foray the Kid begged to go along, but the boss of the gang said, "No Sirree. We need a good shot like you to stay and guard the camp, and if any damned sheriff comes snooping around here you just take a crack at him." The gang rode off snickering (sic) and the kid stayed at the camp, feeling quite important over his responsibility. He sat outside the sod shanty with his trusty old gun on his knees and scanned the skyline above the cut bank like a hawk. All day he watched seriously but along towards sundown he began to think that a mighty tiresome job had been palmed off on him, and he pictured with envy his companions having an exciting time chasing horses or celebrating in some trading post. He grew sleepy and was about to nod off when he was aroused by the snorting of horses in the corral.

Instantly alert he looked up to see a horse and rider appear on the rim of the cut bank. He saw the rider was none of his companions so he up and blazed away with his old rifle. The horse reared and the rider dropped limply to the ground.

The kid was on the qui-vive (*sic*) now: he was actually guarding the camp. In a few minutes another shape appeared on the horizon, but this time it was a lone man creeping cautiously to peer over the rim. Just his head and shoulders were visible but that was enough to make a good target for the Kid. He whanged away again and the head disappeared. Some moments passed by and the Kid relaxed his scrutiny of the skyline and was wondering if he should cut two new notches on the stock of his rifle and thus add to the long line of scars already there when his quick eye caught the gleam of metal in the setting sun.

It flashed from the top of the bank and looking closer he saw that two clumps of sage brush had suddenly grown there, and the gleam came from them. Quick as a thought he squatted down and at the same time raised his rifle. Bang! Bang! Right into the sage brush and not an instant too soon, for just as he stopped a bullet whistled over his head and thudded into the sod wall of the dugout, and another kicked up the dirt just a few paces ahead of him. He leaped up and ran to the side of the dugout and as he crowded close to the dirt mound he poured bullet after bullet into the clumps of sage brush until no more shots came from there.

Soon he heard familiar cowboy yells, and the pounding of hoofs. A large herd of horses came galloping down into the corral, and he knew that his companions were returning with a good "haul." He went out to meet them, proudly displaying the four new notches on his gun and bragging how he had guarded the camp.

Even the thieves were astonished when they found the Kid had shot down four sheriffs from Deadwood, a job that the toughest outlaw had never accomplished before. He became quite a hero among them, but his glory was short-lived, for it was not long until the whole gang was rounded up and one by one they did the dance of death at the end of a long rope.

48 A Woman's Wiles

This story was told by an eye-witness of the incident. It happened when the narrator was a small boy eight or nine years old. The boy's parents had a ranch on Bear Butte Creek and that region was then very wild and isolated. Near the ranch in a big grove of spruce trees was a log cabin and here lived "Horse Thief" Sudon and his young wife. The two families were not exactly friendly but in those days people adopted a live-and-let-live policy and took pride in minding their own business, which after all was a healthy creed to live by. So for some years the peaceful monotony of the backwoods reigned over the ranch and the neighboring cabin in the grove.

The Sudons bought milk from the Simonsens and it was the duty of the two little Simonsen boys to carry the milk to the cabin. This was a chore they enjoyed for they liked little Mrs. Sudon. She always gave them nick-nacks (*sic*) to eat on the way home and thus kept up their enthusiasm for delivering the milk on time.

One nice evening when the boys stepped up to the door of the cabin they noticed a strange horse tied to a tree nearby and heard an unfamiliar voice within. Curious as children always are they edged nearer the door and when Mrs. Sudon had taken the milk from them they peeked in and were astonished to see a man sitting by the kitchen table pointing a gun at Mr. Sudon, and Mr. Sudon had handcuffs fastened with chains to his wrists. The boys stood popeyed, taking it all in, but the big folks didn't seem to pay any attention to them at all. They just kept arguing. The boys didn't know that the man with the gun was Sheriff Captain Knight of Deadwood and that he had come to pay a surprise visit at the little cabin in the spruces. Mrs. Sudon was pleading with the man, "Oh, Mr. Knight, please won't you let me fix supper for my husband before you take him away? It's such a long way to town and I have supper almost ready. Maybe you will eat a bit too?"

"No, thanks, Ma'am," said the sheriff. "I've had my supper and we'll be going as soon as I find out a few things."

But poor Mrs. Sudon kept on pleading as she scurried back and forth, putting dishes on the table and tending the cooking. She was a pert, pretty little woman, and you must remember that the days of chivalry were not as yet dead, for men still looked upon women as tender, delicate creatures to be shielded from the harsh realities of the world. A few stifled sniffs and surreptitious dabs with her apron at the tears in her eyes were enough to penetrate the hard crust of the sheriff, so he dropped the gun to his knee and conceded grudgingly, "Well, he can eat his supper before we start, I guess, if you hurry it up." From the tail of his eye he watched the little feet rushing back and forth between the stove and the table.

Suddenly she stumbled and lurched against him and the revolver went slithering across the floor. Before he could even realize what had happened she had pounced on the gun and he was looking into the muzzle end. Her eyes were cold as the blue steel and she said in a steady voice, "Take those handcuffs off my husband while I count ten or I'll put a bullet through your brain."

He knew there was no use arguing so he hastened to unlock the handcuffs.

"Now, John," she ordered, "Get the clothesline rope and tie him up." The sheriff could not make a move for he knew she would as soon kill him as look at him.

They left Knight laying on the floor of the cabin with his hands and feet tied while they got their horses and rode off into the woods, taking the sheriff's horse with them. The disgruntled officer squirmed about on the floor and wondered how he would ever be able to save his face if the story got out. In the dusk he saw two little faces peering curiously at him through the cabin door. He called to them and with help from the boys he managed to get loose and make it over to the Simonsen ranch. There he borrowed a horse from one of Mr. Simonsen's woodcutters and started for town. As he plugged slowly along on the heavy old draft horse he had plenty of time to reflect on the perfidy of women, but he no doubt took consolation in the thought that he was not the first man to be fooled by a woman's wiles.

49 The Legend of the Indian Princess Ah-ho-ap-pa, Daughter of Chief Spotted Tail, or Shan-tag-a-lisk

The story of Ah-ho-ap-pa is a white man's tale about the Indians with whom he was in bitter conflict. It is therefore a priceless social document. We can see in the remnants of the romanticist's concept of the Noble Savage the frontiersman's attraction to Indian women and his inability to imagine anyone finding another way of life as natural as he found his own. Indeed, we have appended here an anecdote from elsewhere in the FWP files that leads the modern reader to wonder with which party after all the precepts of human dignity were truly at home.

In August of 1928 as we were with John Hunton going over the grounds and site of Old Fort Laramie he pointed out to the north of the old hospital building, saying, "The daughter of Spotted Tail was buried and remained there for many years."

There are many stories about this wonderful maiden but none so charming as that given by the Kansas poet, Eugene Ware. Few stories are however more poignant.

Spotted Tail's Indian name was Shan-tag-a-lisk, and he was one of the best friends the whites ever had among the Plains Indians. The name of his daughter was Ah-ho-ap-pa, meaning "beautiful in the extreme," but she was not like other Indian maidens nor did she want to be like the others of her own people. Upon a certain occasion when rations were being distributed at the old fort she held aloof and refused to go into the circle whereby she might share in the distribution. Upon being urged she finally said calmly, "I am the daughter of Shan-tag-a-lisk. I do not care to go into the ring. I have plenty to eat."

She was generally seen alone and would often go to the store and sit on a bench and watch all that went on. She was particularly fond of watching guard mount, which was made more spectacular for her benefit. Major Wood, Post Commander, would see that the officer of the day wore the dashing red silk sash, ostrich plumes, and gorgeous regalia. She seemed altogether absorbed and captivated by this performance and although the men knew who she was she never spoke to any of them, and they seemingly did not dare to speak to her but gave her the name

"The Princess." She maintained that fine reserve also that gave her great dignity and she gazed always with no surprise or emotion.

After some days her father with his people went away up on the Powder River and the soldiers saw her no more. Then one evening as the officers at the fort had gathered together for the evening's chat one of them said that he had known Ah-ho-ap-pa since her babyhood. He told of some earlier years she had spent at the squaw camp around Fort Laramie and declared that she had always maintained that same reserve almost to the extent of being "stuck up," as he put it. She had declared that she would not marry an Indian, although Shan-tag-a-lisk had been offered as many as two hundred ponies for her. She had learned the Spanish name for officer, "captain," and although not knowing just the rank of the various men she had repeatedly declared that she would not marry anyone but a "captain." She always carried a knife and one day a Blackfoot soldier in her father's band tried to carry her off and she almost cut him to pieces and he barely escaped with his life. Her father was greatly pleased with his daughter's ability to defend herself.

General Harney had given her a little red book years before and this the daughter now carried around always with her. Ah-ho-ap-pa had tried also to learn English from a captive white man but the boy ran away before she had made any progress. She dressed like the bucks of her tribe and refused to do the menial work performed by the squaws but preferred to carry a gun like her father.

Two grasses and two snows have passed away on the Powder River and the "Princes" is stricken with consumption and lies in her chilly and lonesome tipi among the pines on the west side of the river. There were terrible days for the tribes on the Plains, for as the whites had been coming in countless numbers and killing the buffalo and pushing along up the Powder River to reach the gold at Virginia City the red man had disputed every inch of the way and there had already been many a sanguinary conflict. Spotted Tail kept well out of these as far as he was able but had been compelled to move with his band up and down the Powder River, across the Rosebud to their old familiar haunts on the Tongue and the Big Horn. Ah-ho-ap-pa had seen no white men now for two years. Her heart was broken.

Her father tried to encourage her by telling her that runners had already been sent out for what was to be the great conference down at the old fort in June of 1866. She told her father that she wanted to go but that it would be too late. She requested that she be buried at the old fort in the place where lay the white soldiers and near the grave of Old Smoke, a distant kinsman. As life slowly ebbed out of the frail body there were prolonged cries of grief from her people. They gathered her up and tenderly wrapped her body in deerskin that had been thoroughly prepared by smoke, bound it with thongs and placed the body upon her two white ponies that had been tied together so that they might thus carry her form to the final resting place of her choice. A runner was sent on ahead by Spotted Tail, who was doubtless sure that his white friends, the officers, would grant the final wish of Ah-ho-ap-pa.

Through the bleak fields of snow they made their way for a week to that old haven on the Laramie which had sheltered so many white men and so many red men in that vast wilderness. Streams were ice and the only feed for the horses was the bark from the willow and cotton wood trees cut at the time of the evening camp. The remainder of the story is so well told by Eugene Ware, an officer present at the time, that the reader will enjoy his words:

"When within 15 miles of Fort Laramie a runner announced to Colonel Maynadier, the approach of the processions. Colonel Maynadier was a natural prince, a good soldier, and a judge of Indian character. He was colonel of the First United States Volunteers. The post commander was Major George M. O'Brien, a graduate of Dublin University, afterward breveted to the rank of general. His honored grave is now in the beautiful cemetery at Omaha.

"A consultation was held among the officers and an ambulance dispatched guarded by a company of cavalry in full uniform, followed by two twelve-pound mountain howitzers, with postilions in her chevrons. The body was placed in the ambulance and behind it were led the girl's two white ponies.

"When the cavalcade had reached the river a couple of miles from the post the garrison turned out and with Colonel Maynadier at the head, met and escorted them into the post and the party was assigned quarters.

The next day a scaffold was erected near the grave of Old Smoke. It was made on tent poles twelve feet long imbedded in the ground and fastened with thongs, over which a buffalo robe was laid, and on which the coffin was to be placed.

"To the poles of the scaffold were nailed the heads and tails of the two white ponies so that Ah-ho-ap-pa could ride through the fair hunting grounds of the skies. A coffin was made and lavishly decorated. The body was not unbound from the deerskin shroud but was draped in a bright red blanket and placed in the coffin. The coffin was mounted on the wheels of an artillery caisson. After the coffin came a twelve-pound howitzer, and the whole was followed to the cemetery by the entire garrison in full uniform. The temperature and chilling weather had moderated somewhat. Mr. Wright, post chaplain, suggested an elaborate burial service. Shan-tag-a-lisk was consulted. He wanted his daughter buried Indian fashion, so that she would go not where the white people went but where the red people went.

"Every request of Shan-tag-a-lisk was met by Colonel Maynadier with a hearty and satisfactory 'yes.' Shan-tag-a-lisk was silent for a long time, then he gave to the chaplain, Mr. Wright, the parfleche which contained the little book that a General Harney had given to her mother many years before. It was a small Episcopal prayer book, such as was used in the regular army. The mother could not read it, but considered it a talisman. Mr. Wright then deposited it in the coffin. Then Colonel Maynadier stepped forward and deposited a pair of white kid gauntlet cavalry gloves to keep her hands warm while she was making the journey. The soldiers formed a large, hollow square, within which the Indians formed a large ring around the coffin. Within the Indian ring and on the four sides of the coffin stood Colonel Maynadier, Major O'Brien, Shan-tag-a-lisk, and the chaplain. The chaplain was at the foot and read the burial services, while on the other side Colonel Maynadier and Major O'Brien made responses. Shan-tag-a-lisk stood at the head, looking into the coffin, the personification of blank grief. When the reading service closed Major O'Brien placed a new, crisp, one-dollar bill in the coffin so that Ah-ho-ap-pa might buy what she wanted on the journey. Then each of the Indian women came up and talked to Ah-ho-ap-pa, some of them whispering to her long and earnestly as if they were sending some hopeful message by her to a lost child.

"Each one put some little remembrance in the coffin; one put a little looking-glass, another a string of beads, another a pine cone with some sort of embroidery of sinew in it. Then the lid was fastened on, the women took the coffin and raised it, and placed it on the scaffold. The Indian men stood mutely and looked on, none of them moved a muscle or tendered any help. A fresh buffalo skin was laid over the coffin and bound down to the sides of the scaffold with thongs. The scaffold was within the military square, as was the twelve-pound howitzer. The sky was leaden and stormy and it began to sleet and grow dark. At the word of command the soldiers faced outward and discharged three volleys in succession. They and their visitors marched back to the post. The howitzer squad remained and built a large fire of pine wood and fired the gun every half hour all night, through the sleet, until daybreak.

"The daughter of Shan-tag-a-lisk was an individual of a type found in all lands, at all times, and among all people. She was misplaced. Her story is the story of the persistent melancholy of the human race, of kings born in hovels and dying there, of geniuses born where genius is a crime, of heroes born before their age and dying unsung, of beauty born where its gift was fatal, of mercy born among wolves and fighting for life, of statesmen born to find society not yet ripe for their labors to begin, and bidding the world adieu from the scaffold."

Comment:

A story runs of later years that a young doctor came to old Fort Laramie and still interested in his studies had taken the skeleton of Ah-ho-ap-pa to his headquarters at the fort for study. Suddenly one afternoon Shan-tag-a-lisk appeared at the fort and said that he had come to take the body of his daughter to the final resting place in the Dakotas. There was much uneasiness and great excitement all at once. Suddenly some of the officers bethought themselves that it was too late for him to leave that evening and he must consent to accept their hospitality for the night at the fort. After some urging the veteran chieftain consented and thus gave the young medical enthusiast an opportunity to place the skeleton in good condition again in the old burying place.

Another version of the same story as outlined by Bert H. Fraser and Ernest A. Rostel in the March 1, 1940 issue of the *Casper Tribune-Herald*, suggested that there was more than a casual attraction between the Princess and the young military officer who led the parades. They wrote,

"While the Princess may have left Fort Laramie, some of the Indians say her spirit never did, her spirit that lingers in the region where life had been its happiest. When the moon is dark she can sometimes be heard with her two horses as they slowly walk up the once busy fort street. The old Indians say the crunchings of the hoofs on the gravel can be heard as the spectral party makes its gliding way past the sutler's store by the parade grounds, and up to 'Old Bedlam.'

"There the Princess pauses and her call mingles with the night breezes out of the north. She seems to hear an answering call. Without the benefit of stairs and doors from the dark, ghostly interior of 'Old Bedlam' comes a shadow which the old Indians say is the brave lieutenant who was killed so many years ago. He is resplendent in his uniform and his step is youthful and gay.

"He leaps on the extra white horse the Princess is leading. She looks at him, her face alight with joy, and he smiles at her as in the day so long ago. The horses start moving, their hoofs making little noise, and soon they are no longer on the ground but climbing into the skies above the trees on the banks of the Laramie and into the horizons beyond."

Ghost Tales

50

Ghost Lights on Old Morrisey Road

When legends are discussed, ghosts cannot be omitted. Ghost stories, with the hint of truth, the certainty of a subjective, first-person narrative, and the validating factors of distinct location and dating, exemplify the archetypical legend. The clear terror that modern man feels toward the ghostly apparition, plain old spook, or more sophisticated UFO suggests unconditional surrender of contemporary technology to superstition. This tale was collected from Bert Beringer.

There is a place three miles south of Newcastle on the Old Morrisey Road that many insist is haunted. A strange phenomenon referred to as "ghost lights" appear within a small area. Some claim that these are automobile lights reflected from far distant hills, other claim that they are emanations from the soil, such as foxfire (*sic*), etc. Anyway, the thrill seeker finds a satisfaction in these lights and many cars are often seen out observing the "ghost lights."

The lights appear at unexpected places and roll over the ground in eerie beams. One tells of his experience with the "ghost lights:"

"I was driving along in my car one night through the "ghost light" area when I suddenly saw what I took to be another car coming toward me on the wrong side of the road. It had only one headlight and was coming directly at me. I turned out of the narrow road, thinking the ditch was better than a collision. My car overturned and when I looked I realized that no other car had been on the road at all."

51 The Hoback River Ghost

This tale was published by the *Jackson Hole Courier* on July 6, 1933, and was entered in the FWP file by Mae Cody.

There is the unverified story of the trapper who at high water period was traveling down the Hoback River when at a point from the north side of the river he saw near the present site of the Michigan Camp a white woman, practically naked, with streaming hair, running and waving her arms in frantic gestures of supplication. The report is that the superstitious trapper thought it a ghost and taking the excuse of the river being too dangerous to ford, rode on without making an investigation.

Just below this place on the Hoback was an old superstition that trappers were beckoned from the shore when the fording was safe by a white woman who appeared on the opposite bank. Whether there is any truth in the former story or not cannot be proven but it would seem quite probably that the beckoning-woman story had foundation of fact from the former incident.

We can picture the agony of a white woman captive escaping from Indians and who supplicates a trapper for help and does not receive it. Yet we can scarcely blame the superstitious trapper who could not picture a white woman alone in this great wilderness. It was but natural that his mind should feature the ghost theory. Again it is quite probable that the story is but the fabrication of some imaginative trapper.

52 The Phantom Scout

Alice Guyol, a FWP worker in Hartville, encountered a situation familiar to many folklore field workers: she collected a fine ghost legend but her informant, fearful or repercussions from this—or another—work, refused to give permission for his or her name to be used with the tale. At any rate, the events occurred near Cheyenne, in the southeastern part of Wyoming, around the turn of the century.

Ed. note: Of all the Wyoming FWP materials excerpted, this is the only piece that has appeared previously in a folklore study. It was published in Levette Davidson's Rocky Mountain Tales (University of Oklahoma Press, 1947).

(More than thirty years ago) a young man lived with his parents in their country home, which was located several miles from the limits of that little city. The family was prominent and well-known and S—— owned a very fine saddle horse which he rode to and from his work in Cheyenne. Usually he would arrive home at night in time for the evening meal, but occasionally he remained in town to enjoy some sort of entertainment, perhaps a show. The motion picture had not as yet been invented but some of the best of the theatrical companies were to be seen in Cheyenne, as they found it profitable to stop there for at least one performance while en route from the East to the West Coast.

It was after one of those performances that S——, riding homeward alone, was to have an experience that he was never able to explain, even to himself. The hour was near midnight and a brilliant moon now and again obscured by scudding clouds lighted the road and the surrounding prairie. S——, riding swiftly along, suddenly discovered that he was not the only rider abroad that night. He could see plainly another horseman, riding like mad across the nearby plain. This rider, bending low in his saddle, was evidently urging his mount on to all of the speed of which it was capable. Instantly S—— concluded that here was someone in desperate trouble and riding for help. As he noted that the rider was coming at an angle that would bring him into the road at some distance ahead of his own position S—— put the spurs to his horse and raced ahead to intercept the other man and offer his aid. He purposely rode some distance ahead of his position where he saw that the oncoming rider would have to enter the road. Then stopping his horse he waited for the man to come up to him.

To his surprise the ride did not slacken his speed as he approached but passed in a rush of icy wind while the horse that S—— was riding snorted, and rearing, plunged into a ditch beside the road where he stood trembling with fear. S—— finally was able to urge his frightened horse into the road and to give chase to the other horseman but he was hopelessly out-distanced and was finally forced to continue on his way home, wondering just what had happened.

S—— was a normal type of young westerner, not especially imaginative, utterly free from superstition, and certainly not wanting in courage. According to his own statement, "The last person in the world who could expect to see a ghost." But, in reconstructing the experience, he recalled that there had been no sound of hoof-beats on the hard road as the rider had passed him, that his own horse had been badly frightened at the thing, whatever it was, that had rushed by to disappear in the distance.

Fearing ridicule he had hesitated to tell of the experience, but he questioned several old settlers, friends of his father and learned that others beside himself had seen the apparition, which was supposed to be that of a pioneer scout who had been killed by the Indians while carrying a message to tell of an uprising among the tribes. Unable to rest while his mission remained unfulfilled he continued to make his hazardous ride, night after night, in the attempt to deliver his message to a little group of phantom men, waiting in vain to receive it.

53 The Specter of Cheyenne Pass

Whatever the reality of the danger, the terror of Indian attack preyed on the minds of trail drivers and settlers alike. The following two tales are remarkably alike in form but the first was published in the *Laramie City (Wyoming Territory) Daily Independent*, June 27, 1874, by A. C. Brackett, and the second appeared in the *Torrington Telegram*, August 8, 1936, as written by Jack McDermott.

In former times immigrants reached the place where Laramie City now stands by traveling on the overland road. From the time they left Camp Walbach at the entrance of Cheyenne Pass until they reached Fort Bridger there were no settlements, only a few stations scattered along the way.

The road was good, but there was monotony about it and a loneliness that was sometimes oppressive. Indians lurked about and occasionally attacked travelers as they were slowly and wearily pursuing their way toward the shores of the Pacific Ocean.

There was considerable talk at one time about the apparitions that were seen in Cheyenne Pass and, in addition to meeting human enemies, it was supposed by many that specters haunted the rocks on either side of the way. Several persons said they had seen these specters and that they were always met with a short time before sunset and about the time the immigrants began to think of going into camp for the night. There was great diversity of opinion in regard to them, and no two men seemed to tell the same story about them. They were seen flitting like ghosts in and out of the rocks, sometimes disappearing among the pine trees and at other vanishing while men were looking at them. A hundred stories were told of their dim and fleeting incomings and outgoings, but all descriptions were vague and unsatisfactory. Perhaps it was only a peculiar kind of mirage they saw and nothing else. These optical illusions (are) quite common in the mountain region.

A man from Missouri with his family was once passing along this road on his way to the newly discovered gold mines in Idaho. He had a large covered wagon, four good horses, some cows and other stock with him. This family consisted of himself and wife, a daughter, and two boys about half grown. He also had two hired men, the whole party being well armed. The daughter was a beauty—one of the handsomest young ladies, in fact, that ever crossed the Plains.

As they approached the pass the horses threw up their heads and snorted and the men who had closed up to the wagon cocked their rifles as if they expected to encounter a dangerous enemy. As yet they saw nothing but all of the animals seemed struck with sudden terror, and it required something of an effort to make them move on. When they reached the narrowest portion of the Pass the Missourian saw a phantom making signs to him as if endeavoring to prevent his further progress. He was a good, old-fashioned church-member and withal very brave man who did not propose being scared off even though every rock in the Pass should show a ghost. He called to one of his hired men, who, by the way, was a colored man who had been raised with him in Missouri and was not afraid of anything, provided his master led, and the two rode on in front of the wagon.

A turn in the road disclosed a scene that was enough to appall the stoutest heart. On each side of the road there was a row of sheeted specters with their hands raised, seeming as if determined to stop the progress of the little party. The day was well advanced and the long shadows on the hillsides threw an additional gloom over everything. As the men went on the specters seemed to dissolve in thin air, though their places were supplied by others farther away in the distance. It must be confessed that every animate thing was overcome with the greatest dread and terror but there was no sound except that made by the feet of the animals and the jolting of the wagon.

For two miles this wonderful succession of specters continued, and a more fearful sight could not be imagined. It was enough to freeze the marrow in one's bones and, after watching it for some time, the young lady was so overcome with fright that she fainted and lay in the bottom of the wagon until they got entirely through the Pass.

As they emerged from the dreadful defile and once more reached the hilly country the specters vanished and no more was seen of them. How to account for the appearance of these weird beings, they were utterly at a loss. They met no Indians and crossed the Laramie River below the place where Laramie City now stands without meeting any accident.

The young lady reached Idaho in safety, where she was for a long time the belle of the Territory, and she eventually married a well-to-do farmer. Her father succeeded in building up a new home in that portion of Idaho which was afterwards created into the Territory of Montana, and now has a flourishing farm not far from Gallatin City.

Though this party got through the Pass in safety the party that followed them was attacked by Indians in the very spot where the specters had been seen, and a lonely grave near the western end of the defile covers the remains of a white man who was slain at the time.

Whether there was any connection between the appearance of the ghostly forms and the attack that was made upon the immigrants of course we can only conjecture. Many people considered that their appearance was intended as a warning and so it would almost seem, as they endeavored by sighs and gestures to keep back the Missourian and his family. These appearances have become exceedingly rare of late years, as there is comparatively little travel on the road and no danger at all from the Indians, who have left this portion of the country.

54 The Laramie Ghost

We are all familiar with ghost stories and some of them become as well known as the policeman on the corner. For example, almost everyone has heard of Marley's Ghost, who came back to tell Ebenezer Scrooge to change his ways or suffer eternal unhappiness. A lesser known ghost but one vastly more pleasing to the eye is the Laramie Ghost. When the sun settled behind Laramie Peak and eerie shadows began to dot the landscape, when the wind began to screech discordantly through the cottonwoods and the sutler's dog lifted his mournful voice to greet the new face of the moon, the soldiers of Fort Laramie would gather around a warm fireplace and repeat the story of the Laramie Ghost.

Colonel P. W. Allison related the story to Superintendent Dave Hieb on May 23, 1931. He in turn had gotten it from his father who had been stationed at Fort Laramie in 1871 and had come face-to-face with the Laramie Ghost.

After graduating from West Point in 1871 young Lieutenant Allison was sent to Fort Laramie. Being a sportsman Allison brought a fine thoroughbred and a large hunting dog with him to the frontier post. Soon after his arrival he joined a small party of young officers on a wolf hunt along the hills southeast of the fort. The dogs soon sighted a wolf, and Allison, being better mounted than his companions, outdistanced and lost them in the ensuing chase.

Failing to bag a wolf Allison began picking his way down from the hills in order to return to the fort. Suddenly he saw a lone rider riding rapidly eastward in such a manner that their paths would intersect. When the rider drew nearer Allison could see it was a beautiful young woman dressed in a long, dark-green riding habit and wearing a feather hat. Thinking that it was a newly arrived visitor at the fort he sought to stop her and warn her against the danger of riding so far away from the post alone. As he drew near the girl raised a jeweled handled quirt and whipped her great black horse. The horse responded to her lash and sped by Allison and disappeared over a rise of ground. Dashing in pursuit Allison was amazed on topping the rise to find no one in sight, and his amazement grew as he examined the little-used trail and found not the slightest trace of tracks. His great wolf hound cowered against him in an unprecedented show of fear.

Somewhat shaken, Allison returned to the fort and attended a dinner along with all the other officers and their wives. Allison attempted to find the face of the mysterious young woman in the crowd, but after careful scrutiny he was certain that she was not here. Fully aware that he might be made the butt of many jokes, he told the assembled group of his queer adventure. Before any jocular comments could be made the commanding officer declared, "Well, Allison, you have just seen the Laramie Ghost."

The commanding officer satisfied the aroused curiosity of the group by telling them the following story: Back in the days when Fort Laramie was a fur trading post the manager of it brought his beautiful daughter back from the East to live with him. She was an accomplished horse-woman but the factor ordered her never to ride alone and commanded his assistants to enforce the dictate in case of his absence.

One day the factor had to be away from the post and his daughter, despite the protests of the factor's assistants, mounted her great black horse and rode eastward down the Oregon Trail. She was never seen again. In the years that followed a legend grew up among the Indians and traders of the valley that every seven years the ghost of the factor's daughter would be seen riding down the old trail.

In spite of the commanding officer's story Lieutenant Allison was still dubious that he had seen a ghost and to settle the matter once and for all he sought out an old Indian woman who had seen the factor's daughter ride out from the fort on the fateful day. He asked the squaw to describe the girl and his mouth opened wide as she chanted, "Wore green dress, hat with feathers, carry whip with handle of jewels, rode black horse," and so on until she had described from head to toe the girl he had seen.

Lieutenant Allison was convinced . . . .

55 The Ghost of Cross Anchor Ranch

Ghost legends were found by the FWP field worker throughout Wyoming, as the following samples illustrate. Crook County is the state's northeastern most county. Jackson Lake is in the extreme northwestern corner. Oakley is in the southwest corner of the state. No wider distribution could be possible. The first tale was collected by Myrtle M. Champ.

The Cross Anchor Ranch was one of the first ranches established in Crook County. Even before the ranch was established there were other inhabitants. The first "cow men" found an old, old cabin on the ranch. On investigating this cabin they found an opening through the floor which led into a series of underground tunnels. In one of these passages was the skeleton of a Negro. No one has ever solved the mystery of this skeleton. But it is thought that the cabin was one of a chain of hideouts for outlaws and horse thieves who operated from the Canadian border to Kansas, Colorado, and Missouri, and from eastern South Dakota to Oregon.

They say that anyone exploring the tunnels will hear moans and groans and low angry voices. Sometimes they can feel a hot breath on their faces or fingers clutching at their throats or clothing. As long as the old cabin stood on the ranch the sound of shuffled cards and the clink of poker chips could be heard at night.

Only the strong of heart or people who do not believe in ghosts ever venture into the tunnels where the old cabin once stood, for it is said the spirits of the outlaws still roam through the old haunts along Horse Thief Trail.

56 The Ghost of Nightcap Bay

This tale was collected by Nellie H. VanDerveer.

Nightcap Bay is a small bay which opens into Jackson Lake. It was named by John D. Sargent, who was one of the pioneer settlers in Jackson Hole in 1887. Sargent located on the east shore of Jackson Lake about ten miles north of the present site of Moran. He called his ranch the Marymere. He gave a name to every little point of interest around the lake.

Sargent is said to have been a well educated and intelligent man, very brilliant but also very erratic, something of a genius. One of the stories told of him is that he could take a pencil in each hand, listen to a conversation on each side of him, and write down both at the same time. Sargent lived an exciting life, full of adventure. As is so often the case with such a brain as Sargent's, it gave way after a time and he shot himself.

At one time a man by the name of Robert R. Hamilton, said to be a descendant of the great Alexander Hamilton, was a partner of Sargent's. One day Hamilton went antelope hunting south of Jackson Lake in the region called the 'pothole country.' When he failed to return within a reasonable length of time Sargent made up a searching party. After seven days Hamilton's body was found where he had been drowned in Snake River. It was buried on the shore of Jackson Lake.

There was some talk of foul play in connection with the death of Hamilton but nothing ever came of it. He was buried and forgotten by most people.

Then Sargent began to tell the story of the apparition which appeared on Nightcap Bay. He said that at midnight of a certain night every year a man in a green coat could be plainly seen rowing around on the waters of the Bay. This story was the cause of considerable speculation and comment among the other old-time residents. It seems that Sargent was the only one to whom the apparition ever appeared.

57 The Oakley Ghost

Contributed to the FWP files by Breta B. Morrow of Evanston in 1938.

I do not believe in ghosts nor does any other member of my family but this incident which I am going to write about took place at Oakley, mining camp about three miles from Kemmerer, when I was about ten years old or perhaps twelve, and I remember every detail distinctly and was willing at that time to believe in ghosts, as most all children do.

It was during the time that my father, Joseph Bird, was State Coal Mine Inspector and we lived at a place called "The Quarry," about a mile from Oakley, where there had once been a rock quarry. There was (sic) a few houses there, a saloon and a dance hall, and a big building that was used as a dining room and kitchen when there was a celebration of any kind wherein they served lunches, ice cream, etc. In the olden days most of the dances had intermission at midnight, at which time a lunch was served. After my father became coal mine inspector we had to give up our company house to the new mine foreman, so we moved over here to the big house, for it was the only house empty at the time.

My sister, Beatrice, was about nineteen or twenty years of age and was taking sewing and millinery lessons, and she had to walk to and from Kemmerer each day to the millinery and dressmaking store, as also did her friend Martha Purdy. Martha lived in the camp row.

On this particular night that I am telling about, instead of my sister coming straight home, she went to her friend's house for dinner; then Martha was to walk home with her afterwards, or part way, I cannot recall just which.

There was a man that worked at the mines at Oakley that they called half goofy, for he was such a peculiar acting fellow and had just been released from the insane hospital at Evanston. He always had a silly grin on his face and would stand and watch people; even after they had passed him he would turn around and watch them for some distance. The children and all the young girls were afraid of him, though I think he was harmless. His name was John D. Martin and when referred to was always called by his full name.

After Beatrice and Martha had had dinner, washed the dishes, played the piano, and killed some time, as the saying is. It was becoming rather late in the evening, about nine-thirty, so they decided to start for the quarry. They were walking along arm in arm and talking, and as they came to the bridge that crosses the Hamsfork River at Oakley, they both screamed and started to run back.

Bea—"Bea" was our nickname for Beatrice—said to Martha, "It was a ghost. Did you see it too?" Martha replied that she had seen it and they both wondered what it was but were too frightened to go back.

They ran on to Martha's home and told her brothers about it and they just laughed at them. Then Martha's brothers accompanied Bea and Martha to the quarry but there was nothing on the bridge then, so when they got home and was telling my mother and the rest of us about it my mother laughed also and said, "Oh, it was just old John D. Martin again following you."

It was about ten-thirty by this time. Soon after, my father received a phone call to say that there had been an accident at the mine and John D. Martin had been killed. My mother jokingly said, "See, I told you it was John D. Martin that you saw tonight. It must have been his ghost." The family all looked at each other, and Bea's eyes opened so wide, for she was quite sure now that it was John D. Martin's ghost.

To this present day she still says she saw a ghost. Beatrice has lived in California for many years and is now about fifty years old and she visited us this last summer, and on going sightseeing over the old grounds she mentioned this incident. I asked her if she still believed in ghosts, to which she replied, "No, I don't believe in ghosts. I know there are no such things, but I know I saw a ghost that night and I will never be able to think it was anything else."

58 Mel Quick's Story

While this looks like a personal reminiscence it is very much like a common modern legend that is told with great frequency among young Americans about a terrified girl who, left alone in a car on a lover's lane, hears a strange sound on the roof of the car and finds the next morning that it is the sound of her lover's feet gently dragging across the top of the car as his hanging body moves in the breeze. This version was collected from Mel Quick by Olaf Kongslie.

Mel Quick, one of the early settlers, often claims that he came here to chase the Indians out of the country so the soldiers could come in. He narrates the following tale:

My friend and I were riding from the new settlement of Custer to Wyoming. We had ridden for that day and as the beautiful spring sunset faded in the west we began to think about supper and our night's lodging. It was nearly dusk when we decided to stop by a little creek that babbled through a grassy draw. A clump of tall pines sheltered the glade and we thought this would be an ideal spot to spend the nights. By this time heavy black clouds and flashes of lightning had appeared on the southern horizon and we thought that the pines would shelter us if the rain came in our direction.

We expected the horses would be glad to stop and crop the new grass but to our surprise they snorted and shied away from the bank leading down to the draw. We thought the oncoming storm and the loud claps of thunder that echoed though the hills was responsible for their nervousness, so we dismounted and led them down the bank, but they rolled their eyes suspiciously and seemed ready to bolt, so we quickly tied them.

We skirmished around and soon made a fire and had the coffee boiling, but there was something in the air that was disturbing. The wind made weird noises in the trees, as though some giant was twirling and swishing an invisible lasso about them. The thunder growled and the lightning lashed its wicked whip. The horses refused to feed steadily but would snatch a bite and raise their heads to snort and sniff the air, for when the wind veered down the draw it brought a faint odor of carrion. We began to wish that we had not stopped in this place but it was too late to go on then.

We hastily swallowed our supper of hardtack, dried beef, and coffee. The wind snuffed out the fire and the darkness settled thick and black about us. By the flares of lightning we managed to undo our bedrolls and tarps. We dragged these to a clump of pines, hoping to find some shelter beneath their wide branches. We crouched there under our tarps on the thick carpet of pine needles and hoped for the best. Soon the rain began to fall in big drops. The wind tore down the draw and the great pines swayed and creaked loudly. Then, as often happens in the hill country the wind went down, the thunder and lightning died away in the distance and a deep silence settled over all.

We were very tired, so we stretched out on our bed rolls, but sleep would not come to our eyes. It seemed as though some awful thing was brooding in the night. We strained our ears at every sound but the stillness was broken only by the thud of our horses' hoofs on the soft turf and their occasional snorts. A creaking sound came from the branches above, as though someone was up there rocking in an old, squeaky chair—rocking, rocking slowly, but the effect was far from soothing to our nerves. We had the "jim-jams" and we could not explain the gooseflesh that broke out down our spines.

The night was unusually warm for that time of year but we felt cold. Finally we got up and built a fire in the open, near the creek. We sat there and drank coffee, but we could not dispel the queer feeling of something unnatural about this beautiful place. We sat there till long after midnight, then completely worn out we sought our bed once more. We fell asleep and I dreamed of a skeleton rocking in my old Grandad's easy chair.

I woke in the first gray light of dawn and was in the middle of a yawn when my sleepy eyes were suddenly snapped open by a surprising sight: two pairs of booted feet dangled above our heads. They rocked in the breeze to the accompaniment of that strange creaking noise. I sprang from the tarps with a yell. Slim awoke and looked wildly about and when he glanced above, the way he scrambled out was nothing slow either:

There, dangling in the morning air, not ten feet above our bed, were two corpses. They were dressed in the full regalia of cowboys, from bandana neckerchieves (sic) to spurs, and their hollow eyes stared down upon us. We did not gaze long on this grisly sight, for our yells had stampeded the horses and we had to keep them from breaking loose. Then, as soon as we could, we bundled our things together and took off down the draw. The horses were only too willing to go and galloped like mad for some distance. We were not in the mood for breakfast and did not stop riding till early noon.

Afterward we learned from a rancher that the hanged men were horse thieves. They had been hanged the previous fall and left to dangle warning before the eyes of others. Such was primitive justice in the early days of this country.

Folk Etymologies

Within the category of legends one of the most common forms is the folk etymology, the tale that explains the origin of a name. By now the "Hartville Rag" is probably forgotten, but thanks to the Federal Writers Project files its story survives, as collect by Alice C. Guyol from Mrs. J. J. Covington and Mrs. Henry T. Miller of Guernsey.

59 The Hartville Rag

On a pleasant evening in the year of 1884 a small group of persons gathered at the ranch house of Mr. and Mrs. Reed on the North Platte for an evening, or to be more exact a night, of dancing. The Reed place was one of the several small ranches that had been located along the river above old Fort Laramie after the danger of attack from wandering war parties of the Sioux had been eliminated. That the day was Monday made little difference, for time was not an element to be given particular consideration in that period and locality. As dancing was the only social recreation possible for the settlers in their isolated homes they danced whenever and wherever the opportunity offered, to the music of the fiddle or even a mouth harp. It was not only possible to dance the square dance, then popular, on the hard packed dirt floor, which was usually found in the log cabins of the settlers, but, if the room was not large enough to accommodate them, the merrymakers often moved all of the furniture out of the house and replaced it when the dance was ended.

As no crops of any kind were raised on these ranches, mostly operated for the breeding of horses at that time, there were no festivals of any kind to bring people together, no churches, no plays, except an occasional home talent performance given by the officers and men at Fort Laramie, to which the settlers came for miles around. And for this reason, no dance, however small, was ever slighted by those who were able to get there.

North of the Reed place, several miles up the river, the Allen homestead lay in the meadows below Register Cliffs. Across the river, where there is now the town of Guernsey, was the home of Henry T. Miller and, above this, J. J. Covington and his young wife had located a homestead. At Fairbank, the site of the copper smelter, lived the Tep Reagans and four miles to the northeast was the mining camp of Hartville.

A young man by the name of Charles Reagan, one of the best-known fiddlers in the entire area, with a repertoire of lively tunes and a knowledge of the most intricate "calls" for the figure of the quadrilles, furnished music for the dance at the Reed ranch, and after dancing the night through the half-dozen couples in attendance decided to dance again on Tuesday night. After a few hours rest the women set to work to prepare the midnight supper for the coming dance. There was at that time no great variety in foods to be had. The regulation supper for social occasions usually consisted of baked beans, potato salad, home-made bread, and coffee. Even at the present time most of these dishes are served at the country dances held at the outlying ranches.

On Tuesday evening the party, accompanied by their musician and carrying their supper, repaired to the Allen ranch. Here they again danced all night and, on Wednesday, crossing the North Platte on rafts, the company, including the Allens went to the home of Henry T. Miller. Here they danced on Wednesday night, and on Thursday, taking Mr. and Mrs. Miller with them, went the mile or more to the Covington place and danced the night through there.

On Friday the same procedure was followed, the women preparing the supper for the following night. On this night they danced at the Tep Reagan place, and on Saturday night, there being by this time about twenty couples, they rode or drove to Hartville for the final dance. Here it was discovered that Reagan had worn out all of the strings on his fiddle except one, but undaunted he managed to evoke a lively dance tune from the one string. He could however play only one air and after a few dances the dancers were forced to return to their homes.

Although the term "Ragtime" was not to be applied to music of a certain type for more than a decade, even at that time a lively dance tune was known as a "rag." The tune that Charles Reagan played on his one fiddle string was henceforth to be known as the "Hartville Rag," and it is still to be heard at times at the country dances in that area.

Most folk etymologies however deal with place names. Occasionally the legends are true but most often the tales are invented and perpetuated to explain an obscure name—a name that has perhaps been warped and changed until it is merely a nonsensical phrase or word with no real meaning at all. The following two legends are folklore, with more claim to interest and belief than to truth. The first was found by Fay Anderson in the March 11, 1897 Saratoga Sun, and the second was collated from several sources by Ida McPherson of Sheridan. Whiskey Gap is about thirty-five miles north of Rawlings; Buffalo is in the northeastern corner of the state.

60 The Story of Whiskey Gap

W. H. Brown was down from Encampment recently. He is an old timer and during his visit to the *Sun* office he gave some interesting reminiscences of early days. Mr. Brown was a lieutenant in Company A., 11th Ohio Cavalry, which was doing frontier work in this country in 1862. It was determined on account of continued depredations by Indians to move the Fort Laramie and South Pass stage line from the Sweetwater country down to a more southern route, and Mr. Brown acted as escort and convoy to the parties making the change. The men owning the road ranches and hunters and trappers on that line had to abandon their habitations and follow the fortunes of the new stage line.

On the way down the soldiers managed to get hold of a good deal of whiskey and as the Indians were troublesome, it was necessary to keep the troops as well in hand as possible, and to accomplish that, Major O. Ferrell, who was in charge of the battalion, gave orders for the destruction of all the whiskey in the entire outfit. Lieutenant Brown was officer of the day and it fell to his lot to execute the order. Camped by a fine spring in a gap a few miles this side of Sweetwater he found a man with part of a barrel of whiskey, which he proceeded to destroy. While doing this the soldiers crowded around with cups and canteens to catch what they could. Almost the entire command got on a regular jamboree and had a high old time as long as the whiskey lasted. The place was called Whiskey Gap and retains that name to this day, but probably few people ever knew how it got its name.

61 The Legend of Crazy Woman Country

(There was a young woman by the name of) Madeline Kindsley, and she was the only child of a wealthy Boston family. She had been reared in the highly cultured, exclusive circles of Boston's aristocracy. She had known no disappointments, no frustrated hopes. Her life had been entwined with the tender tendrils of love and devotion.

But life is greater than plans or hopes. Early, so early in her life that she grew up with the idea, she became engaged to a young lad of her social standing. Whether or not she loved him had never really entered her mind. She had accepted her parents' scheme of things as a matter of course, as girls were wont to do in those days and in her particular strata of society. But in the summer of her eighteenth year there came upon the Kindsley estate a young, strong, handsome boy of twenty summers. Madeline met him one day as she wandered through the orchard.

They stood looking at each other, the boy awkward and ill at ease in the presence of the flowerlike loveliness of the girl, the girl looking into the eyes of the boy, which were wide open and held a strange fascination for her. That first time they met Madeline noticed those eyes that drew her and held her to this boy who was so strangely a part of a world of which she knew nothing.

The girl was the first to speak that day, when wealth and poverty met under an apple tree; "You are working here?" she asked.

"Yes," he told her, regaining something of his poise.

"I am Miss Kindsley," she told him. The girl smiled and the boy returned the smile with eyes that were unafraid. Then the girl walked away and the boy went on with his work believing that he would never see her again.

But he did, because Madeline Kindsley returned the next day and the next and the next, until there came a time when they met each day at an appointed hour and place. And they just sat in the protection of the forest-like orchard with her hand in his, and each knew a happiness they had never known before.

As the fruit budded and blossomed and matured, so did their young, pure love. Then there came a day when Madeline's mother found her daughter sitting with her hand in the hand of a laborer. She stood rooted to the ground as fixed as the trees about her. The young couple stood up and faced this woman, who had never overstepped the bonds of aristocracy. There was no scene, no exchange of words, no loss of temper. Quietly, unprotesting, proudly, Madeline stepped beside her mother and they walked away.

But love is not so easily quieted, not so easily stilled. Long into the night Madeline tossed and rolled on an unruffled bed. With the break of day there came to her a resolution from which she never swerved during the years that came to pass.

And that day, at the appointed hour, she was at their trysting place. But Ben was not there. Fear gripped her heart and she dropped to the rustic seat under the apple tree. Hot tears, for the first time in her life, burned her cold colorless cheeks. The next morning the young lad appeared. "I knew you'd come," he said, as he sat down beside her. "I knew you'd come to say 'good-bye.'"

Terror struck at her heart. She wound her lovely arms about the boy's neck and drew his head down and buried her face in the dark mass of his wavy hair. In a voice that shook with emotion she said, "Oh, don't say that. Don't say 'good-bye,' not ever."

The boy jerked his head up and seized her small, frail hands in his large, strong hands. "Do you mean that, dear? Do you mean that?"

"I will go wherever you go," she said.

The boy's deep, frank eyes grew very large. "It doesn't seem possible. Seems like it can't be true," he hesitated and then went on, "that you love me."

"Love, Ben, does not single out palaces nor hovels to seek admittance. Love, Ben, enters unbidden whither it is meant to go. I know that, now, since I met you. I never knew what love was until I met you and now it has enveloped me, encompassed me, captured me. I am very happy."

Then young Ben knew that this girl, whom he had regarded all through these happy weeks as a love that could never be his, loved him as only those love who give love full rein. Then a cloud of thought shut out the sunshine and shadowed in his face. "But I could never give you any of the things you have."

The girl spoke and she was very serious. "I have thought of that, have thought it all over, thought it all out. But what does it all amount to, Ben? Happiness? No. I have had everything—everything that a human being could ask for—everything but happiness. I never knew what it was to be happy, really happy, until I met you. Love, happiness, there can not be one without the other. I want to be happy, I want love, I want you."

"Let's go west, sweetheart. Let's go west, where a man can get a home for the trying—a home, cattle, riches."

The girl looked at him earnestly. "West?" she asked, not understanding.

"Yes, dear, west. You know, they say there's millions and millions of acres of land west of the Mississippi and the government wants it settled so they give a man all the land he wants for a home. Folks get together and get wagons, covered wagons, and oxen, and grub and strike out for the west and a fortune."

The girl listened and was enraptured. "That'll be fun," she told this boy who knew so little about the hardships of the slightly broken trail west of the Mississippi.

Young Ben drew the girl very close to him. "I'll get work and save my money and . . . "

"Get work?"

"Yes, your mother fired me last night."

"But where will you go?"

"Oh, I'm not afraid. I can work at anything. I'll soon find another job and. . . ."

A strange look came into the girl's eyes, a look that the boy was to learn was one of fear. "Oh," she pleaded, "Don't go. Don't leave me, not ever, Ben."

"But I must go. I must get work, dear, it will take money, lots of money, to get a wagon and grub."

"How much?"

"Most folks like to have a couple of hundred, nearly a couple of hundred."

The girl smiled tenderly and stroked back the lad's hair. "Two hundred is so little. I will have five hundred for you tonight." She thought a moment and then went on, "Tonight, dear, at midnight. Come to my window and I will give you a package with five hundred dollars."

The boy held her very close to him and their lips met in a true lovers' kiss.

That night at the appointed hour Ben stood under the girl's window and received the package containing five hundred dollars. He kissed the hand that reached out to him and then whispered, "A wagon train is leaving the day after tomorrow, dear. I'll be here tomorrow night at this time. Be ready."

"I will," the girl whispered back, and Ben fled into the night.

And the day following the next, just as the sun nodded to the world, Ben Brown, the laborer, and Madeline Kindsley, the frail flower of aristocracy, rode on a rough seat under a canvas cover behind a team of slow, plodding oxen. They were one of fifty-three wagons that were going west to build an empire. As the wagons rolled along and away from civilization and out into the bleak unknown, Madeline cuddled very close to the boy beside her and clutched his arm tightly, for the girl began to fear this thing that was so strangely new to her.

The boy looked down at her tenderly and thought that he understood. "There's a preacher along," he reassured her. "They always take a preacher along to marry folks and to bury them."

"Oh," and a cold chill shook her frail body.

"I mean," and the boy smiled with affections, "I mean, he marries some and buries some. We're going to be married tonight with the first stop."

The girl snuggled closer to the boy and his strength surged into her body and buoyed her up. It came to be the one thing that sustained her in this long strange journey that made strong men totter.

That first day took them into sparsely settled country but it was when the week was up that Madeline's heart grew heavy and a look came into her eyes that the boy was to fear more than he feared the unknown vastness ahead of them. Slowly, hour by hour, day by day, week by week, the covered-wagon train trekked on over a slightly broken trail.

They met with the usual trials of the immigrant trains—the hostile Red man, the beasts of prey, the treachery of the elements, the dissensions of fifty-three different wagons—all the dangers that beset the men and women who broke the trail across the vast unknown that men might follow to build an empire.

For most of the men and women in this train this breaking trails was not a new experience but for Madeline it was a thing of which she had not even heard before. She sat erect and very close to the boy whose fortune she had vowed to share, but there came a look of wistful longing into her eyes that haunted the boy until a great fear gripped his heart.

It was late summer when the wagon train reached the foot hills of the Rockies. They had not made as good time as they had expected. Their oxen were footsore and weary. Their ranks had been depleted by nearly half. Autumn had sent out her signals of warning. Oregon seemed so far away, and so a vote was taken and it was decided to remain here in a country that seemed to offer all the advantages of a land twice distant. And here, in what was one day to become the great and glorious state of Wyoming, men and women worked side by side and in groups to build homes before winter set in.

The first snow found Madeline and Ben in a little, one-room log cabin but no palace or hut or hovel ever housed a happier couple. Here the color came back into the cheeks of Madeline and the haunted expression left her eyes and the boy whistled about his work, because he was not afraid.

Madeline watched the other women in the little settlement and tried to learn from them. She tried to be the helpmate to her husband that they were to theirs, but it was not easy. Reared among the superlative luxuries of life it was not easy to sleep to the cry of the wild, to eat coarse food, to wear home-spun clothes, and to help clear the land of rock and stubble. But for Madeline these things were nothing compared to the long days she must stay alone while her husband helped the other men build their homes, break virgin soil, and hunt for game, and that look of fear returned to her eyes. And the boy dreaded those days when he must leave his wife because he knew that when he came back there would be that strange, haunted look that made him afraid.

Then Madeline was with child and that strange expression never left her eyes again. After many weary months she awakened her young husband one night and he went for the woman who was to be this frail girl's only attendant. When they returned Madeline was in travail and she was living again those months in which she had been so happy but in which she had known so much fear.

When the wee mite of humanity, the miracle of human existence lay beside its mother the young lad, who had grown into an old man during the hours of its birth, sat beside the bed and took his young wife's hand in his a spoke with deep emotion: "I am sorry, dear—that we came west."

All the love and sympathy of the woman for her mate rose up within her breast and she drew him very close to her. "I am glad. I have been very happy, but I am afraid."

"I know," he told her, "I know. As soon as we can we are going back."

"No," she told him, "we are the empire builders. We can not turn back."

But the look, the look of the haunted beast, the look of fear of the unknown, the look of the mother who scents the lurking foe became more intense in Madeline's eyes each day until Ben knew fear too. Fear, not of the visible, but fear of the unseen enemy.

Then the end came unexpectedly, swiftly, cruelly. In the faltering dusk of a summer's evening a tribe of Indians on the warpath swooped down upon the little settlement and killed all but a handful of men, whom they took captive. Madeline must have gone stark mad in that moment of fear. No man will ever know, but when the soldiers came to quell the uprising they found her wandering aimlessly about, emitting at regular intervals a maniacal cry that held the Indians terror stricken and at bay.

The soldiers caught her and in that last supreme effort to fight the thing that had held her fear bound for two years Madeline fought four stalwart soldiers. The soldiers started with her to the fort but the last supreme struggle she had had with the demon fear had used the little strength that had been left in a body that was from the start unfit for the life of a pioneer.

They buried her with Christian rites in a grave that they dared not mark, they had not known what to have written on a marker. No one knew at the time that a section of country of a great commonwealth would come to be named after a woman who sleeps in an unknown grave. For years after the soldiers found her people referred to the area where she was wandering as "the country where the crazy woman was." This finally came to be abbreviated to "the Crazy Woman Country," and this it is called today. It has always been for the most part used for cattle range and in its bleak, sparsely settled vastness it still holds for women a strange, unfathomable fear.

62 The Story of Rawhide Butte

This story rings of truth but it is told throughout the west about every creek and river, hill and butte called "rawhide." Many of the creeks were called "Rawhide" because they were used by tanners to rinse treated hides; with other features perhaps it was the texture of the color of the land that gave it its name. The tale must have given many a back chill, however, to the pioneer children who heard it.

A man coming from Missouri . . . made the statement he was going to kill the first Indian he saw. He traveled for many days with a train of covered wagons before he fulfilled his statement. The first Indian he saw was a squaw, whom he killed.

This enraged the other members of the Indian party greatly. They followed the wagon train for many days. Finally they came upon the train near the Rawhide Buttes. They made it understood they would attack the entire party unless this man who had committed the crime was given to them.

The legend tells us they skinned the man alive in place of scalping him. He became unconscious several times but was conscious until the savage punishment was almost completed.

Several narrators insist his skin was spread on the side of one of the buttes and thus we have the name of Rawhide Buttes.

63 The Legend of Fanny's Peak

The threat of Indian attack was more imagined that real. Now, in retrospect, we can see that in any encounter between the white man and the Indian it was the Indian who had the most to fear, for the savagery was distinctly one-sided. The Indians did indeed kill men and adopt white women as wives, but if scalping is to be taken into account, it should be remembered that the practice was standard for the soldiers, who did not exclude women and who did not limit themselves to heads. The Indians, it must be noted, were shocked and terrified by the unlimited and unprincipled savagery displayed by white soldiers. This legend was collected from Julius Dewing and Mel Quick.

This is a legend of how the Missourians first came to the Wyoming Black Hills, as told by one of our respected citizens, who came here in the early days from Missouri.

"I came to this country from Missouri. It was a long, hard trip overland with a team and a wagon, but we made it, and all unbeknownst to us we left a trail across that trackless prairie which was to influence the population of this new country. There was roughlock chain on the hindermost wagon, that dragged on the ground all the way from 'Mizzouri' and cut a trail over the sod. Other Mizzourians, looking for a trail to follow west, saw the mark and followed it right up the end and that's how there came to be so many sons of Mizzouri in the Black Hills."

'Way back in the early seventies a small group of people trekked to the Black Hills and made a settlement at the foot of what is now called Fanny's Peak. How this peak received its name is one of the favorite tales of the old timers here about.

Among this small group of pioneers was a young husband and wife. Legend records only the name of the wife, Fanny. This handful of people set to work to build for themselves and their stock warm log shelters against the coming winter and to wrest a living from the untamed country. The Indians as yet were not completely subdued, and their fierce resentment against the encroaching whites often burst out in unexpected and bloody attacks; yet in the face of hardship and danger these people set bravely to work to carve out homes and advance the outposts of civilization.

One morning the men had gone to the timber to hew out logs and had left their little settlement unguarded. Fanny was left alone to do the myriad chores of the camp and prepare the dinner of venison and hardtack. She was going about her work in a light-hearted way when a clatter of hoofs aroused her and she looked up to see a band of Indians, all decked out in war paint and feathers, bearing down on camp. She leaped up and ran to the timber with the speed of a deer but too late; the Indians had caught sight of her. Yelling like demons several made after her, while the rest remained to plunder and set fire to the camp. Abandoning all hope of reaching her husband, the desperate girl bent all her efforts to reach the summit of the peak, where she thought, no doubt, she could signal to the men at work in the woods.

Up she scrambled over huge boulders, but the Indians left their horses and came after her with fierce, hoarse cries. Then, when the plucky girl had almost reached the top, the Indians seized her and started to drag her back, but she was strong and agile and managed to break away, and a few swift bounds carried her to a pinnacle that overlooked a sheer precipice.

For an instant she stood screaming a warning to her husband and the others; then, as her pursuers came on with hands outstretched to seize her, she gave one last, wild cry and plunged over the cliff to her death on the rocks far below. She had chosen death that way in preference to the cruel tomahawks of the Indians. Her screams warned the men of their danger but the Indians, satisfied with their vengeful work and thinking they had played enough mischief on the white man, galloped away with loud war whoops.

Fanny's Peak will ever be remembered in this region as a monument to a brave pioneer girl and ever serve to recall the tragedies and sufferings of the early settlers.

III

Indian Folktales

By the time firm white contact had been established in Wyoming eleven Indian tribes dominated the area: The Crow to the north, Cheyenne and Arapaho in the east and southeast, Blackfeet and Flathead in the north, Shoshone and Nez Perce in the west, and the Utes and Gros Ventre in the south. The relentless pressure of the advancing frontier, the completion of the Union Pacific Railroad in 1869, the boom of rich mineral finds, the extermination of the buffalo herds, the growing pressure of southern settlement in the Colorado gold fields, and western pressures from the Mormon settlements extinguished some tribes like the Nez Perce and drove from Wyoming others like the Crow (to Montana) and the Utes (to Utah), until only the Shoshone were left, on the Wind River Reservation.

The Shoshone (also mistakenly called the Snakes) were the northern-most group of the Shoshone tribes. In 1868 as the result of a treaty concluded at Fort Laramie, the Arapaho, a branch of the Algonquin family and therefore of a culture considerably different from that of the Shoshone, ceded their Wyoming land claims in favor of a new reservation in South Dakota—land already granted to and firmly held by the awesome Sioux, who were yet to teach the United States a few lessons in military tactics. The federal government had pulled the same trick on the Ponca Tribe in Nebraska, but the Arapaho, like the Ponca, were smart enough to resist the cruel ploy.

The Arapaho were to be removed to the Oklahoma Indian Territory then but instead settled with the Shoshone on the Wind River Reservation and asked permission of the government to winter there. The tribe is still there; however, it must be noted that the two tribes are culturally disparate and have maintained that integrity to a great degree. The Federal Writers Project files noted that at the time of their collecting there were 1,184 Shoshone and 1,198 Arapaho at the Reservation.

As we have noted in the general introduction to this collection, the FWP operated within professional and cultural standards that have since become obsolete, but the materials themselves remain of interest and use. Another caveat is necessary in any collection of Indian tales, no matter what the date or professional standards of the work: Indian materials collected by white field workers pass through a cultural filter that necessarily affects them.

Creation Myths

All men have wondered from where they individually and collectively might have come, and every people have a creation story to explain that origin. The creation myths of the Wyoming Indians are representative of the type.

64 Arapaho [1] and Arapaho [2]

In regard to the creation the Arapahos say that long ago, before there were any animals, the earth was covered with water, with the exception of one mountain, and seated on this mountain was an Arapaho, crying and poor and in distress. The gods looked at him and pitied him and they created three ducks and sent them to him.

The Arapaho told the ducks to dive down into the waters and find some dirt. One went down in the deep waters and was gone a long time, but failed. The second went down and was gone a still longer time, and he also came up, having failed. The third then tried; he was gone a long time. The waters where he went down had become still and quiet and the Arapaho believed him to be dead, when he arose to the surface and had a little dirt in his mouth. Suddenly the waters subsided and disappeared and left the Arapaho the sole possessor of the land. The water had gone so far that it could not be seen from the highest mountains but it still surrounded the earth, and does to this day.

Then the Arapaho made the rivers and the woods, placing a great deal near the streams. The whites were made beyond the ocean. There were then all different people, the same as at the present day. Then the Arapaho created buffalo, elk, deer, antelope, wolves, foxes, all the animals that are on the earth, all the birds of the air, all the fishes in the streams, the grasses, fruit, trees, bushes, all that is grown by planting seeds in the ground.

This Arapaho was a god. He had a pipe and he gave it to the people.

He showed them how to make bows and arrows and how to make fire, by rubbing two sticks, how to talk with their hands, in fact, how to live. His head and his heart were good, and he told all the other people, all the surrounding tribes, to live at peace with the Arapahos. They came there poor and on foot, and the Arapahos gave them of their goods, gave them ponies. The Sioux, Cheyenne, Snakes, all came. The Cheyenne came first and were given ponies[,] these ponies were "prairie gifts." The Snakes had no lodges and with the ponies they gave them skin tipis. The Arapahos never let their hearts get tired of giving. Then all the tribes loved the Arapahos.

Arapaho [2]

From the *Kemmerer Reporter*, May 27, 1927.

The Arapahos have a definite tradition that they came to this "new earth" by the way of the northwest, crossing on the ice, that they left the old world because their country was taken and they themselves cruelly treated by a people they called the "Neau-thau. . . ." While crossing this frozen water it broke and the bulk of the tribe was drowned. Those who reached the land on this side, after mourning their loss, continued their journey, traveling toward the south. When they reached this region they found it inhabited by a people they called the "He-wuch-a-wu-the," or "the dwellers in grass houses," their name for the Shoshones. They also found a pygmy race of cannibals living in the cliffs.

That portion of the tribe that had not reached the frozen water to cross to this country, when they heard of the disaster that had befallen part of the tribe, turned back. So the Arapahos claim that it is their kindred who now inhabit "the old earth."

In the tribe the Arapahos have always had self-government, electing their own chiefs, and the only office among them that was entailed was that of guardian of the sacred pipe, as they call it, the "Chariot of God." This sacred pipe they revere as we do the Liberty Bell and they firmly believe it was given to the tribe as a token of the Creator's favor and protection. They place all their hopes and fears in it. It may be interesting to hear the origin of this pipe.

In the beginning the earth was covered by the water of a flood, except the topmost peak of a high mountain, on which sat the first Arapaho that was created, weeping. Looking up he saw Je-sau-ue-au-thau (the Great Spirit) coming to him, walking on the water. Being asked why he wept, he replied that he was lonely and homeless. God then commanded a dove to find a country for the Arapaho.

Returning after a fruitless search the dove said, "The water is over all." A turtle was then bidden to go on the same quest. It dived at once into the water and presently brought up some mud in its mouth and said, "The earth is under water." God then said, "Let the waters flow away to the big seas and let the dry land appear.

Then, as they walked about in this beautiful place, God threw some pebbles in the deep lake. Seeing them sink into the depths the Arapaho cried, "Oh, are my children to die?"

To comfort him God presented him the flat pipe and said to him, "Preserve this most carefully, for it will be through the ages to your children during life a guide and blessing and when they die it will carry their souls safely to 'our home.' When at last it wastes away I, the Deliverer, will come from the northwest to be chief over my people forever. Be kind to your friends, fight bravely your enemies. Farewell."

Where the pipe led the way the whole tribe followed. Where it stopped there they camped. It was too sacred to carry on horseback, so the custodian had to go on foot and carry the pipe in his arms. It led their hosts to battle and gained them victory. Dying Arapahos, gazing on the pipe were led safely to "our home," hence its name, "Chariot of the God."

65 Shoshone

Collected on the Wind River Reservation from Venerable Shoshones by
A. F. C. Greene in 1936.

The origin of the Shoshone Indians is lost in the mists of antiquity. The
native legend is to the effect that there was a great flood at sometime
in the Earth's history which covered all the dry land. The streaks or
discolored strata to be seen in the bluffs bordering the different streams
is proof that water once covered them.

During the flood a water bird of some kind swam about on the surface
of the water looking for a place to rest. After many days he appeared
with a tuft of grass in his bill which he divided in two parts and twisted
around in his bill, laying them side by side on the ground. The Great
Spirit appeared and breathed into these tufts of grass the breath of life,
one of them becoming a man, the other a woman. These people were
very beautiful and were as white as snow. The Great Spirit told them
that he had created all kinds of animals, birds, and fruits for their suste-
nance and enjoyment.

These people wore no clothing, being absolutely unconscious of their
nakedness. In course of time they had several children.

One day, as the first man was starting out on a trip to get food, he talked
at some length to his wife. He said, "You are a most beautiful woman.
There is a devil in human form who is determined to entice you to do
wrongful things. Beware of him. Have nothing to do with him. Do not
speak to him and do not accept anything he may offer you."

While the man was absent this devil appeared to the woman in the
form of a very handsome young man. He offered her some fruit, most
beautiful in color and texture and of a variety which she had never before
seen. She steadfastly refused to accept the fruit but his cunning speeches
finally wore down her resistance and she ate some of it. Immediately all
of her flesh turned brown.

When her husband and children returned she induced all of them
to partake of some of the fruit. Like herself they all took on the brown-
colored skin, which Indians have worn from that day. These people

were the first Shoshones. They eventually became a large and powerful people. The Comanches and Shawnees were a part of this tribe, each with a powerful chief at the head. Controversies later arose, which resulted in these three bands splitting up into separate tribes. The Comanches and Shawnees betook themselves to other regions. The Shoshones selected the territory where they have since resided.

Tales and Legends

66 Axe Brown's Stories

These two legends are fragmentary but are clearly field collected and are therefore of particular value.

Axe Brown, Arapaho Indian, forty years of age, tells of a giant petrified lizard that lay within the river bottom near a gravel bar, about one-half mile below the old highway bridge over the Big Wind River at Riverton. He says his attention had been drawn to the thing by happening upon quite profuse a collection of silken handkerchiefs, neckerchiefs, strings of beads, necklaces, wristlets, rings, and various forms of Indian made jewelry brought there as a token of worship by the Indians. This he says occurred when he was eight or nine years of age, and he remembers it quite distinctly.

The immense fossil with the earth and surrounding willow growth, he says, has been torn away by flood waters and washed away many years ago.

Brown . . . also revealed a story passed down by old Indians of a band of Shoshones who had lived at Devil's Battleground (Hell's Half Acre). This band of Indians were on the verge of starvation, just about completely out of provisions. What little food remained was apportioned among them and they started out to seek relief and succor, leaving behind an old woman incapacitated from travel. They had no horses which could have been killed for food or which could have been used to carry their burden, so everything was left behind.

After considerable torture and starvation they came upon another band of Indians encamped, who fortunately had killed several buffalo. Here they were given food and several of the younger and stronger men then started back, taking food with them to get the old woman who had been left behind. Arriving at the old campsite they found her sitting upon a rock, having turned into stone. She had petrified in this sitting posture and there she sat for years in that resigned state of fossilization.

67 Lone Bear's Story

This tale has perhaps the highest degree of integrity (*sic*) of the Arapaho stories retold here. It is taken from the Shoshone Agency newspaper, *The Indian Guide* vol. 2, no. 4 (September 1897). It displays its authenticity not only in the union of man and nature but also in the recurrence of the number four, an analog to the Anglo-European tradition of the mystic number three.

Few of the Indians on this reservation are better known or more highly esteemed than our friend Lone Bear, the second chief of the Arapahos. He is now about fifty years of age, of fine physical powers, and noble, commanding face, with an expression full of kindness and intelligence. Years ago when he was an Indian of the Indians few could equal and none excel him in all the arts and practices, which the Indians used to esteem. He was a mighty nimrod in his day and there are those of his tribe now living who have seen him kill two buffalo with one arrow, and he was also one who could perform the seemingly impossible feat of driving his arrow completely through a buffalo so that it fell out on the other side. Now however he has abandoned all thoughts of such pastimes and devotes himself earnestly and successfully to learning the arts and practices of the white men and is one of our most successful farmers.

The following story we heard him tell to a party of white men and Indians seated around a campfire near the place on the banks of the Big Horn River, which the Arapahos call "Ah-can-can-ah-mes-thai," or "where we left our lodge poles." Here it was in 1874 that they abandoned their lodge poles when they left the reservation and went on the warpath for the last time.

His story was heard very attentively by his auditors and all of the Indians seemed to be familiar with it. It may be that it has some foundation in fact. Here it is just as he told it, and Tom Crispin interpreted it.

Long ago some Indians of the Comanche Tribe, who live a long way south from here and speak the same language as the Shoshone, were out hunting once, and there was a young squaw along with them. They were running buffalo and at night the squaw was missing. She had fallen off her horse or been thrown or had lost her way—at any rate, she could not be found. The next day all the party looked for her but they could not find her. Many days after they looked but they could not find her, so they went back to their lodges without her and everybody thought she was dead.

Two snows after, while hunting wild horses, they saw a herd and rode as near to them as they could. The horses ran away and the Indians chased them. They saw in the herd a strange animal such as they had never seen before but they could not get near enough to tell what it was. They went home and told what they had seen and the tribe held a council and said, "We will send forty of our young men on our best horses to catch or kill this animal." Two days later the young men rode out of the village.

They rode to the place where the wild horses had been and spent three days looking for them. At noon on the third day they saw the herd grazing a long way off. They did not disturb them that day but the next, at the first light, the young men started out to chase them. When they were about half a mile from the herd it started to run and the Indians put their ponies to the top of their speed.

Leading the herd was the strange animal and they saw that it looked like a man. No horse was so fast as it was and they saw that they could not catch it on their horses.

They stopped chasing it then and held a council. They said, "We will surround the herd tomorrow and maybe we can catch the animal that way." In the afternoon they surrounded the herd a long way off and placed six of the best riders along a ravine through which it would have to go. Then the riders began to drive the herd toward the ravine and it passed near to one of the young men who was there.

The animal was leading the herd and running fast—faster than any horse can run. The young man rode towards it as fast as this horse could go and as the animal ran past him he saw that it was a man or a woman. He had his lasso ready and threw it around the man's breast, but before he could tighten it the man caught it in his hands and pushed it off over his head.

Several other of the young men rode across the ravine in front and they surrounded the animal, and it stood still. Its eyebrows were so long that it pushed them up with its hands and looked up at the young men and they saw that it was a woman. Her hair hung down to her feet. They tied her with ropes and took her with them. When they came to the village one of the squaws said, "That is the woman who was lost two snows ago."

They said, "How do you know her?"

She said, "Look on her leg and you will see a scar. She was dressing a buffalo robe one day and the scraper slipped and cut her."

They looked and saw it was the woman. They kept her for three days but she would not eat, neither would she wear clothes. The third day her brother came into the tent and saw that she had torn her clothes off and he killed her.

68 The Nin'am-bea, or "Little People"

These are infinitesimal people who inhabit the recesses of the mountains. They are not visible to everyone. The Great Spirit has given the power to some medicine men to see and converse with them. Long, long ago a medicine man was traveling through the mountains. He became weary and sat down to rest. He saw a large eagle making swoop after swoop toward something on the ground which was not visible to him but it aroused his curiosity. The eagle seemed to be in some distress and occasionally feathers could be seen floating down to the ground from his wings and tail.

The Indian made a careful stalk towards the conflict but still could not discern the object attached. He prayed to the Great Spirit to let him be permitted to see what was going on.

His wish was granted. The Great Spirit opened his eyes so that he could see that the opponent of the eagle was one of the "little men." Having been empowered by the Great Spirit to talk to these "little people" he asked this one what all the fuss was about. He was informed that the eagle was the deadly enemy of the "little people" and that they always tried to kill an eagle when they caught sight of one. They used their minute bows and arrows for this purpose and if the eagle was ever pierced by one of these arrows he would surely die.

This "little man" informed the medicine man that they were normally friendly to the Shoshones but that occasionally one of the latter would ridicule their existence or pick up one of the sharp-edged flints which are so commonly found in these mountains. Either of these actions enraged the "little men" and the offender payed for his temerity with his life. He would be shot under the arm with one of the little arrows of these people and no one, except a medicine man who had the sanction of the Great Spirit, could extract the arrow.

A few of these medicine men have the power to see and converse with these "little people." If you see a Shoshone with one of these flints you may know that he is a medicine man clothed with the required power. The flints are bad medicine in other hands and none of the old full-blood Shoshones could be induced to touch one.

69 The Mouthless People
Collected by A. F. C. Greene.

After the human race became Indian there were many tribes and all varieties of game. A peculiar people once made a visit to the Shoshones and the latter, as is the Indian custom, prepared a well-cooked meal before them. They were surprised to notice that these people had no mouths but snuffed the odor of the food through their nostrils. They seemed to thoroughly enjoy it. The Shoshones told them, in signs, that they were not getting half of the enjoyment possible from the food, and a medicine man offered to provide them with mouths. To this they willingly agreed.

The medicine man took one of the sharp "little people" flints and cut a slit under the nose of each of these mouthless people. The latter then gorged themselves with the food set before them and testified by their actions to the fact that they had missed some of the best things of life.

The old Shoshones say it is plain to be seen that this is a true story because the mouth is nothing more than a slit under the nose.

70 A Shoshone Legend

Collected by A. F. C. Greene, June 1936.

Many years ago a war party of Shoshone was returning home from the east. They came to the top of a hill in sight of the place now called Thermopolis. They saw what they thought was smoke from a large prairie fire. After talking the matter over for a time a few of them approached the smoke and discovered it to be steam from an enormous hot water spring, which at intervals would spout a column of steam and water into the clouds.

As they approached the edge of the spring they saw a large reptile, which immediately plunged into the center of the hot water and disappeared. The Indians thought it must be some evil spirit which inhabited the spring.

They were very much afraid and prayed to the Great Spirit to deliver them from any harm. The Great Spirit told them to consult the "little men," who would give them good advice. One of the medicine men then hunted through the adjoining hills until he located one of the "little men." The latter told him that the springs were given to the Shoshone Indians by the Great Spirit. The "little men" said, "Tell your people that if they will offer their respects to the Great Spirit before bathing in these waters they will be healed of all their ailments but they must have faith in the power of the Great Spirit. No unbeliever would receive any benefit from the waters.

71 The Fort Washakie Hot Spring

The Shoshone say that the hot spring located one and one-half miles east of Fort Washakie is fed by the same waters as these at the Big Hot Springs at Thermopolis, which run underground to reach the surface again at the local spring. The same virtues are attributed to this spring as to the larger one, and all of the older Indians go through the same ceremony of offering a prayer to the Great Spirit before they enter the water.

72 The Story of the Cottontail and the Sun (Shoshone)

The Trickster, in the form of a rabbit, coyote, or semi-human, is a fascinating character of North American Indian tales. He is simultaneously a hero and villain, saving the tribe at one moment and then slyly outraging an innocent maiden the next. He is simultaneously clever and outrageously stupid. He is, in short, a compilation of all the contradictions that are mankind. The story of the sun-snarer is one of the most popular and most frequently collected among American Indians. This version was collected for the FWP files by Charles Fowkes Jr.

Long ago, the story runs, the sun was so close to the ground that all the Indians were getting burned. In their extremity they held a council and appointed the cottontail rabbit to shoot the sun and make him behave. Accordingly, the cottontail went toward the sunrise and dug a deep pit there, in which he hid to await the appearance of the sun. No sooner had he caught sight of the sun than he let fly arrow after arrow, all of which however fell burnt and harmless to the ground.

At last he took the stick with which he drilled fire in the old Indian fashion and discharged that from his bow. The shot took instant effect and the sun fell into the pit. The new sun that arose from the old one has always kept a respectful distance for the earth and the cottontail carried off as a sign of his adventure the marks on his body where the falling sun struck him.

Indian Legends of Jackson Hole

The following four tales were recorded by Nellie H. VanDerveer in Jackson, Wyoming. While they display considerable cultural influence from the white frontier they also retain characteristics that mark their fundamental authenticity.

73 The Sheep-eaters

Handed down through many generations is the story of the "sheep-eaters," one of the numerous bands of the Shoshone Indians that wandered around the country which is now Jackson Hole. Other bands of the sheep-eaters were known of in various other portions of the country immediately surrounding Jackson Hole.

The sheep-eaters were very timid and very much afraid of all the other Indians, even the other bands of Shoshones. They had no real weapons, either of offense or defense, so they did their best to keep out of the way of the other Indians. Sometimes they hid in caves or in any out of the way place they could find. Sometimes they built crude shelters and hideouts of rocks on the mountain sides or other places where they were not likely to be discovered. One of these retreats has been found on the west slope of the Teton Range. Others have been discovered in other parts of the country.

There were many mountain sheep or Bighorns at that time and they inhabited mainly the mountainous parts of the country.

The sheep-eaters, being so timid and having no weapons of any account, had to subsist on vegetation and on whatever animals they could kill with rocks. The sheep-eaters hid on the upper rock ledges and dropped rocks on the sheep as they were traveling along the lower ledges. This was their easiest way of obtaining good meat and sheep meat was their favorite, hence the name, sheep-eaters.

74 The Happy Hunting Ground

From time immemorial the Indian has believed in the Great Spirit and in the Happy Hunting Ground. The idea of the location of the latter varied, of course, with the different tribes. Tradition says that many of the western Indians believed that Jackson Hole was the Happy Hunting Ground for all good Indians. Wonderful tales were told amongst them of the great numbers of wild game, the beautiful mountains and lakes and streams, the pleasant summer days and the cool nights, and many other things to make Jackson Hole a paradise to be looked forward to with longing.

On the other hand, Yellowstone National Park, immediately to the north, was looked upon by the Indians with fear and awe and superstition. They avoided it always as a fearsome place and the abode of evil spirits. The tradition among them was that it was the future place of evil where all bad Indians would have to spend their time when they died, thus corresponding to the white man's idea of hell.

The Indian said that all good Indians, when they died, would go to Jackson Hole, the Happy Hunting Ground, but that all bad Indians would be allowed to travel through Jackson Hole and see all its beauties, after which they must travel on to Yellowstone National Park and stay forever there, tormented by the evil spirits of that dreadful place and thinking with increasing longing of the wonderful place through which they had passed and where they might have stayed had they been good Indians.

75 The Legend of Sheep Mountain

Many thousands of years ago a great Indian Chief ruled all of the western tribes of Indians in a wise and kind manner and there was no strife or killing amongst them, only peace and plenty and contentment. It was only after many centuries that strife and trouble began, and more particularly after the coming of the white man.

This famous Indian chief who ruled so wisely and so well often went to the highest mountain peaks where he could look far out over the valleys and ranges of the wonderful country over which he ruled. Sheep Mountain, the slopes of which border Jackson Hole on the east, was one of his favorite places and many days he spent on its broad summit contemplating his domains and their future. In a spirit of contentment and meditation he gazed down upon Jackson Hole, the Happy Hunting Ground of all good Indians. To the north was a fearful region of boiling water and steam and disturbing noises but in Jackson Hole there was peace and quiet and an abundance of fish, wild game, and birds. The climate was ideal, the scenery beautiful—in every way it was the Indian's idea of Paradise.

When the good old chief finally knew that his time on earth was short and that soon he would go to the Happy Hunting Ground he wished that he might forever remain on top of Sheep Mountain where he could look down forever into Jackson Hole and guide the spirits of his followers as one by one they entered in the Happy Hunting Ground.

One day as he was lying peacefully on the mountain top with his arms folded on his breast and dressed in his war bonnet and his ceremonial robes the Great Spirit who grants the wishes of good Indians waved his hand gently over the old chief and he passed from this earth and was turned into stone as he lay on the summit of Sheep Mountain and there he is to this day.

76 The Legend of "One-Eye"

One-Eye was a great hunter who lived in the mountains to the east of Jackson Hole many centuries ago, but he had two eyes then. His lodge was never without meat because he was such a successful hunter. He used to hide out particularly in Sheep Creek Canyon where was a favorite trail of the Bighorns and other wild game in their journeys from the mountains down into the valley and many of them were killed by One-Eye.

He became obsessed however with his own skill so that he killed more than he needed for food; he killed just to show his prowess. The gods finally became angry with this hunter and said he should have but one eye instead of two so that he could not see so many wild things. They put him to sleep and when he awoke he had but one eye instead of two so that he could not see as well land that was in the middle of his forehead. So he became known as "One-Eye."

When One-Eye died he was not allowed to mingle with the other spirits in the Happy Hunting Ground but was turned into stone on a point of rock in Sheep Creek Canyon where he had so often lain in wait for an unwary animal. Having only one eye he would not kill too many and he was too good an Indian and too great a hunter to be sent on north to the region of evil spirits.

To this very day One-Eye may be seen on a point of rock looking out into Sheep Creek Canyon.

Indian Place Name Legends

The cultural concepts of the white settler and the native Indian differed (and to a great degree still do differ) so profoundly that only rarely could tales—and never songs—combine into a hybrid representation of the two disparate cultures. However this is not true in the case of place name legends. Hot springs, bizarre geological formations, dramatic mountain peaks, all catch the eye of the white man and Indian alike and excite explanatory narratives. Moreover, the white man has shown a centuries-long proclivity for adding mystery to his own place name legends by attributing them to the Indians, even where that might not have been the case at all. For these reasons we combine in this section the place names of the Indian and the white man's tales that have been attributed to the Indian.

77 The Legend of Big Springs

The FWP files' version of the Big Springs place name legend groans heavily under its burden of romantic, white rhetoric but the files also have documentation that purports to authenticate the tale. It was reputedly recorded by L. J. Duhig, co-editor of the *Thermopolis Record*, in its July 18, 1903, issue, "as based on legend as related to him by the Indians."

The second part of the tale, dealing with the thunder ground, rings much truer, having living analogues yet today among other tribes, notably the Lakota, and the tale is directly attributed by Duhig to White Antelope, an Arapaho.

The early folklore of the southern portion of the Big Horn Basin largely centered around the Big Horn Hot Springs, this being the main natural attraction of that part of the country. Since time immemorial Indian tribes have visited the Springs, the last ones to occupy this section of the Basin surrounding the Springs being the Arapahos and Shoshones. The legends of this are of Indian origin.

The Big Spring of this group, said to be the largest hot mineral spring in the world, flowing 18,600,000 gallons of water every 24 hours at a temperature of 135 degrees Fahrenheit, is believed by the Indians to have been created by the Great Spirit or the Great God of the Medicine Men, and the legend of its origin is as follows:

Ages ago the Great God of the Medicine Men stood on the mountains that overlook the valley of the winding river that has its birth in the eternal snows and flows into the distance beyond the land of the savage Sioux. He was contemplating the works of nature and he saw that they were good. Great herds of buffalo fed on the hills and slaked their thirst at the peaceful river; bands of graceful antelope, watchful deer, and majestic elk wandered where their fancy led them; the noble bighorn stood guard on the rocky crags to see that the mothers and young of his flock were not molested. All these nature had given to the Arapaho, whose villages he could see at intervals in the pleasant places by the river's side. His heart swelled with pride, for he loved his people.

But sadness overcame him. Nature had done much for them but they had many physical ills that human skill could not cure. He said, "If nature has done so much for my people, she can do more," so he called the other gods in council and told them of the needs of the people. It was decreed in the councils of Deity that by the banks of the beautiful river there should burst forth a stream in whose waters human infirmities would be cured and the afflicted of mankind could find relief. To the God of the Medicine Men they gave the task.

At the foot of a great, flat-topped hill he found a cave whose depths had never yet been reached. In its hidden chambers he placed the things that will cure the ills of man—the things that the gods alone know—enough to last to the end of time. He kindled the mysterious fires that water will not quench, and he caused a living stream to issue from the cavern.

The people heard of the miracle and they came from far and near. They were made whole and they worshiped the god who had wrought the wonder. The tradition of our people tells us that though human eyes cannot see him the God of Medicine Men forever stands guard on the flat-topped hill that shelters the Spring where he had used the most subtle of his arts.

While the Indians believe the Great Spirit sent the healing water they also think there is a place at the Springs which is the abode of evil spirits. According to a legend in connection with the Devil's Punch Bowl, an immense crater of an extinct spring which now has a blackish water in the bottom of its crater and around the edge of which rushes grow.

This, according to the legend, they call the "Thunder Ground," probably because of the ground surrounding this crater being of "formation," a mineral deposit from the hot water, having a hollow sound when it is traveled over. The legend tells that they believe a herd of buffalo which they were hunting vanished into this crater.

78 Shoshone Version of the Legend of the Big Spring

Submitted to the Wyoming files by Orville S. Johnson of Basin, and described by the documentation as "told by a Shoshone youth one 24th of July when he was taking part in a Pioneer Day celebration in Lovell."

Many years ago this Big Horn Basin was but a great sea. Around it roamed the animals who love water and green grass. To the south and west was the land of the people of the Moon, fore-bearers of the Shoshones. They came to the shores of the inland sea to hunt and fish. The animals were intelligent in those days and refused to be killed. The fish refused to be caught.

The Indians became hungry and then thin. If the Great Spirit made the animals and fish so smart, he should provide other means of food for the Indians whom he loved as much if not more than the beasts. The whole tribe prayed.

Suddenly the waters of the great inland sea began to lower. Down they went, with the Indians following, until they were so low the fish were piled on top of each other. It was easy then to eat fish, to dry fish.

Finally the great sea completely disappeared, and the Indians stood on the banks of a river roaring through a crack in the mountains. The river was full of fish. It was crooked and lined with trees and brush where the Indians could hide and wait for the animals to come and drink. There was not as much shoreline as the sea had had and hunting became easier. The hungry people had grown plump and happy again. Until the white man came, they stayed that way.

79 The Legend of Wind River Canyon

Wind River Canyon abounds in legends. One begins with an Indian lover and his sweetheart. Beloved of the Great Spirit because of their tribal customs, many favors had followed the tribe from its beginning. It was a small tribe and the lover was the last of its chieftain blood. The youth's father had died of old age not long before.

The girl was the loveliest creature in the whole Big Horn Basin at the time. The plans of the lovers included a new chieftain's son soon, and some special feasts to the Great Spirit for his goodness to the tribe.

Suddenly a gust of wind came up and blew one of the eagle feathers from the hair of the maid. Both started in pursuit. Down the deep canyon the feather floated, just out of reach, until they had passed through the entire canyon. About where Thermopolis now stands the feather drifted to the ground and they picked it up. They looked around. They saw steam and other wonders, but knowing then that the Great Spirit had led them there for that very purpose they feared not to investigate.

The water of the springs were hot but smelled clean and they bathed in one of the springs. The results were extremely to their liking. The whole tribe presently moved down there where they became famous for their strength and endurance.

To this day the wind will guide a weary traveler down to the springs if he will but loose a feather at the head of the canyon and follow that feather as did the Indian brave and his maid in the days when nobody knew of the existence of the springs except the Great Creator.

Another legend has to do with the coming forth of the springs themselves. War was among all the tribes in this section. Bitter war. A chief's daughter had been stolen and no effort had been made to satisfy the father with horses or robes or anything of value.

Suns rose; moons waned. The war went on until the chief who had no daughter found his band terribly thinned. Of course the other band thinned too but the Chief-with-no-daughter did not seem to think of this.

Then one spring morning the two hands met on a high hill. The sun was red with anger because of so much fighting among his children. Chief-with-no-daughter felt a twinge of conscience. He looked below to the west and saw a swirl of white smoke suddenly begin to curl upward. He drew the attention of his warriors to it. Then he called to the chief who had stolen his daughter to look below.

"It is the Great Spirit," Chief-who-stole-the-maiden declared. "He is telling us to smoke the pipe of peace."

They descended. The odor was unpleasant to their nostrils. "This is no peace pipe," declared Chief-with-no-daughter. But he resisted ordering his warriors to start fighting again and walked down beside Chief-who-stole-a-maiden. Presently the odor became less unpleasant. And then the smoke became a great cloud and was not unpleasant at all. The warriors of both tribes sat about the smoking spring and passed the pipe of peace amongst themselves.

80 The Legend of Chugwater Creek

A name like "Chugwater" is certain to excite curiosity and wonderment. After a time residents of the area developed a story to answer the questions and whether true or not it became the official version. This etymology appeared in the *Chugwater Record* on July 15, 1937; it was collected from Mr. S. W. McGinley, who said that the story had been told to him by "a very old Indian."

When old Wacash, the Mandan chief, was one day unhorsed, gored, and trampled by a buffalo bull it put him in a very bad way to lead the buffalo hunt, which was the main source of the food for the tribe. (He had) only one son and he was not yet a warrior but the only brave on which Wacash depended to succeed him in power and take his place in the tribe when he was no more.

This only son was called Ahwiprie (The Dreamer) (and he) could sit for hours by himself absorbing sunshine and never seeming to have a care or give a hoot as to where the next meal was coming from, but he always managed to be on hand when the cooking pot was removed from the fire.

The old chief in his crippled condition called his son and told him to make ready and lead the fall hunt in the manner as heretofore led by himself, to get the best buffalos, runners together and join in the chase for the winter meat. But to all the old chief's entreaties, orders, and urgent solicitations, all he received was a nod or a grunt—nothing more.

Still the boy continued to lay in the sun and dream. As they were still in summer camp on a clear, beautiful stream, the son persuaded the tribe to remain where they were for a time, regardless of his grouchy old father's orders.

Now, just toward the sunrise from camp was a very high cliff that rose from the valley below two hundred feet in the air. (The cliff) was all of a mile up and down the stream and only a fourth of a mile from the campsite, coming to a V-shape point at the camp. Now, the dreamer had spent many days looking up at the bluff and dreaming dreams which kept him entirely to himself.

As cooler weather approached he called together a few scouts and after a short ceremonial smoke spoke to them in this way: "Listen to my plans for gathering winter meat and many robes for tipi covers and general use of our tribe. You all know the customary way is to ride into the herds on the range and kill as many as possible or needed, to pack the meat and hides to camp where curing and tanning is done by the squaws. Then later it all has to be re-packed again to our winter camp on some sheltered stream, thereby making double the work for the squaws and children.

"As I am soon to become your chief, long and careful thought have I given to my first duty to my people. Now listen carefully. Before the sun shows its face in the morning, three of you ride south, three north. The balance toward the rising sun. See that you pass by and through all herds without disturbing them.

"You that go north travel to the river (the Laramie River); you that go south go to the Big Sand Grass (Fox Creek); and you that go east stop at the rim of the sunken lands (Goshen Hole). Then for two days slowly work toward camp but do nothing to alarm the buffalo. On the third sunrise close in on the buffalo, herding them toward camp and the V-shaped cliff that drops from the sky to the camp grounds below.

On the morning of the third day all the young braves mounted on the best horses of the tribe, were lined up ten miles each side of the jump-off.

When the herd was headed right and going fast they all joined in the chases, driving and scaring the buffalo in one solid mass.

The leaders were not able to see the break in the level, high prairies until they were on the very edge of the precipice. Then, unable to stop or turn they were crowded over by the massive weight behind them, (and) thus countless hundred went to their doom.

Falling from such a great height, striking the rocks below, many of them burst on reaching earth, and from the "chug," "chug," "chug," as the bodies bounced to earth the stream on which the camp was located was called Waters of the "Chug," or Chugwater.

The V-shaped bluff still stands as a landmark visible for many miles . . . , near Slater, eight miles north of the town of Chugwater, which is named after the creek.

81 Legends of Lake DeSmet

Lake DeSmet lies five miles north of Buffalo in the north-central part of Wyoming very near the site of Fort Phil Kearney. The material given here were reportedly collected by Ida McPherren from oral sources at the University of Wyoming.

The first day the lake was discovered a band of Indians camped upon its banks. They tried to use the water for drinking and cooking purposes but found it to have a very bitter, unpalatable taste. This was a great disappointment and shock to them because they had no way of knowing what was wrong with it and believed its bitterness to be due to the presence of an evil spirit.

That night, when they slept under the stars beside this great, cool lake, there must have been something terrifying in the weird, uncanny sounds of the night, even to the Indian, accustomed as he was to the desolate wilds. The lake was infested by great hordes of sea gulls. They flew about during the day and returned to the lake after dusk and all night long they soared and droned (sic) and swarmed. They rose en masse with the break of day and flew away out of sight. They were not to be found on any other waters familiar to the Indian and they must have made hideous noises and presented a gruesome sight as they rose and fell in their great numbers.

But it was with the dawn that the real terrifying experience came to this band of Indians who had found a great lake. After breakfast the champion swimmer among them ran to the lake's edge, gave a happy war whoop and plunged into the waters. The Indians who were watching him saw him turn about as if to return to shore, open his mouth as if to call out, and widen his eyes with horror and despair, and then disappear below the surface of the water. The Indians became panic-stricken and circled about the lake waiting for him to re-appear but he did not come to the surface again. When they had waited for what they knew to be a long enough time for him to come to the top of the waters and he did not, they grabbed their belongings and fled in terror from the lake and no Indian ever skirted it again.

It lay isolated from man and unfrequented by beast, and queer, uncanny tales grew up about it, and many strange legends. One legend in particular is interesting because it is illustrative of the customs and beliefs of the Indian of that day.

A band of Indians were camped on the shores of the lake and a young warrior called Little Moon asked his sweetheart, whose name was Star Dust, to meet him at the edge of the lake when the camp had gone to sleep. Little Moon arrived at their trysting place before Star Dust and as he stood waiting for her the beautiful face of a maiden formed in the heavy mist that hung over the lake and smilingly beckoned to him. As she smiled beguilingly Star Dust appeared and tried to wind her arms around her lover's neck, but Little Moon, held spell-bound by the strange apparition beckoning to him pushed Star Dust from him angrily. When he turned again to the lake the vision had dissipated. The next morning, when the Indians broke camp, they found the body of the drowned Star Dust (at) the red bluff north of the lake. Star Dust must have cast herself into the lake and abandoned herself to its waters when repulsed by her lover. The father of Star Dust demanded vengeance and Little Moon was bound to the rock and left to the tortures of the elements.

With Lake DeSmet as with all things in life if we look for the ugliness we cannot see the beauty. A half century ago the lake was visited by men who had heard of its bad reputation and who were trying to fathom the reason. Each party of explorers came away with a tale more weird than that of their predecessors. Some of these tales were based upon truth and some were only the wild imaginings of minds that were given to morbid exaggeration, based on ever so insignificant an incident, and some were honest opinions of men who were easily influenced by the mysterious.

Perhaps the thing that influenced honest men the most into believing something mysteriously gloomy cast its shadow over the lake (was the fact that) unnatural noises pervaded its nights, for which the horses had an aversion. They were always nervous, irritable, and uncontrollable when in close proximity to it.

A story is told about two men who went duck hunting at the lake. They drove over late one night in order to be there early the next morning before the ducks left the water. The men slept in a small tent beside the horses and the wagon. About midnight the horses snorted, reared, and then quieted. The men took their guns and the next time the horses snorted and reared they shot into the air for the purpose of frightening whatever was the cause of the horses' restlessness. After that the horses were quiet the remainder of the night but in the morning the men found that the horses had dragged the wagon about fifty feet from where they had been standing.

Another story that lent credence to the idea of mystery and weirdness is about a bird dog. In 1914 Arthur Burkhart went duck hunting on the lake in a canvas canoe. He had his bird dog with him. When Mr. Burkhart shot a duck the dog jumped into the lake and swam out to retrieve it. When he was half way to where the duck was, the dog suddenly barked and stared back to the boat, but instead of returning in a straight line he circled around whatever it was that had frightened him and returned from the opposite direction. Whenever Mr. Burkhart took the dog to the lake the animal acted frightened when he came to this spot and always circled around it.

There were tales that went the rounds in the early days in Wyoming in regard to sea serpents having been seen in the waters of the lake. Mr. Seneff, who was a civil engineer and worked a great deal in the vicinity of Lake DeSmet thought of running pleasure boats on the lake but one day he saw a sea serpent rise from its waters and splash waves large enough to swamp a rowboat.

At another time, Mr. Barkey, the father of Reuben and Roy Barkey, the famous rodeo performers, whose home is near the lake, rose early one morning and went into the fields. He heard a strange noise coming from the lake and turned to see a huge sea serpent rise from the lake, rose a second in midair and then disappear from sight, presumably having returned to the waters. Mr. Barkey's description of the animal more nearly approaches that of a dinosauer (*sic*) than any other description of the sea animals given, but his resemblance is mostly connected with the serpents's size.

There were many people who believed the (the conversion of the waters of Lake DeSmet into a great irrigation project) would be a terrible disaster to the valley through which the waters would have to go because they believed that the alkali in the water would destroy all the vegetation on the land through which it would flow.

82 Lovers' Leap

Wyoming's Lovers' Leap, as reported in this article extracted from the *Laramie Daily Sun*, July 6, 1875, is validated by a white man's tale, attributed to the Indians, and is thus the archetypical version of the traditional "Indian" love story.

A beautiful and dark maiden of the Ute Tribe became enamored with an Arapaho chief and warrior. She, being the first of the female sex in the wild west to exercise what is now known as "woman's rights," abandoned her tribe and sought her lover on the Plains. By some unaccountable instinct the Arapaho at the same time left his tribe and fled to the mountains. A party of both tribes followed these two truants to watch their maneuvers and soon met in mortal combat near the Lovers' Leap.

The chief and the maiden met and were soon locked in each other's embrace and each told the strange story of their love. Yet their happiness was of short duration. The war hosts of the two tribes were soon assembled and both attempted to recover the two lovers, whereupon a conflict of arms ensued.

While the fight was being bitterly waged these two lovers escaped for safety to the top of this conically shaped mountain with a yawning precipice on one side. The Arapahos won the battle and were ascending the mountain and some of the young warriors were about to capture these two lovers when all of a sudden they rose to their feet, poised themselves on the over-hanging cliff, entwined their arms around each other, gave a look of revenge on the vanquished and victorious hosts, and then disappeared from sight over the precipice. When these two lovers first met is not accounted for, but that some such a legend as this exists among the Indians there is no doubt, and that this cliff has from time out of mind been called Lovers' Leap is a fact.

83 The Legend of Bull Lake

Bull Lake is slightly northwest of the center of the state. The Shoshone legend was recorded by Nellie VanDerveer of Jackson.

Many years ago a great herd of buffalo inhabited the region surrounding the lake. The leader of the herd was an enormous white buffalo bull. Of course the Indians from time immemorial have held a white buffalo in awe and reverence. Anyone who succeeded in killing one was thought to be a super-human—almost a god.

So the Shoshone hunted this herd around Bull Lake constantly, hoping to get the great white leader. Finally, in fear and desperation, the herd tried to get away from their tormentors by crossing the lake on the ice. It was not strong enough to hold the weight of the animals. They broke through the ice and went down to their death with a great plunging and roaring. Above all the others could be heard the cry of the big white leader as he went down in the icy water.

To this very day a roar can be heard coming up from the depths of the lake. It is the spirit of the old white bull roaring on and on forever in protest at the tragic fate that befell him and his herd. And so it is called Bull Lake, the lake that roars.

84 The Great Medicine Wheel

The Great Medicine Wheel, located about fourteen miles south of the Montana border, is still a mystery and has been designated a historic area by the State of Wyoming. It may indeed have fulfilled the religious functions outlined here (although it seems more likely that the number of "lodges" was determined by clans or tribal affiliations than "planets") or as is so often the case with "mysteries," the truth may simply still be hidden from us. It might be noted that another paper in the same section of the FWP files that refers to the "mystery" of nineteen stone "medicine rings" with an opening inevitably to the east interpreted the formations as religious sites. Now we know that the stones were used to hold down tipi skins, the door flap of which was always faced to the east for functional and traditional reasons. Perhaps some day the purpose or concept of this Great Medicine Wheel will also be understood.

The Medicine Wheel is located on Medicine Mountain in the Big Horn Mountains of Wyoming. It is about seventy miles west of Sheridan, near the Sheridan-Lovell Highway which crosses the Big Horn Mountains. The elevation of the wheel is 9,956 feet. It is supposed that the wheel was built by prehistoric races, as the Indians have not even any traditions as to the origin of the wheel. This race was evidently a sun worshiping race. They worshiped mountains and peculiarly shaped rocks as well as the sun and the planets. It is about one thousand feet to water in every direction from the Medicine Wheel, so when they come to worship at the Wheel they must have come to fast also.

The Crow Indians say it was built to look like a medicine lodge to the gods above, the spokes of the Wheel looking like the poles of a tipi. The center cairn of rocks is the largest of all and probably represented the sun. The spokes, made of rocks, all radiate from this shelter of rocks to the outer rim of the Wheel. There are twenty-eight of these spokes for the twenty-eight lunar days. Around the edges of the Wheel are six medicine tipis (so called by the Crows) for the different planets. Three of these are different distances from the center, or the sun. One is at the end of a long spoke which extends from the edge of the Wheel. One is a short spoke, and the third is inside the rim of the Wheel. The three other medicine tipis are on the outer rim of the Wheel. Then, there is one medicine tipi perhaps fifteen feet from the Wheel, and it might represent the seventh planet. These medicine tipis were probably the shelters for the chiefs or medicine men of the different tribes in time of worship. These shelters were very low and had a slab of rock across the top. They must have been propped up by heavy pine logs, as now the logs are mixed with these piles of stone. It is some distance to timber. Years ago there was a large excavation under each of these medicine tipis. The wheel is about seventy-six feet in diameter and 245 feet in circumference. In 1925 the Forestry Service built a rock wall around the wheel to keep livestock away from it.

The Indians who came into this country realized that this place was for worship and on top of the large rocks at the edge of Medicine Mountain they built little shelters of rock with a hole just large enough to crawl into. There they would go to fast until they had a vision of how to make their medicine. They claimed that the "little people" lived in these dream houses and so they left offerings of beads and wampum for them. (See pages 167–68 for a further discussion of the "Little People.")

For a more intimate knowledge of the future the Indian depends upon a process of making medicine: earth or sand of different colors, ashes of certain plants, particular bones or portions of birds, animals, or reptiles, varying with the special superstition of each individual Indian. These are mixed together in a shallow dish and stirred with a stick. From the combination of colors the Indian believes he can infallibly divine which god is to him in the ascendant at that time. At least one ingredient in the medicine of each Indian must be special to himself and a secret from the rest of the world.

On an Indian's initiation as a warrior he would go alone to a dream-house on Medicine Mountain and spend long, anxious hours in deep religious meditation of the question, the most momentous of his life, "What shall the ingredients of my medicine be?" When hunger and thirst had exhausted his vital powers he would fall into a trance during which the important secret would be revealed to him. After that he was not only a man and a warrior but priest for himself and his family. He made his own medicine by oft-repeated experiments and became an expert in reading the secret involved. The special and secret ingredient used by each Indian in his medicine is kept in a little pouch on his person and always carefully concealed, even from his wife and most intimate friends.

A Crow legend tells that Red Feather, a famous chief over a hundred years old, went to the Medicine Wheel to obtain his vision for his medicine. He stayed in one of those dreamhouses fasting for four days and nights. The third night the "little people" came to him and told him that he had not fasted long enough. On the fourth night they came and took him with them into a cave in the top of Medicine Mountain. He remained there for a week and was instructed by them in the art of warfare and leading his people. He was told that the Red Eagle would be his powerful medicine and would guide him and be his protector all through life, also that he should always wear on his person as an emblem of his medicine the soft little feather which grows above the eagle's tail. This gave him his name and he rose to be the biggest war chief the Crows have ever had.

That the Wheel was visited by countless numbers of people is shown by the old, worn travois trail that is visible for two or three miles. Medicine Mountain is really a twin mountain, united by a magnificent causeway, which is called "The Devil's Causeway." This is barely wide enough for a wagon way, the walls running sheer to the valley below. From the edge of the Wheel one can follow out the pattern of a paved floor, which extends towards the Causeway and there ends in terraces of rock. On the north side of the floor are also terraces and at the foot of these terraces there was evidently at one time an underground passage which extended across the top of the mountain to a cave. This has all caved in but can be seen very plainly.

Medicine Wheel Legends

Collected by Ida McPherrer.

One story runs that about the time Lewis and Clark were in this section of the country a young Indian came upon the stone wheel and implored it to give him medicine to make him a great and noble warrior. He fasted there for three days and nights and on the fourth night two men and a woman came up through an underground channel from the center shrine and conducted him back through this channel and told him that if he would always wear the little red feather that grows upon the tail of the eagle he would be a great warrior and chief. This the Indian lad did and he became a great chieftain and was known as Red Plume. When Red Plume died he told his people that his spirit would occupy the shrine at the Medicine Wheel and that they could get in touch with him there.

Another legend is to the effect that when the Crows first visited the Big Horns they sent two of their braves out to explore the newly occupied territory. There two lads found the great stone wheel and regarded it as the work of the Great Spirit. The Crows then and ever after held it in the greatest reverence. Whenever they pass the Wheel they stop and offer thanksgiving to the Great Spirit and give as a sacrifice the best of their kill.

85 Legends of the Devil's Tower

The Devil's Tower is a singular basalt tower jutting out of the Plains, a remnant of a volcanic core from which the surrounding materials have been eroded. Its sides carry long scars that are the result of the cooling processes of many millennia ago, but the Indians' legends suggest another cause. One of the most interesting of the legends was told to Dick Stone in 1933. First praying to the Great Spirit to "look down upon me so that I shall speak straight and true," Medicine Top, speaking through an interpreter, told the following story.

There were seven brothers. One day when the wife of the oldest brother went out to fix the smoke wings of her tipi a big bear carried her off to his cave. The man mourned her loss greatly and would go out and cry defiantly to the bear.

The youngest brother, who had great power, then told the oldest one to make a bow and four blunt arrows. Two arrows were to be painted red and set with eagle feathers; the other two were to be painted black and set with buzzard feathers. The youngest brother then took the bow and four arrows, told the other brothers to fill their quivers with arrows, and they all set out after the big bear.

At the cave the youngest brother told his brothers to sit down and wait. Then he turned himself into a gopher and dug a big hole to the bear's den. He crawled in and found the bear lying with its head in the woman's lap. The young Indian put the bear to sleep and changed himself back into an Indian. He then told the woman that her man was in mourning and that he had come to take her back. He told her to make a pillow of her blanket and put it under the bear's head. Then he had her crawl backwards through the hole he had dug. So he got her out to where the six brothers were waiting. Then the hole was closed up.

The woman now told the brothers they should hurry away as arrows would not go into this bear. After they had all gone the bear woke up, went out of his den, and walked around it. He found the trail of the Indians. He started after them, taking with him all the bears of which he was the leader.

The youngest brother with the four arrows kept looking back. Soon they came to the place where Bear Lodge (Mato Tipi, the Indian name for Devil's Tower) now stands. He told the six brothers and the woman to close their eyes. He sang a song; (he) finished it. When the eyes of the others opened the rock had grown. He sang four times, and when he had finished, the rock was just as high as it is today. This the younger brother could do because he was a holy man.

When the bears reached the Bear Lodge they all sat down in a line, but the leader stood out in front. He called, "Let my wife come down!" The young Indian mocked the bear, saying that he might be a holy being but he couldn't get her.

Then the brothers killed all of the bears except the leader. It growled and kept jumping high against the rock. His claws made the marks that are on the rock today. While he was doing this the youngest brother shot the black arrow at him. They did not hurt him, and by taking a run the bear went further with every jump. The third time he jumped the young Indian shot a red arrow at him but it did not enter the bear. At the fourth jump the bear almost got up on the Tower. The Indian then shot his last arrow. It went into the top of the bear's head and came out below his jaw and the bear fell dead.

The youngest brother then made a noise like a bald eagle and four eagles came. They took hold of the eagles' legs and were carried to the ground.

Now the young Indian told his brothers to pack in wood and pile it on top of the body of the bear leader. This was set on fire. When the bear got hot it burst and small pieces, like beads of different colors, flew off. The youngest brother told the rest to put these back in the fire with a stick. (If they had picked up these pieces with their hands, Medicine Top said, the bear would have come to life again.) Finally, the bear was burned to ashes.

After this there was a great many young bears running around. The Indians killed all but two. The youngest brother told these two not to bother people any more and he cut off their ears and tails. That is why bears have short ears and no tails to this day.

86 A Kiowa Legend of the Devil's Tower

The recent death of I*See-o (*sic*), the last of the Kiowa Army scouts at Fort Sill, Oklahoma, brought to the recollection of Mrs. Cyrus Beard, Wyoming State Historian, the Indian legend which this famous scout told an army officer several years ago concerning the origin of this great mass of rock.

I*See-o was the last of the great Kiowa Indian scouts and the only sergeant in the United States Army holding his position for life. A copy of his story told to Major General H. L. Scott of Fort Sill, Oklahoma Territory, in 1897 is preserved by the state historian of Wyoming.

I*See-o himself never saw the Devil's Tower but he told the legend as it had been handed down in his tribe. The story is about the seven star girls and Tso-sa—Tree Rock, also known as Bear Lodge, the Devil's Tower.

"Before the Kiowa came south," he said, "they were camped on a stream in the far north where there were a great many bears—many of them. One day seven little girls were playing at a distance from the village and were chased by some bears. The girls ran toward the village and the bears were just about to catch them when they jumped upon a low rock about three feet high. One of them prayed to the rock, "Rock, take pity upon us," and it heard them. It began to elongate itself upwards, pushing the children higher and higher. When the bears jumped at them they scratched the rock, broke their claws, and fell back upon the ground. The rock rose higher and higher, the bears still jumping at them until the children were pushed up into the sky, where they are now, seven little stars in a group—the Pleiades. In the winter when they are just overhead it is the middle of the night.

"The marks of the bears' claws are there yet—just like the side of the Medicine Bluff (at Townsite, Oklahoma). No Kiowa alive now has even seen this rock (the Devil's Tower) but the old men have told about it. It is very far north, where the Kiowa used to live. It is a single rock with scratched sides rising up straight to a great height."

IV

Folk Belief, Custom, and Speech

Man has always wanted to know and control the future, that most uncontrollable of commodities. *Traditional belief is dominated by the efforts man has made to affect and divine his future—how to predict the weather or a lover, how to recognize personality in physical traits, how to avoid bad luck or court good luck, when to plant or harvest, how to ward off or heal illness, omens, and signs.*

It is difficult—if not impossible—to separate the recognized genres of folklore in general. Is the legend, which is usually based on an item of traditional belief, a part of folk belief or folk narrative? And the task is doubly hard with folk belief and custom, and to a slightly less degree, folk speech. Belief and custom are inextricably tangled: is avoidance of passing under a ladder an act of belief or a belief-act? Considering the problem of folk speech, is a proverb like "Possession is nine points of the law" primarily a speech formula (based incidentally on a traditional belief) or is it principally a belief formularized incidentally in a set speech pattern?

Perhaps the most important thing is not so much that the three categories—belief, custom, and speech—be distinguished from each other, but that their mutual relationships and interdependence be recognized.

Folk Belief

87 Weather

Within the category of folk belief one of the most prevalent sections in any collection deals with weather, for the actions of men—from those of sailors and farmers to cowboys and bar girls, from horse thieves to railroaders—is governed in part, at least, by the weather. To be able to predict that fickle element would be an envied power indeed.

Can accurate predictions result from the application of these traditional methods? Many observe that folk meteorology certainly cannot be any less accurate than the televised variety. Indeed, some of these forecasting methods are based on long term observations and are at least as accurate as barometric readings or satellite photography.

Winter weather and storms hold a particular threat for Wyoming because they come swiftly and brutally along the east slope of the Rocky Mountains, and snowfall and cold can reach depth and degree that offer immediate and mortal danger. Little wonder then that the WPA file contained three full pages of signs of approaching hard winters and storms.

When a sow carries straw to make her bed it is a sign of cold weather and deep snow.

When blackbirds bunch up early in the fall it is a sure sign that the winter will not only be severe but will begin early and last a long time.

The earlier the coyotes get their winter coat and the thicker it is, the longer and harder will be the winter.

When the domestic animals get an unusually thick coat early in the fall and it stands on end and looks like fur, watch out for a long, hard winter.

Some years hordes of robins come to Jackson Hole for a few days in the fall after most of the summer robins are gone. They make a brief visit and then they too are gone. The weather prophets say, "Get ready early for winter. It will sure be a long, hard one."

When the leaves turn brown and the trees get bare and gray early in the fall it is another sure sign of an early winter.

When the mice and the pack rats persist in moving in and establishing winter quarters, the old timers say they sure know that a long, hard winter is coming.

Another sign that never fails, they claim, is the date when the ground squirrels hole up. If earlier than usual, an early and severe winter may be expected. But if now and then one is seen throughout the fall, they say that the winter will be light because the squirrels always know.

When the elk and other wild game stay high up in the hills until late in the fall that is an indication that the winter will be short and mild. If they come down to the lower ranges early and in bunches the winter is sure to be a severe one.

When the wild geese pause but briefly during their fall migration to the south the old timers shake their heads and say that the birds know when a hard winter is coming. But if the geese stay for months and play around as if carefree and happy then the wise old ones smile and prophesy a nice, mild winter of short duration.

Coyotes howling in the daytime or early evening means a storm that night.

If the cattle are lowing more than usual it is a sign of a storm. If the cattle are very frolicsome it is a sign of a storm. If range stock scatter out over the range from shelter early in the morning, however, it is a sign of good weather.

Horses running about the pasture, cattle trailing in a long, slow file, dogs or cats eating grass during the day, or roosters crowing during the day all indicate an approaching storm.

When puffs of snow cling to the tree branches, the storm is not yet over.

A peculiar wailing of the wind in the chimney indicates snow.

When the Great Horned Owls hoot in the woods they prophesy snow.

When "sun dogs" or northern lights appear in the sky they foretell snow and cold weather.

If snow fleas blacken the drifts beneath the pine trees it is a sign of a thaw with more deep snow to follow.

A white Christmas ushers in a winter with copious snowfall.

"A black winter brings a full graveyard" is a favorite Wyoming expression.

A peculiar blue-purple cast on the hills presages a spell of extremely cold weather.

When flies and gnats bite viciously it is a sure sign of a thunder storm.

When the Yellow Hammers (large woodpeckers) make their peculiar flickering call it will rain before evening.

If chickens go in their coop when the rain begins to fall it is a sign the storm will soon be over, but if they stay outdoors to receive a drenching the rain will last for several days.

Rain that falls in big drops or snow that floats down in large flakes means the storm will be of short duration, but when the moisture falls in fine precipitation the farmers know a good rain or snowfall is due.

To ranchers living in remote sections the distant rumble of trains and the sound of whistles becoming noticeable louder and more reverberating indicate an atmosphere heavy with storm.

To those living in the hill country the peculiar soughing of the pines and the faint, greenish tint on the landscape presages a violent thunderstorm.

When fish leap clear from the water to snatch at a low flying insect or continually send up air bubbles the fisherman knows a shower is near at hand.

"If it rains while the sun is shining it will rain tomorrow" is a popular Wyoming saying.

The hill dweller firmly believes that when the wind blows "up the creek" there will surely be a storm.

The stockman dreads the cold east wind, for he believes it will bring a blizzard or a cold spell of weather.

A sudden change of the wind from cold to warm westerly currents may mean a "chinook" with accompanying thaw.

An extremely brilliant red sunset may mean the following day will be windy.

The rancher says, "A dry, windy April means a dry, windy summer."

The cry of the rain-crow from a very high treetop is supposed to mean rain within three or four days.

There is a general belief that if it starts raining before seven a.m. it will quit before eleven.

Fleecy clouds in the sky foretell calm, clear weather.

Smoke hanging low over the ground means a storm in the offing.

When the moon is on its back, it denotes weather wet or mild; when on the end, it denotes frost.

Should the new moon lie on its back it is a sign it will be dry that month, for the moon would hold water. The hunter says he can hang his powder-horn on it. But should the new moon stand vertically it will be a wet month, for the moon will not hold water and the powder-horn would slip off. (In some areas of the state these signs are reversed.)

The moon changing in the west denotes that fine weather will prevail during that moon. If the moon changes near midnight there will be fine weather. The nearer to midnight the finer the weather.

A disk or ring around the moon indicates bad weather, rain or snow. In some localities the number of stars inside the circle denotes the number of days until it will rain. Whichever way the ring opens the wind will blow in. If it does not open there will be fine weather. The bigger the ring, the nearer the bad weather.

If the new moon is of light color there will be a frost; if it is red it will be mild for a month.

The weather of the new moon governs the month's weather, at least during the first quarter, after which it remains the same.

The moon being red near midnight with blunted corners or horns portends mild weather for that month; if the corners are white and sharp there will be frosty weather.

The Indians told the first settlers that if the moon lay well on her back the weather during that moon would be dry. "Big snow, little snow" is a common Indian saying, and they also believe that if the weather is unusually hot there will be rain within the week.

88 Love

Next to weather the most constant and unpredictable of the world's elements is love. But here the admirer of folk technology cannot afford to be smug: it seems doubtful that traditional indicators are any more reliable than modern ones, like computer dating. Perhaps the lovelorn, seeking whatever solace they can get, can find some in remembering this.

Dropping hairpins from your hair means that your beau is thinking of you.

Two spoons in a cup is the sign of a wedding.

If a couple out walking together stumble it is a sign that they will be married.

If you want to sneeze and can't it is a sign that someone loves you and doesn't dare tell it.

If you can't drink a cup of tea you must be love-sick.

If a gentleman and lady are driving and are tipped out they will be married.

If you are cross when you are young you will be an old maid.

If you fall upstairs you will have a new beau.

Stumbling either up or down stairs means you will be married inside a year.

If a lady dons a gentleman's hat it is a sign that she wants a kiss.

If a girl puts a two-leaved clover in her shoe the first man who comes on the side where the clover is will be her future husband.

Put a four-leaved clover over the door; the first person to pass beneath it will be your future husband.

Hang a wishbone over the door; the first one who enters will be your lover.

Two girls break a wishbone together; the one who gets the longest bit will remain longest unmarried, or as the familiar rhyme runs

"Shortest to marry,
Longest to tarry."

Blow seeds from the dandelion until none remain, counting each puff as a letter of the alphabet; the letter which ends the blowing is the initial of the name of the person the blower will marry.

If you are a bridesmaid three times you will never stand in the middle.

Light a match and the way the flame goes shows where you future husband lives.

Repeat, looking at the new moon the first time you see it,

"New moon, true, tell unto me
Who my true love is to be,
The color of his hair, the clothes he is to wear,
And when he'll be married to me."

If you see the new moon over the right shoulder, take three steps backward and repeat

"New moon, true moon, true and bright,
If I have a lover let me dream of him tonight.
If I'm to marry far, let me hear a bird cry;
If I'm to marry near, let me hear a cow low;
If I'm never to marry, let me hear a hammer knock."

One of these sounds is always heard.

The first time you see the moon in the New Year look at it and say

"Whose table shall I spread?

For whom make the bed?
Whose name shall I carry?
And whom shall I marry?

Then think of one you would like to marry and go your way. Ask some questions of the first person you meet and if the answer is affirmative it indicates that you will marry your choice; if negative it means you will not.

Look over the right shoulder at the new moon and count nine stars; pick up whatever is under your right foot, such as a stick, pebble, or what-not; put it under your pillow and you will dream of whoever is to be your husband.

If you take your engagement ring off your finger your engagement will be broken.

You will be unhappy if you lose your wedding ring.

Runaway matches will prove unlucky.

To be married in a brown dress is good luck, black is bad.

The two days before the wedding are the bride's days. If they are pleasant she will have good luck.

A double wedding is unlucky; one of the marriages will be unhappy.

Some think that to be married when the weather is gloomy will lead to a gloomy married life; on the other hand, to be married in the rain foreordains prosperity. To be married in the spring sunshine means to be happily united while to be married in a storm signifies a quarrelsome, troublesome marriage.

Marriage in the fall is said to lend toward frugality and saving. To be wedded in the spring, when nature is most prolific, leads to numerous offspring.

A glamorous wedding will often end in disaster while simpler weddings lend to simplicity and contentment in married life.

If the bridegroom drops the wedding ring when attempting to place it on the bride's finger the couple will separate.

89 Good Luck

Lucky day is Wednesday. Friday is lucky unless it falls on the 13th, which is unlucky, of course. Monday is often called Blue Monday or Hard Monday, being hard to get back into the routine after Saturday and Sunday.

If your right hand itches you are going to get money; if your left hand itches you will shake hands with a friend; if your nose itches a friend is coming.

If two persons wash their hands at the same time it is a sign that they will be friends forever.

To see a rainbow early in the morning indicates happiness; late in the day means disappointment.

The moon seen over the right shoulder brings good luck; over the left shoulder, ill luck. If you should see the moon over your left shoulder and should without speaking turn around and look at it over you right shoulder your ill luck will disappear, and you will be as well off as if you had seen it over your right shoulder first.

If you have money in your pocket when you first see the new moon turn it over and you'll have plenty all the rest of the month. If you have money in your pocket the first time you see the new moon and it is seen over you right shoulder you will have money all the year.

Take out money and shake it in your hand on first seeing the new moon and it will increase your wealth.

Look at the new moon through a ring, wish something while doing so, and your wish will come true. If you first see the new moon with full hands—that is, with busy hands—you will be busy, full of work, all the month; if idle, the reverse.

If you see the new moon face on, you will go headlong through the month.

If the stars appear unusually bright you will soon receive good news.

To find money when you are seeking employment means you will be successful.

Finding an old shoe indicates that you will soon take a journey.

Carry a grub worm with your bait and use it last. Never throw the first fish back, no matter how small. Spitting on bait brings good luck and keeps fish on the hook. It is bad luck to lose the first fish caught.

Putting a big hook on the line catches big fish.

If a mouse is unusually ambitious within the walls of your house it denotes that you are, or soon will be, hoarding away money. If a mouse drowns in your cream bowl your table shall be bounteously supplied with eatables.

If a sick person has vivid dreams of horses he or she will quickly recover.

90 Bad Luck

If you see the new moon through trees or brush you will have trouble that month. One who chances to have a cup in his hand when he first sees the new moon is destined to wait on the sick until another new month appears.

If you are sensitive to the sun your pleasures in life will be dulled when the days are sunless.

If your shadow falls across the thresh hold of a new dwelling place you intend to move into you will have reverses and misfortune in that house.

Losing money from your pockets means you will soon be in want.

Two persons wiping hands on the same towel and twisting it occasions a quarrel. From another source, if two persons wipe their hands at the same time they will be foes forever.

Never look after a friend who is leaving you till he is quite out of sight or you will never see him or her again; but turn your eyes away while he is still visible so that he or she may return.

If you sing (laugh) before breakfast you will cry before supper.

If a child sings before breakfast it will get a whipping before night.

To sing after you go to bed is a sign that tears will come before breakfast.

If a rooster crows before midnight it is a sign of bad luck.

Friday is a very unlucky day. Housekeepers will prefer paying a quarter's rent extra to going into a house on that day. It is of course most unlucky to be married on Friday; Wednesday is the day considered most favorable for the purpose. It is unlucky to travel or begin a piece of work on Friday. If you begin work on Friday it will be a very short or very long job. It is bad luck to cut your fingernails on Friday. If you cut your nails on Sunday you'll do something you're ashamed of before the week is out.

If business is transacted on Sunday you will lose it on the coming week.

Pancake Day is Shrove Tuesday and if you do not eat pancakes on that day you will have no luck throughout the year; the hens won't lay, etc.

Whistling girls and crowing hens are not to be trusted.

It is unlucky to turn back after having once started out.

To get out of bed on the wrong side puts one out all day.

Whoever eats the last piece of bread will be an old maid.

If you break something you will break two other things.

To twirl a chair on one leg means that you are going to fight with someone.

When a shoestring breaks in the morning while you are lacing your shoes you will be nettled throughout the day. If it breaks while you are walking you are heading into something disagreeable. If it happens while you are in search of work you will be unsuccessful.

Crossing hands, when three or more persons shake hands, is supposed to bring bad luck. It is said to bring good luck to shake hands over a coffin in which a body lies. To shake hands over a coffin means that a vow shall be fulfilled.

When a lamp or candle flame becomes extinguished for no apparent reason it presages the death of a relative. If a lamp or candle flame flickers it denotes trials and tribulations.

When a clock runs down it presages death. Some believe that when a clock runs down a piece of work they are doing will remain unfulfilled. There is an old saying that if a clock stops near the end of the week you shall have the weekend free to yourself.

A falling star presages the death of someone in the community.

If a strange dog follows you and howls there will be a death in your immediate family. Should you see a white dove near you, you will receive news of a death of a very good friend.

Gypsies believe that when an owl hoots someone is dying but if a penny is thrown towards the owl a life is saved.

If birds enter the house and fly around it is a sign of death.

A dog howling continuously signifies death in the neighborhood. Never sweep under a sick person's bed; it will cause death. If a sick person lives until two a.m. he will live till ten.

If the moon shines on your face as you lie in the bed at night you will die inside of a year. It is a general belief that it is dangerous to sleep with the moon shining on your face. If the moon shines on fish they will spoil.

91 Wishes

Two people who speak the same thing at the same time should make a wish and it will come true.

Some of the new eastern settlers of the Riverton Valley believed in making a wish when they saw a strange white horse.

If you break a mirror close your eyes, step over the broken pieces, and make a wish. This is supposed to counteract the bad luck of mirror breaking.

Making a wish in a cemetery at midnight is said to bring gratifying results.

Count nine evening stars in succession and you will have your wish.

Make wishes when the moon is seen over the left shoulder, when crossing a new bridge, when four people shake hands by crossing, when the knob is broken from a wishbone.

Wish the first time you see the moon and your wish will come true.

Bow to the new moon seven times the first time you see it and you will get a present, or wish and you will get your wish. If you shake your dress at the new moon you will get a new one.

92 Medicines

The Wyoming WPA files offer a very interesting item in the area of folk medicines: a list of remedies as practiced by an early settler in the 1860s. All too often folk cures are picked up one by one and it is not possible then to know what any one person's repertoire of cures might have been. But here, in a list contributed by Mrs. Dolly Ingebretson in 1936, we see her mother's medical list as practiced in Uinta County, Utah, just a mile or two west of the Wyoming border.

Remedies of Mary Elizabeth Simmons Robison

For granulated eye-lids: rub with white dust of chicken droppings.

Soda to sponge off fevers, burns, and as a use for an antiseptic. A weak solution of salt water for sore eyes or cold tea leaves for a cold pack

Something in the eye: a horse hair as a loop put in under the eyelid, then pulled down gently will remove the foreign substance.

For a very bad burn: lard and soot and bind on.

Fine black earth many times for piles.

Black mud or bluing for bee stings.

Some other herbs for teas and medicine are Indian root, hickory bark, wild cherry bark, ginger root, and birch-tree bark.

Fresh cuts: turpentine.

Boils: bread and milk poultices, bean poultices, soap and sugar salve and flaxseed poultices.

Hops tea for cold and nervous headaches.

Cooked dandelion greens, also watercress, for liver trouble.

Wild sage tea as a spring tonic.

Tame sage tea to break up colds.

Saffron tea to clear up complexion of very young babies.

Catnip tea for colic and nervousness.

Peppermint tea for colic and indigestion.

Plant leaf bruised for bruises.

Sheep berries, steeped and given rather warm to the children, to bring out measles.

Pig poultices for quinzy.

Sugar, tobacco, and turpentine mixed together and bound on for blood poison.

Buttermilk pancakes for a gathered breast.

Spirits of camphor for fainting or headache.

Alum for sore throat, sore mouth, or canker, also gunpowder for canker.

Whooping cough: kill, clean, and cook a mouse as you would a chicken. For an infant feed them only the broth. A larger child should be fed the meat of the mouse and broth too. Repeat in a couple of days.

For pneumonia: chop head off a chicken, split the chicken in half lengthwise and while still warm clap on breast of sufferer. Sometimes a second chicken is applied. It will turn quite black after being applied to the chest and the patient is cured.

Anemic persons: boil red beets. Slice and cover with gin. Let stand all night. Take one tablespoon every morning.

Diphtheria or Pneumonia: Give a laxative first. Slice onions in a skillet with hot lard, and when warm enough so you can hold your elbow in them without burning they are ready to be applied as a poultice. When they get cold or turn black renew poultice and it won't be long until the patient is relieved.

Cures from Other Wyoming Sources

Cupping for headaches: a cup is placed on the forehead and a piece of paper ignited to heat the cup and raise a blister. The blister is then cut and the headache is cured.

To cure or prevent rheumatism: carry a copper coin in one shoe and a piece of zinc in the other; carry a buckeye or a potato in the pocket. [A WPA worker noted at this point that he once " . . . saw a potato that had been carried about by a rheumatic for several weeks and it resembled a stone."] A common custom among cowboys is to wear a leather strap about the wrist as a cure of rheumatism, sprains, etc., and to give general strength.

A black yarn around a child's neck will ward off croup.

A red yarn around a child's neck will ward off nose bleed. In case of nose bleed put a key down the back or place a wad of paper between the upper lip and the gum.

Onion poultices in your shoe will cure a cold.

Asafetida worn around the neck will ward and cure diphtheria, small-pox, and other contagious diseases, asafetida being an excellent tonic and blood purifier.

To cure whooping cough: tie a toad to the head of the person's bed.

To cure a wart: steal a person's dishrag and the owner of the rag will inherit the wart in time. Warts may be charmed away by rubbing them with a piece of meat three days in succession but you must then bury the beefsteak.

A sty can be cured by rubbing it with an old ring, especially a wedding ring.

A string of amber gold beads worn around the neck will cure or prevent goiter, will cure or prevent quinsy.

A sore throat can be cured by binding about the neck on going to bed one of the stockings which the patient has been wearing. No other will do.

If a child is bitten by a mad dog, the dog must be killed before the child will get well.

If you sleep with your head towards the north it will prevent sickness.

Rub a corn, wen, etc., with the sun if by day, and with moon if by night. The sun or moon will draw all the pain away.

To rub for "sweeney," rub the diseased part of the horse's shoulder with a corncob with the sun every third morning.

93 Physiognomy, Reading Character and Omens by Physical Features

Do not marry a girl with a pointed nose; she will nag you.

A large nose is a sign of stability of accomplishment, good nature,. wisdom, or good, common sense.

A vein across the nose is an omen of short life.

If you have a mole on the left side of your nose it is lucky.

Small ears indicate that a person is stingy; large ones that he is generous. Large ears are a mark of a liar, small of a truthful person.

Long, slim ears are a sign you will steal.

Ears bent away from the head indicate generosity; lying close against the head they indicate a penurious nature.

If the protuberance behind the ear is large it indicates generosity.

Hazel eyes betoken a good disposition.

Blue-eye beauty, do your mammy's duty.

Black eye, pick a pie, run around and tell a lie. Gray-eye greedy gut, eat all the world up.

Large, somber eyes indicate a passive nature whereas small, sharp eyes indicate an active disposition, cunning, and shrewdness.

If the left ear itches, hear good news; if left eye itches, hear sad news.

Heavy eyebrows are a sign of long life.

If your eyebrows meet you are ill-tempered. If the eyebrows are far apart you will live away from home; if near together you will live near home or at home.

If there is a blue vein in the child's forehead extending down upon the nose it is one of the surest signs of early death.

Vertical wrinkles in the brow show the number of husbands one will have, horizontal ones the number of children.

A high, broad forehead is indicative of learning and knowledge, heralding intuitive characteristics.

According to different informants a space between the two front upper teeth signifies wealth, that you will die of consumption, that you are a liar, or that you can't keep a secret; if they are overlapping you are close-mouthed.

Broad front teeth are a sign of generosity, but one must never trust anyone with pointed teeth.

A lump on the tongue is a sign that one has told a lie. If you bite your tongue suddenly while you are eating it is a sign that someone is coming hungry. To bite your tongue while talking means that you have told a lie.

A double chin is a sign of wealth, whether it be money or health. A heavy jaw, square, out-thrust, indicates boldness, courage, and determination.

Coarse hair indicates good nature; fine hair a quick temper. Red hair indicates a "spit-fire." Beware of that man, be he friend or brother, whose hair is one color and moustache another.

When a woman's hair parts where it should not it is a sure sign she will be a widow.

A single white hair means genius; it must not be pulled out. If you pull out a white hair two will come in its place.

Put some of your hair in the fire. If it burns slowly you will have a long life, if quickly, a short one.

Draw a single hair from the head strongly between the thumb and the fingernail; if it curls up you are proud. (Another source says that if it curls up by the third draw the person is high tempered.)

The color of the hair growing on the neck indicates the color of the hair of one's future husband.

Hair growing on the upper lip of a woman means riches.

Hairy arms mean strength.

A dimple is the mark left by the angel's finger in turning up the face to kiss it while the person is asleep. A dimple in the chin is lucky; some say it shows you're no fool.

Dimple in chin, Devil within.

If a person is very handsome it is a sign that he will have one of the infections of childhood (measles, whooping cough, etc.) more than once.

If your right hand itches you will shake hands soon; if your left had itches you will soon come to money.

The number of folds on your wrist as you bend your hand shows the number of thirties you are to live.

If the ends of the fingers are capable of being bent far back it indicates a thief.

Large hands with thick fingers indicate a leaning toward muscular activity or hard labor. Slender fingers and delicate hands are indicators of an inclination toward the playing of musical instruments. Among the lawless it indicates cleverness at thievery, shop lifting, picking pockets, or the expert manipulation of locks and safe combinations.

If you cannot make your thumb and one finger meet around your wrist you are a glutton.

If you cannot touch the tips of your little finger and first finger together behind the two middle fingers on both hands then you will not marry the man you want to marry.

Clasp your fingers and if the right thumb laps over the left you were born in the daytime; if the left overlaps you were born at night.

If your thumb sticks up in a closed fist you are either capable or honest, probably the latter, as thieves are said to double theirs in.

In clasping your own hand you put uppermost either your right or left thumb; if the former you are to rule, vice versa to yield.

A person with an initial in his hand will be very fortunate in selecting a companion for life.

The letter formed by the veins on the inside of the wrist is the initial of the name of the future husband or wife.

A straight line in the palm of the hand is an omen of early death.

Anyone who habitually bites his nails is ill-natured.

Always keep your fingernails clean and you will be rich.

A white spot on the nail means a present; you get the present when it grows to the end and is cut. White spots on the nails of the left hand denote the number of lies one had told.

Count on fingernail spots: Friends, foes, money, beaux. Begin with the first nail spotted and the noun falling to the last nail thus marked gives the sign.

Another formula: A friend, a foe, a gift, a beau, a journey to go.

Broad nails show the person to be bashful, fearful, but of gentle nature; narrow nails denote the person to be inclined to mischief and to do injury to his neighbor.

Long nails show the person to be good-natured but mistrustful and loves reconciliation rather than differences.

Oblique nails signify deceit and want of courage.

Round nails show a choleric person, yet soon reconciled, honest, and a lover of secret sciences.

Fleshy fingernails denote the person to be mild in his temper, idle and lazy.

If the sole of either foot itches you will walk on strange ground.

If you stumble with the right foot it means a glad surprise.

If your instep is high enough to have water flow under it you are of good descent.

A mole on the sole of the left foot means trouble and hardships during life.

A mole on the eyebrow denotes that one will be hanged; on the ear that he will be drowned. A mole on the neck means a death by hanging too.

A mole on the arm indicates riches.

Mole on your arm, live on a farm.

A mole on the arm means that you will fight many battles and will be very successful in them.

Mole above breast means wealth.

Mole on the neck, money by the peck.

94 Dream Interpretations

In the world of folklore, dreams have always been a route to the understanding of personality and perceptions of the world through the mind's filter. Only fairly recently has the sophisticated world, through Freud, accepted the dream as a message.

Cod: sign of rain.

Good catch of fish: rain.

Catching fish: good luck; sign you will make a good bargain according to the size of the fish; money.

Flies: sickness; good luck.

Lice: sign of death; enemies; approaching wealth; sickness in the family.

Snakes: enemies. If you kill a snake in your dream it is interpreted in some localities as being a sign that you will conquer your enemies.

Pigs: luck.

Rats: especially in number, a sign of death; enemies; thieves.

Fresh earth: misfortune.

Digging ground or white potatoes: death.

Seeing ground unseasonably plowed: death.

Eggs: a beating; anger; if broken, the anger will pass.

Nest full of eggs and a bird sitting on them: something new.

Fire: bad luck; sickness; trouble in the family; an argument; anger; hasty news.

Dream of flame out of season, you will be angry without reason.

Large blaze: unexpected money.

Smoke: trouble; death.

Baby: death; bad luck; trouble.

Priest: bad luck.

Negro: a quarrel.

Kiss or intimacy with a woman friend: disagreement.

If you dream of a person of the opposite sex three nights in succession you are sure to marry him.

If you dream of a gentleman you will never marry him.

If you dream of a person as going two ways at once it is a sign that the person dreamed of will die before the year is out.

Naked man: death of a woman, and vice versa.

Drunken husband or man: bad luck.

Men: lucky.

Women: unlucky.

Walking through snow: sickness.

Snowstorm: speedy death of a relative.

Snow in the spring (May): a good catch of fish.

If a fisherman dreams of rain it is a sign of a good catch of fish.

Anything dreamed "on the east wind"—that is, when the east wind is blowing—will come true.

Silver money: sickness.

Small change: bad luck.

Gold or silver: good luck; and increase of property.

Paper money: bad luck.

Teeth: unlucky; falling out, death, bad luck; being pulled: sickness; losing: losing a friend.

If you dream of having a front tooth drop out you will lose a near relative within a year; if a back tooth, a distant relative.

Marriage: funeral.

Funeral: marriage.

Dream of a piece of wedding cake. Write names on slips of paper and pull them out. The one you pull twice is the one you will marry. The one you dream about will be your future partner in life. If you have the same dream three nights in succession it will come true.

Eating meat: sickness.

Blood: sickness; someone will scandalize you.

Cherries: evil.

Ship: while you are on land, a funeral.

Whatever you dream the first night you are in a strange house will come true. If you dream the first night you are in a strange bed the dream will come to pass. If the dream was of a sweetheart you will be married.

Saturday night's dream, Sunday morning told, will come to pass before it's a week old.

Relate a dream before breakfast and it will come true.

If you dream the same thing three times it will come true.

Dreaming of handling new-made boards is a sign of a coffin.

If you dream that you see an empty coffin, you will see it filled within one year.

Dough in a bread-pan: coffin.

Bread: good luck.

Riding in a carriage: travel with a friend.

Pick up a stone in a strange place and put it under the pillow for three nights; if you dream it will come true.

To dream of being in a new house is a sign of death.

To dream you are a fool is good luck and an increase of wealth.

Dreaming of persons being sick is a sign of being well.

To dream you cry means you will laugh.

Clear water: good news.

Muddy water: bad news.

Flying birds: a wedding in the family.

95 Miscellaneous Beliefs and Omens

In building of log cabins, whatever object is taken in first the most will be done with these articles. It is usually good practice in the interest of keeping the cabin clean to put the broom and mop in first. If it is a chair or bed the persons will be inclined to be of a lazy nature. To build a house of stone denotes settling down in contentment; of lumber from a storm-felled tree, bad luck. Building a house in the spring indicates future happiness. Leaving a house unfinished indicates struggles and uncertainties ahead.

If a log falls from the wall during construction of a log house it foretells an early death in the family that will now occupy the house.

A journey, if it is to be a long one, will be most pleasant and successful if it is started in the new moon; a journey will be well rounded out if started in the full of the moon; a journey for a favor will prove disappointing if begun when the moon is on the wane.

A journey started very early in the morning holds forth success. To begin a journey immediately following a heated argument will prove to be full of disappointments.

Plant potatoes in the dark of the moon; this is to prevent them from growing to tops with small yield. Some plant them at the new moon to hasten their growth.

When table silver falls to the floor the housewife assumes that visitors will arrive before the day is ended. When a cat jumps to the table and laps cream visitors are coming to stay a spell. Among some families of the local German settlers is the belief that if a cow insists upon remaining in the barnyard and does not go out to pasture and moos consistently she is calling friends of the family to come visiting.

Rattlesnake rattles placed inside a violin improves the tone of the instrument.

When a cat is moved to a new home the owner can make it stay by rubbing butter on the cat's feet.

A horse is thought to be dangerous and treacherous if it shows much of the white of its eye. If a horse rolls entirely over during its rolling exercise it is considered a valuable animal.

To make a good bread stir it with the sun; to make good yeast make it as near sunrise as possible. If you wish to secure lightness you must always stir cake and eggs the way the sun goes, you change and turn the other way it will undo all the churning you have done.

When the two figures that tell one's age are alike—as 22, 33, 44, etc.— some great change in life is to be expected.

96 Indian Beliefs

Rain is considered an omen of good fortune, wind the reverse. Snow suggests a bright future ahead. Hot weather forecasts bad luck. An early cold spell is a warning to prepare for a harder winter than usual. If a chinook comes early in January there will be an early and warm spring.

If muskrats or beaver show a lack of activity in the fall the approaching winter will be severe. On the other hand, should these creatures show an unusual zest in adding material to the walls of their houses the winter will be unusually severe and of long duration.

An eclipse of the moon in the spring, planting time, means a crop failure, and if it comes in the fall there will be want and famine throughout the winter.

If an Indian sees a fireball in the night he believes that a departed dear one is coming to communicate with him. He therefore goes away and sits in solitude to await the message. If several see the same fireball it is a sign that a friendly spirit is coming to impart information to them all.

If sun-dogs are seen upon the horizon in the morning it signifies cold weather is coming. If they are seen in the evening warmer weather is on the way.

If a tree near the village withers for no apparent reason sickness and pestilence will fall on the village. If a watercourse or spring near the village goes dry the villagers will suffer famine and great discomfort. If there is drought the winter supply of meat will be hard to get.

Beds of quicksand, as found along some streams, and sometimes called "suck beds," are believed to be tentacles of evil spirits that pull one down to a horrible death. The victim of such a suck hole must have committed some great wrong. But if the person is innocent he will be allowed to escape, the experience being a warning not to participate in any evil doing.

Swamps are traps made by evil spirits and inhabited by beasts and reptiles that lie in wait for someone to venture into them so that they might be pounced on and devoured as a reward for their rashness.

Hot springs too are the works of evil spirits and in early days the Indians shunned them as bearing an evil omen.

Rivers were made by evil spirits scratching the earth with sticks, thereby leading water down upon people they disliked to wreak vengeance on them.

An albino buffalo was a very rare animal even when there were millions of buffalo roaming over the western Plains. Such an animal was held in the greatest awe and reverence by the Blackfeet Indians. The white or albino buffalo was indeed a sacred animal: it belonged to the sun. Anyone who killed such and animal assumed part of its sacred character. His whole tribe also shared in this with him to a great extent. (*Collected by Nellie VanDerveer*)

On the very rare occasions when a white buffalo was killed by the Blackfeet an elaborate ceremony took place. All of the members of the tribe arrayed themselves in their finest ceremonial garments. They wore their choicest embroidered shirts and leggings, their fringed and beaded moccasins, their gorgeous robes, and especially their crowns and bonnets of erect eagle feathers with tails that extended down to the ground.

The chief of the trip knelt on the ground. Materials for a fire were placed before him. He lighted the fire with steel and flint and then washed his hands in the smoke as if he were using water. He then arose and stretched upward, holding his knife toward the sun. At this movement of the chief a vast, solemn silence descended over the whole tribe. Not a sound broke the stillness. All stood in awe and reverence.

The chief then went to the dead buffalo and cut out its tongue, after which he stepped away to make room for the other warriors, who then proceeded to skin the sacred animal very carefully. Before beginning this, each one reverently placed his hands and his knife through the cleansing smoke just as the chief had done.

During the entire time that the sacred buffalo was being skinned the chief held the tongue at arm's length toward the sun. He remained perfectly rigid until the long task was completed. Then the chief solemnly chanted, in the language of the Blackfeet, "O Sun! To you I give this sacred buffalo. It is yours. Take it."

The flesh of the white buffalo was never touched. It did not belong to the Indians. It had been given by the chief—to the sun, so to the sun it belonged.

The Shoshone and Bannock Indians are extremely superstitious in regard to the coyote. For no reason whatsoever would a member of these tribes kill one. The killing of a coyote by any other person is regarded by these Indians as an act to be looked upon with fear and superstition.

A coyote is supposed to be inhabited by a "spirit." Therefore it must not be molested in any way lest evil befall the tribe or one of its members.

The unearthly wailing and shrieking of the coyotes is said to be the anguished and despairing cries of lost souls in hell. They can never be in peace but must always cry out their despair, especially when the weather is unsettled and a storm is approaching. Then their spirits are more uneasy. Those who do not believe this say that the coyotes howl when a storm is approaching because they sense the disturbance and it makes them uneasy.

Some say that it is because spirits are embodied in the coyotes that the latter hold their own against all attempts to exterminate them. Sometimes they seem to disappear when warfare is waged against them, but as soon as it lets up they come back more numerous than ever.

Another thing which almost anybody will admit about coyotes is that they seem to know whether or not a person is carrying a gun. Many instances have been reported of some person seeing the same coyote many times without it showing a sign of fear. It would even come near or play around like a dog, but if that same person carried a gun the coyote would run for its life and keep out of range.

To have cheated your brother or a relative is to invoke the wrath of evil spirits. To have executed some commendable deed is to thwart the design of evil spirits.

Among the Indians if a number of their saddle horses come to the lodge and graze about in the vicinity it signifies a call upon friends. In the early days it signified that warriors would soon set out for a hunt or a raid.

When an Indian squaw's shoulders ache and she feels lassitude coming over her she believes that soon she will have a heavy burden to bear. If her hands itch she will soon have much work to do. If her hands go numb she will have nothing to do. If her eyes are tired and smart she will see sorrow in her family. If her feet itch or feel uncomfortable she will have to go a great distance.

Visiting friends are often given tobacco as a token of friendship. When friendly hunting parties met on the Plains or in the mountains they often exchanged knives or arrows as a token of good hunting.

Indian girls used to make up small pouches of softly tanned doeskin that were then filled with dried and crushed aromatic herbs and given to a chosen young brave as a token of their love.

There were established businesses of barter and trade among the tribe or between friendly tribes. This barter and trade was often a token by which friendly relations were established among neighboring tribes or these en route through the region.

There was a type of barter established by a class of people whose sole object was the making of pottery, which was a distinctive art requiring a certain skill in the making and of choosing soils or clays that only certain localities would yield. These wares were then bartered to other tribes for hunting implements, tipis, robes, and dressed skins for the making of clothing, and even for clothing already made up. There were also those who fashioned beads and who exchanged their handiwork for other commodities.

An arrow wrapped with the skin of a snake was a token of death to whomever it was sent. A broken arrow sent to someone was a token of misfortune and meant bad luck in hunting.

Folk Speech

97 Glossary of Terms, Nicknames, and Folk Speech
Cowboy Terms

The items starred in the list below were collected for the WPA by Ludwig Stanley Landmichl. Those items followed by a + were submitted by Nellie VanDerveer. All others appear in the WPA's *Wyoming: A Guide to Its History, Highways, and People* (New York: Oxford University Press, 1941).

Arbuckle: Adjective applied to a cowboy, implying that the boss must have got him by mail order with Arbuckle Coffee premium stamps.

Barefooted: Unshod (of a horse).

Bed down: To lie down for the night on the bed ground.

Bed ground: The place where livestock such as sheep or cattle are held for a halt on the trail or on the range.

Bed roll: The blankets and bedding owned by each cowpuncher; they are usually rolled up with a tarpaulin around them.

Beefing: Complaining.

Bicycling: Holding one foot down or under the surcingle while "scratching" with the spur on the other foot, and then alternating.

Big boss: The owner of the cattle outfit. His first lieutenant is called *Right-hand man*, sometimes *top screw*.

Biscuit shooter: The cook.

Biting the dust: Being thrown from a horse.

*Black snake**: Long tapering whip of braided leather used for driving cattle or horses.

Blow: To lose a stirrup while riding. Also to let a horse stop for breath in high altitude.

Bogged down: Trapped in a swamp or bog. Sometimes used when a person is swamped with work.

Bogging them in: Holding a tight spur in the animal's belly.

Bounce: To turn animals.

Box canyon*: An abrupt wall within a canyon that prevents passage up or down the canyon.

Brand blotting*: Disfiguring or altering brands on livestock, usually applied to stolen stock.

Bronc*: Horse.

Bronc peeler*: Man who breaks range horses for riding purposes.

Broomtail*: Horse.

Buckaroo*: Dude-ranch hand, usually a dude wrangler or horse wrangler, who is a good rider and can put on a show of horsemanship for the benefit of the ranch guests.

Buckstrap: Strap attached to the fork of a saddle by which a rider may hold while riding a bucking horse to lessen the jolts.

Bucking rolls: Leather covered swells attached to a saddle to make the rider's seat more secure.

Bunch quitter: An animal that strays frequently.

Bush popper+: Cow.

Bust: To throw an animal by the forefeet.

Camp*: When applied to a ranch means a house, unless the wagon is understood. Large ranches have a headquarters and two or three "camps."

Cantle-boarding: Riding loosely and hitting the cantle or back of the saddle.

Cavvy: A string of horses used in ranch work such as roundups.

Cayuse: Originally and Indian pony bred by the Cayuse Indians of Eastern Oregon; hence any broncho or inferior breed of horse raised on the range. Generally speaking, *cayuse* has a slightly more derogatory meaning than bronco, although the words are often used interchangeably.

Chaps: Short for *chaparejos*, leggings worn by cowboys for warmth and protection when riding in brush.

Chinook: Warm wind named from the Chinook Indians.

Choke down: To subdue an animal by choking with rope.

Circle horse: One selected for his stamina to cover territory in the roundup.

Clodhopper: Farmer.

Coffin nails: Cigarettes.

Coffin varnish: Liquor.

Conchas: Metal ornaments adorning saddles, chaps, bridles, etc.

Cookie★: Camp cook.

Corporal: See *Old man*.

Coulee: Bed of a stream, even when dry, when steep and having inclined sides.

Cows★: All cattle, collectively speaking, regardless of age or sex, are cows on a ranch. The term *she-stuff* is used in referring to those exclusively of the female gender.

Coyote★: Range rider.

Critter★: Cow or horse.

Crow-hopping: Mild bucking.

Cut horse: Horse used to cut animals out of a herd.

Cut out: To separate an animal or a group from the main herd.

Dally: To *take a dally* is to circle the rope around a post (*snubbing post*) or saddle horn in order to hold a roped animal.

Devil's jig★: To hang horse thieves or cattle rustlers without ceremony.

Dewlap: A strip of hide cut and left hanging under an animal's neck for identification purposes.

Dog-fall: To throw a steer with his feet under him.

Dogie: Motherless calf which trails behind the herd and causes no end of trouble.

Double underbit: Two triangular cuts in the under part of an animal's ear for identification purposes.

Doughbelly: See *Dogie*.

Drag★: The rear of a herd.

Draw: Gully or ravine.

Drift: Animals *drift* in a storm away from their regular feeding grounds.

Drift fence: Fence separating different ranges.

Dry gulched: To shoot or hang a man from surprise.

Dude: Formerly applied to an Eastern novice. The term is now used as the general and comradely expression of greeting to the visitor.

Dudine: Feminine of *dude*.

Fantail: Wild horse.

Flank: Side of the herd.

Foot: To throw an animal by the foot.

Forefoot: To rope an animal by the front feet in order to throw it for handling.

Go over the range: To die.

Grabbing the apple: Hanging on to the saddle horn.

Graveyard step: Milktoast.

Greaser: Mexican.

Grubber: An animal that noses about the roots of the loco weed to eat them is said to be *grubbing loco*.

Grubstake: To furnish food for a person for a definite time or in a certain amount, usually for a prospecting venture.

Hackamore: A halter of rawhide, braided and snug-fitting.

Hairbrand: A temporary brand made by burning or picking out the hair. If skillfully done it looks like an old brand.

Hammerhead+: Horse.

Hardpan*: A tough-looking character.

Hawse*: Horse.

Hay cribs: Log walls without a roof enclosing haystacks.

Hay hand: Man employed during haying season on a ranch.

Haze: To ride at the side of an obstreperous broncho in an effort to keep the horse from running into a fence or some obstruction. Term used in breaking horses.

Hazer: An assistant to keep horses from the fences.

Heeling: Roping cattle by the hind feet.

High roller: A high bucker.

Hit the hay: Go to bed.

Hobbled stirrups: Stirrups tied down to surcingle to aid a rider in keeping his feet in them.

Hog tie: To tie the feet of a steer or horse or calf after it has been thrown.

Hold-up man: Man stationed at crossroads, on a hill, or at critical points to keep the herd from leaving the trail.

Hondo: Leather or metal loop at the end of a lariat.

Hoodlum wagon: A second wagon used in the roundup for carrying extra beds and bringing wood.

Hoof: To walk.

Horse talk★: Conversation with plenty of common sense.

Hoss★: Horse.

Hot rocks: Biscuits.

Hot rolls★: Bedrolls.

Hull★: Saddle.

Jinglebob: To split the ear of a calf or cow to the head, leaving the pieces flap.

Jingler: The man who takes care of the Cavvy.

Jug handle: A slit in the loose hide under an animal's throat made sometimes for identification.

To *juice*: To milk.

Kak★: Saddle.

Lass rope★: A lariat or saddle rope, usually of four-strand, hard twisted rope and neatly coiled and attached to the swell of the saddle with a strap.

Latigo: A strap for lacing the saddle on.

Lead poisoning: The condition of someone who has been shot.

Leggings case★: A case where a man has broken some cowboy rule of etiquette and is held over the wagon tongue while he is given so many strokes with a pair of chaps.

Line camp★: A cabin some distance from the home ranch, situated on the border of the ranch.

Line rider★: A man who rides the line or border of the ranch to prevent livestock from straying too far off.

Loco: Crazy.

Lone wolf★: Range rider.

Makin's: Tobacco for filling a cigarette paper.

Man-killer: A vicious horse that will kick, strike, and bite.

Martingale: A strap from the bridle to the surcingle, between the forelegs, for control of the head of a horse.

Maverick: An unbranded calf or critter.

Mooer+: Steer.

Moon-eyed: A horse with white, glassy eyes.

*Native**: Guest from the surrounding country, a neighbor, used primarily on dude ranches.

Necking: Tying an unruly cow or a wanderer to the neck of a more tractable animal.

Nester: A man who squats on the land and fences it in.

Nice kitty: Skunk.

Nighthawk: Cowboy on night duty.

Oklahoma Rain: Sand- or duststorm.

Old man: Ranch owner.

Old woman: A wife.

Open winter: A mild winter with the range free of snow.

Outlaw: A horse that cannot be broken.

Overbit: A semicircular cut in the upper part of an animal's ear for identification.

Pack horse: Horse trained to carry a pack rather than to ride.

Pack saddle: Framework especially designed for pack animals.

*Palaver**: To have a talk.

*Patch**: Spotted horse.

Pegging: Holding one horn of a steer in the ground to hold him down.

Pilgrim: A newcomer.

*Pinnacle**: Any hill or promontory.

Pinto: Spotted pony.

Plaster+: Saddle

Plumb loco: Quite crazy.

Poison: Liquor.

Poke: See *Warbag*.

Poultice+: Saddle.

Pound leather: To ride.

Prairie lawyers: Coyotes.

Prayer book: Book of cigarettes.

Prod pole: At once.

*Pulling leather**: Holding onto the saddle.

Rake: To scratch a horse with spurs or drag the spurs long his neck to make him buck.

Rawhiding*: Chafing or bantering someone.

Red-eyed: Mad.

Remuda: A term applied to all of the horses in a particular outfit.

Renegade*: A critter that won't stay in the herd or confinement.

Ride the grub line: To visit various ranches to gain free food and lodging.

Riding cuffs*: Leather cuffs six to eight inches long.

Rig: Saddle.

Right-hand man: Chief foreman of a cattle outfit.

Rodeo: A western celebration featuring bucking, roping, and bull-dogging.

Rocky mountain canary: A burro.

Roll in: To go to bed.

Rope horse: Animal good for roping activities.

Rope in: To take in, to trick.

Rope shy: An animal that jumps away from the rope when the rider is trying to lasso him in.

Roundup: Gathering of the herd.

Roustabout: A man of all work about the camp.

Running iron: Ring or bar or even a piece of wire or any tool used for branding in an emergency.

Rusty+: A poor steer, not much good for beef.

Sabe*: Do you understand? Do you get it?

Salty: Mean (applied to a horse).

Savvy: To understand (from *sabe*).

Sawbones: A doctor.

Scratching: Raking a horse with spurs while the animal is bucking.

Seam squirrels: Lice.

Seeing daylight: Said of a rider who bounces high in the saddle, showing light between the rider and the horse.

Shep*: Sheepherder.

Shindig: Dance.

Skin mules: To drive mules.

Sky pilot: Preacher.

Sleeper*: A calf ear-marked by a cattle thief who intends to come back later and steal the animal. Thus, during a roundup should a ranch hand find such an animal he would probably leave it behind as not belonging to his outfit. The thief would return later and carry the calf off, probably killing the mother so that her bellowing for her lost offspring would not attract attention.

Slick: Unbranded.

Slough: See *Slug*.

Slug: A large amount.

Slow elk: A cow that is stolen and butchered and the meat eaten or sold.

Smooth: Unshod (of a horse).

Snake+: Steer.

Snake juice: Liquor.

Snubbing post: Post around which a cowboy takes a "dally," "dally wel-tie," or "hitch" to hold an animal. Usually in a corral between the center and the fence.

Soft: A horse that tires easily.

Sop: Gravy.

Sougan: Originally a blanket of thick weave used to keep out rain or cold. With the coming of the tarpaulin the word came to mean any cheap or old worn blanket used on the trail.

Sowbelly: Salt pork.

Squeezer or *Snappin' turtle*: A chute for branding.

Starve out*: A pasture of very few acres at a permanent camp, usually without water and with the grass used up, into which the horses are thrown overnight to avoid catching or rustling them in the morning.

Stetson: Broad-brimmed, high-crowned hat.

Stinging a whizzer: A tall tale as told by the personnel of a dude ranch to a group of guests.

String: Horses assigned to each rider.

Sunday hoss*: A horse with an easy saddle gait. Usually a single footer with some style.

Sunfisher: A horse that darts from one side to another when bucking giving the effect of switching ends.

Swallow fork: A V-shaped cut from the ear for identification purposes.

Tail: To throw a calf after the rope has dragged the animal near the branding fire.

Tail-up: To pull a cow from a mudhole by the tail.

Talk turkey: To mean business.

Tarp: Tarpaulin, a large piece of canvas, often used as a component of the sleeping roll.

Tender: Said of a horse that shows signs of getting saddle or harness sores or sore feet.

Tenderfoot: A newcomer.

Ten-gallon hat: Cowboy hat, Stetson.

Tie-down: A strap to hold down the head of a horse that habitually carries its head so high he might fall into a hole without seeing it.

Tight legging: Gripping legs tightly around a horse.

Top hand: A good all-round cowboy.

Top screw+: The boss.

Tracing iron*: See *Running iron*.

Trap wagon*: Spare wagon, often towed along behind the chuck wagon, carrying bedrolls and all other paraphernalia used on roundups and cattle drives, including firewood.

Turn-out time: Time in the spring to turn the cattle out to grass.

Twine+: Lariat.

Under bit: Angular cut in under part of ear for identification purposes.

Vamoose: To move along.

W: To put a form of hobble on a bad horse.

Waddy*: In the fall and spring when some ranches were shorthanded they would take on anyone able to ride a horse and use them for day herding; hence the word *waddy*, such as wadding—anything to fill in with.

Wahwah*: To talk.

Warbag: Usually a canvas bag or tarpaulin used for carrying clothing and possessions.

Wattle: A dewlap which forms a bunch instead of a string. Made for identification.

Whizzing*: Spinning yarns.

Winter horse: A sturdy horse kept ready and trained in winter for heavy work.

Yamping: Ordinary stealing.

Loggers' Folk Speech from the Wind River Valley and South Pass Region

Collected in Riverton, Wyoming by Ludwig Stanley Landmichl.

Beans: Food, a meal; "Let's go get some beans."

Bearcats: Small crew of daring men who do the risky work of driving the logs through narrow canyons.

Boom: Place in a stream where logs or railroad ties or mining props are being held.

Breaking boom: Opening the boom to let the logs out.

Breaking jam: Breaking loose the jam formed in the stream, often a difficult undertaking owing to the terrific pressure of water behind the jam.

Breaking landings: At driving time in the spring the driving crew breaks loose the piles of railroad ties along the banks of streams.

Broad axe: A heavy axe with a ten-inch blade or more, weighing over nine pounds, used for hewing purposes.

Broadway: The main road through the woods.

Camp cook: The cook at the choppers' camp, hauling camp, or sawmill.

Carriage: The man who rides the carriage holding the log and who makes the adjustments for sawing various thicknesses of boards.

Come-along: Team and wagon on large truck that gathers the men and brings them to the drive camp at the end of the day.

Corduroy: Small logs laid side by side close together over swampy ground as a road.

Crowding: See *Hauling*.

Double cut: To sit astride a couple of railroad ties or a log and ride them through a canyon or around the bend of a river to save time and hard walking over boulders and rough going. It is considered a risky trick.

Drive cook: Cook of a log and railroad tie crew.

Dutch oven: Cast-iron pots with heavy lids used for cooking food and baking bread on tie and log drives.

Flumkey: See *Flunkie*.

Flunkie: The cook's assistant, the dish washer.

Greenstuff: Green slabs from the saw used as boiler fuel.

Hand banking: Cutting logs close enough to a stream that they may be piled directly along the banks without being hauled by horses.

Hot and heavy: Coffee made over a campfire in the woods and extra strong. It is usually drunk scalding hot, without sugar or cream.

Hauling: When water pressure moves logs or ties held at the boom and piles them atop each other. Also called *crowding*.

Hauling contract: Taken to mean having horses and sleighs who do not chop but only haul the cut ties to the stream and pile them at the landings.

Jam: When ties or logs pile up at some point in the stream.

Kettle: Steam boiler at the saw mill.

Key log: The main log or logs (or railroad ties) that have caused the jam and are holding it.

Landing: A pile of logs piled beside a stream so that it may readily be broken, sending them into the water when it is high in the spring.

Mill crew: Crew that works the saw mill.

Pike or *pike pole*: Long, slender pole with an iron spike and hook, used by the log or tie drivers to push or pull ties along the streams.

Plume (sic): Where a stream bed is extremely restricted or strewn with large boulders a trough of planks is built; the water is turned into it and the logs or ties are sent along through it.

Powderman: Man experienced in the use of dynamite who does the shooting of jams or obstruction in the streams that might cause jams.

Rear: Small crew of men who follow the main drive crew to see that all logs missed by the main crew are sent downstream.

Roughlock: A chain that is fastened under and around the runners of the heavy sleds used in hauling logs or railroad ties; the chains cut into the ice and snow of the road and prevent the sleds from gaining too much momentum down the hills. Also cheese and cheese products.

Sawyer: Head man at the sawmill.

Scoring: Chopping along one side of a log with an ordinary axe, making cuts eight or ten inches apart, the purpose of which is to make the hewing of railroad ties faster, easier, and smoother.

Shooting: Using dynamite to blow out the key logs to break loose a jam.

Skids: Heavy poles used in loading logs or building skid paths on creek banks.

Snow chute: A path made in huge, late snowdrifts for sliding logs down the bank into a stream.

Sowbelly: Pork or salt pork.

Stoker: The man who fires the boiler.

Swamper: The man who constructs roads through the forest and across bogs and swamps.

Tail: The rear-end of a drive.

Tender: Man with a team of horses (or with a large truck) who moves the drive camp from place to place as the drive progresses downstream.

Timber cruiser: An experienced woodsman who seeks out new locations for lumbering operations.

Game Hunters' Terms

Collected by Ludwig Stanley Landmichl.

Back bush: The back-of-beyond country; any isolated region beyond camp.

Boil the pot: To stop along the trail and brew a pot of coffee or tea.

Breaking trail: Making a trail through deep, fresh snow.

Camp meat: As soon as a hunting camp is established one of the guides kills an elk, usually a fat cow, to be used as camp provisions—Camp Meat.

Camp robber: A bird of the jay family that stays close about a hunting camp.

Chuckaluck: A hastily gotten together meal of leftovers.

Deerlick: A place where deer frequently come to lick the salt put out for them only to be shot at night, which is of course unlawful.

Drift: The direction game takes when feeding or grazing.

Flag: Game of the deer family throw up their tails when they run, and hunters speak of this as "showing the flag."

Game crossing: Wild game have certain places where they cross ridges separating valleys; hunters often take advantage of this by posting themselves at such position.

Hikers' roaster: Slender, green stick that can be thrust through small game to rotate it over a bed of coals.

Jerky: Game meat cut into strips, salted, and then smoked and dried.

Lean-to: Shelter hastily constructed by leaning small poles against a horizontal pole and covering this frame with pine boughs placed upside down to shed rain and snow.

Lying-out: Hunters sometimes get so far away from their main camp during a day's hunt that they cannot return, so they make themselves as comfortable as possible, building a fire, putting up a lean-to, and resting until daylight.

Moose meadow: Swampy place overgrown with willow thickets where moose browse.

Moose wallow: Small pond within the mountain meadows where moose feed on aquatic growth.

Night fire: A log fire so arranged that it burns slowly and steadily throughout the night when a woodsman is forced to spend a night out without bedding. On cold nights two such fires are built, one on each side of the sleeper.

Packer: A man who packs in provisions to the hunting camps using horses.

Potshot: Shooting at game that is not moving or shooting into a bunch of quail or other birds that are huddled together.

Shake down: A bed made of pine boughs or a layer of pine needles.

Still hunting: Hunting by a sort of prowling method, working against the wind as much as possible to prevent the game from scenting the hunter.

Tidbits: The heart and liver of freshly killed game.

Trailing: Following fresh game tracks along a trail or tracking over fresh snow.

Mechanics' Terms

Collected for the Wyoming WPA by Charles M. Fowkes Jr.

Anchors: Brakes.
Bucket: Pistons.
Clunk: Used car.
Grease monkey: Mechanic.
Junkpile: Used car.
Knucklebuster: Hammer.
Old irons: Used car.
Persuader: Hammer.
Puddle jumper: Old car.
Steeper: Creeper.
Tin lizzie: Model T Ford.
Thumb skinner: Hammer.
Whoopie: Old car.

Road or Bridge Construction Terms

Collected for the Wyoming WPA by Charles M. Fowkes Jr.

Bar Tender: Paymaster.
Bush Whacker: Man who cleans brush from road right-of-way.
Cat Skinner: Caterpillar tractor operator.
Flunkey: Camp tender.
Grade-stiff: Man who works on dirt road construction.
Hammer Head: Pile driver operator.
Owl Man: Night watchman.
Truck Skinner: Truck driver.

Restaurant Terms

Collected for the Wyoming WPA by Charles M. Fowkes Jr.

Adam and eve on a raft: Poached eggs on toast.
Beanery: Restaurant.
Cheese on: Cheese sandwich.
Eggs fried with their eyes open: Fried but not turned.
Hasher: Waitress.

Prison Terms

Beet-ies: The disease afflicting the convict laborer who is supposed to be hoeing beets but is slacking.

College: Prison, as opposed to School, the state reformatory.

Fish: A new convict.

Hay: Tobacco.

Hole: A cell.

The man: Superintendent or warden.

Paste: Breakfast oatmeal.

School: See *College*.

Screw: An unpopular guard.

Second-loser: A man serving his second term in prison.

Painters' Terms

Collected for the Wyoming WPA by Charles M. Fowkes Jr.

Cub: An apprentice.

Holiday: A spot skipped while painting.

Quill: Sign paintbrush.

Skyhooks: Swingstage.

Tears: Bumps or runs made from not brushing paint careful.

Sheep-shearers' Terms

Cherry picker: New man with a crew.

High roller: A fast and good shearer.

Hootenanny: Device for holding shears during sharpening.

Keno: Someone able to shear one hundred or more sheep in a day's time.

Stone breaker: A very slow shearer.

Dairy Workers' Terms

Collected for the Wyoming WPA by Charles M. Fowkes Jr.

Butter toad: Butter wrap.

Creamery dick: The big boss.

Railroaders' Terms

Collected for the Wyoming WPA by Charles M. Fowkes Jr.

Bend the rail: Throw the switch for another track.
Hot rail: A line on which a train is approaching.
Varnished cars: Passenger trains.

Printers' Terms

Collected for the Wyoming WPA by Charles M. Fowkes Jr.

Slang-whanger: A writer who uses a lot of slang.
Type lice: Mythical creatures used to confuse greenhorns in the shop.

Department Store Terms

Collected for the Wyoming WPA by Charles M. Fowkes Jr.

Chatter: Sales pitch.
Counter jumper: Store clerk.

Folk Speech from Jackson Hole

Collected by Nellie VanDerveer.

Dude money: One-dollar bills.
Dude wranglers: Those who guide and otherwise "herd" dudes.
Grub: Food.
Jackson hole bible: Montgomery Ward Catalog.
Jackson hole Courier: Gossiping woman, the grapevine.
Jerry: Stove.
School dad: A school teacher, female as well as male.
Snowshoes: Skis.
Take the top off: Ride a horse for the first time.
Trembling jimmy: Jello.
Wolf moon: January's full moon.

Nicknames

Backlag: Slow woman.
Bag: See *Backlag*.

Biscuit Shooter: Waitress.

Bull: Policeman.

Cross-Legged Button-Hole Puncher: Tailor.

Deadhead: Slow man.

Dick: Detective.

Dizzy: Fast woman.

Doughslinger: Baker.

Driller: Dentist.

Dynamite: Slow man.

Fast Baby: Fast woman.

Flatfoot: Policeman.

Flat Tire: Slow man.

General: Old man.

Golddigger: Fast woman.

Graybeard: Old man.

Hot Mamma: Fast woman.

Hot papa: Fast man.

Judge: Old man.

Kitchen mechanic: Cook.

Knowledge dispenser: Teacher.

Lone wolf: Bachelor.

Mortar mixer: Barber.

Nailer: Policeman.

Needle pusher: Tailor.

Never-sweat: Slow man.

Old poke: Old woman.

Painkiller: Dentist.

Pearldiver: Cook, dishwasher.

Pie builder: Baker.

Roller: Single man.

Sawbones: Doctor.

Scraper: Barber.

Single footer: Single woman.

Slewfoot: Policeman.

Slick: Servant girl.

Squeeze: Fast woman.
Stew: Cook.
Stick: Slow man.
Town clown: Policeman.
Trimmer: Barber.
Wielder of the birch: Teacher.
Wild rooster: Fast man.

98 Cheap Thunder! An Example of Folk Speech in Action

An article from the May 28, 1875, Cheyenne *Daily News*.

"Idaho Bill"—Preaches ignorance to the natives of Rawlins.
"Coyote Jack" and "Polliwog Jim" come to the front.
They hang their banners upon the outer walls and the cry is
"Bust Head for Three."

There is great excitement at Rawlins. All the people, both old and young, are prancing around in joyful glee and shouting like Modoc Indians on the warpath in honor of "Idaho Bill," who, arrayed in his awful paraphernalia of blood, thunder, and blue blazes, sits by day and night in close communion with "Polliwog Jim," "Coyote Jack," and a keg of "buck"—the noblest Roman of them all—and tells dreadful stories of war scalps, blood, bones and death to the prancing and wonder-inflated Rawlinites; and he tells them too of the wonderful, wonderful advantages and facilities Rawlins possesses as an outfitting and starting point for the Big Horn Country. He tells them that when the Lord built the Big Horn country he stuck it down purposely so near to Rawlins that it is now, with the help of an elastic imagination, not more than six or seven hundred miles into that country. He tells his story to all classes of people and they rush out to hear him in wonderment. The old men turn out, the young men come to hear him, the old ladies souse around most monstrously to hear this great wigglety-woggelty mugwump "tark" (*sic*) in great glory of the wondrous things with which his mind is burdened, while a good many of the ancient and honorable old maidens of Rawlins in great desperation buckle on their gorgeous furbelows, fol de rols, and toggery, and sail out with a sort of Grecian ben-Kangaroonian swagger in the vain hope of captivating this prince on wheels. In fact, speaking in a general way—

> The lightenings flash,
> The thunders roll from pole to pole,
> And the cattle stick up their tales and run—
> and all on account of the glorious and gorgeous "Idaho Bill."

Meanwhile, "Idaho," "Coyote," and "Polliwog" continue to drink their "buck" and "bust-head" and puke just as natural as can be.

These worthies propose to organize and lead a great expedition from Rawlins to the Big Horn Mountains; and there is not the slightest doubt but they will do it, provided they don't have to go farther than the out-skirts of that place to find them.

But they are going to do it according to the Rawlins people, and the astonishing announcement is made that from that place, which is more than 200 miles west of Cheyenne, it is twenty days' march nearer to the gold region of the Big Horn country than this place; and they seem to be willing to swallow all this "hefty" mountaineer sayings, when, in fact, any twelve-year-old school boy can see at a glance that it is at least three hundred miles further to that very desirable little patch of earth from Rawlins than from here, and, furthermore, it is only twenty days' march from this city to the Big Horn Mountains.

But the facts of the case don't at all interfere with the situation as por-trayed to the credulous natives of Rawlins; they propose to send out an expedition. Just how many thousand there will be in the expedition that will make the grand advance under "Idaho" and his aides it is not known, but there will be a good many; and the only trouble to be apprehended now is that there won't be room enough between Rawlins and the Big Horn Mountains for the expedition to move. And then too, Rawlins is a great outfitting point according to the illustrious "Idaho"; in fact, it is a big thing all round, and there is no doubt at all on this point.

Speaking about "outfits," if the people of Rawlins will take "Idaho" and supply him with the fit, he will put on the "out" himself; in fact, he is pretty good at this thing, and we would like to suggest to the people up there that it would be a pretty good idea to look out for him as there is no telling when his "expedition" may start. It is possible that the "expedition" he will lead may strike right out promiscuously, unbeknown to many people, just as he did here in Cheyenne. When "Idaho" once gets up an "expedition" it generally turns out to be an uncertain sort of animal.

This "Idaho Bill" came to Cheyenne and after having been puffed up to an alarming extent by the *Leader* he all at once became a very great and ponderous character, and of course had to sling on a little style. So round he goes among his friends and admirers, and got them to "shell out" a little and eventually obtained thirty dollars from Colonel Carpenter to get a horse. Then as a man who is liable to strike out to the Big Horn country or any other foreign pot with an "expedition" it was necessary for him to borrow a watch, so as to tell the time of day (or night, as the case might demand), by which means he would know just when it would be best to start.

After this "Idaho" got a livery team and made up his mind to make the grand advance on his own hook for the Big Horn; and he got there. Not only that, but he got into the "Horn." It was a pretty old "Horn," and it had cells and iron doors; but still as it was an expedition, it was all right.

Thirty dollars and costs got him out of the "Horn" and "Idaho" at once began to subside, and he kept on subsiding and subsiding, and paying no attention to anything but his "expedition" until at last everything being in readiness "Idaho" went like the old maid—"afoot and alone"—and nobody down here had heard a word about the missing watch, etc., or "Bill" himself, until the gratifying intelligence came that the aforesaid gentleman is at Rawlins with "Coyote Jack" and "Polliwog Jim," preparing for another grand advance.

If Mr. "Idaho" doesn't get an invitation to come back to Cheyenne and perhaps make a little speech of one or two words to Judge Fisher and a jury of twelve men on the charge of larceny, then certain things will not be done which are now talked of somewhat.

We will take our leave however of this illustrious "scout" with the suggestion that the Rawlins expedition may take to its heels and become a little more expeditious in its movement than some of the people up there expect.

Breinigsville, PA USA
14 January 2011
253316BV00002B/2/P